LBSC'S
SHOP, SHED
AND ROAD

LBSC'S SHOP, SHED AND ROAD

Originally published in 1929—reprinted
as *The Live Steam Book* and now completely revised and with new drawings
and plates together with additional
chapters it appears again under its
original title

Edited by

MARTIN EVANS

MODEL & ALLIED PUBLICATIONS LIMITED
13/35 Bridge Street, Hemel Hempstead, Hertfordshire
ENGLAND

Model and Allied Publications Limited
Book Division,
Station Road, Kings Langley, Hertfordshire,
England

First Published as *The Live Steam Book*, 1950
Second Impression (Revised) 1954
First Published under the original title 1969
Second Impression 1974

ISBN 0 85344 017 4

Printed by
Unwin Brothers Limited
The Gresham Press, Old Woking, Surrey

Contents

AUTHOR'S PREFACE TO HIS ORIGINAL LIVE STEAM BOOK "SHOP, SHED, AND ROAD"

I HAVE ALWAYS had a reputation for being unconventional in all things, so guess I'll maintain it by apologising for the appearance of this book at all! However, just listen here before you start shooting. Between the advent of the "Live Steam" columns in *Model Engineer* in 1924, and September, 1929 (date of last count), my list of correspondents reached the respectable total of 1,031; and 90 per cent of that total had at one time or another severely slated me for constantly referring to 'back notes", saying that they couldn't be bothered to wade through back numbers for odd details, and quoted one of my own pet sayings that "Life's too short". They suggested that the notes be published as a book. I didn't like the idea of it, as in miniature locomotive work we are always improving, just like full-size practice, and much of the work described is out of date; but an argument was put forward which finally settled the matter.

I may, perhaps, be permitted to say, without any idea of blowing my own whistle, that the popularity of the "Live Steam" notes is mainly due to the fact that the jobs described, and the methods employed, HAVE ACTUALLY BEEN CARRIED OUT with very successful results. Therefore, anyone "following the directions on the label" will have the satisfaction of knowing what sort of a result they are going to get, which is a far different proposition from making up a "design" which has never taken the road. I can speak from experience on that subject, having been a victim very many years ago, when I built an engine "out of a book". There was very little of the original "design" left by the time I got the engine to go as it should. Anyway, our worthy friend, Mr. Marshall, suggested that if he combed out the "Live Steam" notes for suitable matter, maybe I would edit them, and satisfy the demands of our brother loco. builders who wanted a book of notes; the result is in your hands. It makes no pretence of finality—we are still steaming along the road of progress—but, if it helps you, the object is attained.

I have often been asked why I have such an intense hatred of the word "model" as applied to little locomotives. Well, a friend asked me the same thing one December afternoon as we were passing a large drapery store in Croydon, one window of which was full of Christmas toys. In answer, I pointed to a child's toy clockwork train in cardboard box with rails complete, labelled "SCALE MODEL RAILWAY, price 2s. 11¾d." 'Nuff sed! Thousands of people saw that toy with its label, and whenever they heard the words "scale model" they instinctively connected it with the toy in the store window. If they heard of anyone making "scale models" they naturally thought that it meant either a maker of kiddies' toys or some poor kite in his second childhood. I have heard them say as much; whereas the building of a little locomotive is really a skilled engineer's job, necessitating the employment of many branches of the mechanic's craft. In fact, the only fundamental difference between my 2½ in. gauge engine *Ayesha* and her 4 ft. 8½ in. gauge sister on the Southern Railway is in the size. They are both working locomotives built to do a specified job on their respective gauges.

To all who build little locomotives: may they turn out powerful, efficient and satisfactory engines is the sincere wish of your old friend and "fellow-conspirator",

"L.B.S.C."

September, 1929

AUTHOR'S PREFACE TO "THE LIVE STEAM BOOK"

MAY I TAKE this opportunity of thanking all the hundreds of readers of *Model Engineer* who found the first edition of this book of use to them, and wrote and told me so. A famous "full-size" locomotive engineer, now alas! passed to the Great Beyond, also told me he found it useful, and it was no leg-pull at that. As stated in the original preface, we still keep making improvements in small locomotive design, and, therefore, the contents of the present book have been thoroughly revised, many of the items being brought up to date, and new material added.

My list of correspondents, given in September, 1929, as 1,031, has now passed five figures, and the good folk are scattered all over the world, as far apart as Honolulu, Valparaiso, Gibraltar, all the British Colonies and Dominions, Canada and U.S.A. and many Continental towns, also in Cyprus and the Middle and Far East. A marine engineer who has travelled extensively and is "at home" in any part of the world, says that the only place in which he hasn't heard "L.B.S.C." locomotives mentioned is in a submarine; and expects the reason is, that he has never been down in one!

I still hate and detest the word "model" being applied to my locomotives; and during the time which has elapsed since the first edition of this book appeared, many things have happened to intensify that hatred—'nuff sed!

I might mention that at time of writing, *Ayesha* is still going strong, and has not yet fulfilled the destiny prophesied for her in the anecdote related in the late Mr. Percival Marshall's foreword. I rather think the little old lady is proud of being the great-great-grand-nanny of very nearly all the locomotives now running on the numerous club tracks which have sprung up in parks, open spaces, club grounds and the like! She sends her love to you all. Finally, your humble servant always endeavours to give credit where due, and so I would like to put on record my great appreciation of the assistance rendered by Mr. W. H. Evans, of the Editorial staff. Without his help in sorting out the various selected items from the hundreds of articles which have appeared in *Model Engineer*, goodness only knows when this edition would have appeared if it appeared at all. He also checked the first proofs, which saved me a lot of extra work, and believe me, I am mighty thankful.

I have known "Brother Bill" for over a quarter-century now, as I made his acquaintance on the day I made my first pilgrimage, at the invitation of the late Mr. Percival Marshall, to the old Farringdon Street offices; and always found him one of the best. Now let me whisper in your ear. Our worthy brother knows more than a bit about racing matters, and has several times pulled me up on a "technical hitch" when I have referred to "two-year-olds", "Derby winners", and so forth, when drawing comparisons in matters concerning speed and performances of my engines; well, let's hope that in his endeavours to speed the production of this book he has "backed a winner"!

Also, I render tribute to Mr. L. J. Hibbert, Principal of the London Polytechnic School of Photography, for his whole-hearted co-operation in realistic shots of *Jeanie Deans* reproduced on the paper cover, and the frontispiece; and "the old gal herself" inside. The trouble he went to in order to get those pictures O.K. was just nobody's business.

Cheerio and good steaming,
"L.B.S.C."

August, 1949

FOREWORD TO THE ORIGINAL EDITION

SINCE SEPTEMBER, 1924, "L.B.S.C." has been a regular weekly contributor to *Model Engineer*, and in his articles he has unfolded to the readers of that journal the secrets of his success. His natural gift for the lucid exposition of technical subjects and his human and often amusing comments on workshop and railroad happenings have made his writings eagerly looked for wherever *Model Engineer* is read. His engines range in character from a very simple working type up to a "Pacific" class engine embodying the latest features of both British and American practice, including the Baker valve gear, and a twelve-coupled goods engine, also Anglo-American in appearance, with four cylinders arranged for eight impulses per revolution, and a tractive effort far exceeding anything else ever built on a similar gauge. He is fond of studying faults in old-time designs, and eliminating them in what he calls "a small edition"; and has promised one or two "real startlers". His work has aroused the interest not only of the private owner, but of some of the foremost locomotive engineers of the country, who have personally inspected his engines under steam and have expressed approval of their experimental and demonstrative value. His whimsical and original outlook on his work is evident from the names he has adopted for some of his productions. There are, for instance, *Simple Sally*, *Helen Long*, *Sir Morris de Cowley*, *Ford Pacific*, and *Ayesha*.

A story is attached to the naming of *Ayesha* which is worth quoting at length. Apart from its interest as the inspiration for the selection of this name, the story as related by "L.B.S.C." himself is a gem of humorous literary condensation, which I feel is deserving of permanent preservation in print. It appears that when *Ayesha* was first constructed, a model engineer looking her over was very sceptical about her wearing qualities. He prophesied an early return to the shops for replacements and repairs. "L.B.S.C.", in referring to this incident, says:

"I guess most of you have read, or anyway heard of Rider Haggard's tale *She*. The lady's name was Ayesha, and through having had a sort of patent firebath in her early days, she 'stayed put' for about 2,000 years without having to bother about lipsticks, face powder, or any other kind of beauty-preserver. With no night clubs, dances, cigarettes, cocktails, etc., her long life was getting a bit tame, when all of a sudden she hit up against the reincarnation of her old lover, whom she had 'done in' in a fit of jealousy all

9

those years ago. 'I had better make sure of keeping him this time,' she thought; and as the firebath department was still going strong she trotted him along to sample it; but not being an engineman who has opened the firehole door without putting the blower on, naturally he felt funky. 'Well,' said Ayesha, 'you're a poor sort of guy, I must say. See here how—if I go in first, will you take a chance?' 'Sure,' said he. 'Then right forward—all aboard!' said Ayesha; and, dressing herself like Lady Godiva, she stepped right into the firebath. But she had forgotten that you can have too much of a good thing; and sad to tell, firebath No. 2 promptly cancelled out the effects of firebath No. 1, so that poor Ayesha just collapsed up into a heap of bones and dust; while her fiance, scared stiff, headed for home with a wide-open throttle. That is how the tale goes—with allowances for 'excessive condensation!' One day the old 'Atlantic' engine was merrily bowling up and down my line at Norbury in charge of a Brighton engineman friend, and I happened to mention about the 'model expert's' pronouncement, at which he laughed heartily. 'Fall to pieces—not she?' said he, emphatically, if ungrammatically. 'Why, bless your soul, she'll be just like Ayesha in Rider Haggard's book— run for 2,000 years before she collapses up into a heap of junk!' Anyway, the name stuck all right, and in due course was consolidated by a pair of little nameplates on the driving splashers."

"L.B.S.C." has inspired hundreds of readers to try their hand at miniature locomotive building, and many hundreds more have profited by his extremely practical workshop hints. This book is produced in response to many requests that the constructive details and data scattered through the locomotive construction articles should be made available for ready reference in a collected form. Here, then, is the result. It does not pretend to be a complete guide to small locomotive building, nor does "L.B.S.C." himself regard it as the last word on the subject. Progress in this field is always being made, and a few of the devices described in the following pages have been improved since they were first designed. They are included, however, partly as a record of "L.B.S.C.'s" original work, and partly because even in their earlier form they have a real practical value. New readers desirous of keeping fully up to date would be well-advised to follow the author's regular weekly notes in *Model Engineer*. The present volume, in addition to being a record of progress during many years, will be found a valuable reference book for details which may be studied with advantage, whatever be the type of locomotive in hand. It will please the several thousand locomotive lovers who already regard "L.B.S.C." as their mentor and their friend. It is hoped that it will bring him many new friends who will admire and profit by his real genius in this fascinating branch of experimental engineering work.

PERCIVAL MARSHALL.

List of Plates

CHAPTER I

Miniature Injectors and Accessories

THERE'S NOTHING AT ALL to be scared of in making, fitting and operating an injector; as a matter of fact, it is easier to make and fit than any pump, and is absolutely "static", having no moving parts. In making it, all you require is care to follow the instructions exactly; in operating, ditto; in maintenance, keep the cones clean. In districts where water is hard, or has been chemically treated, the cones gradually fur up, or become coated with a greenish deposit. This is exactly in accordance with full-size practice, and the big engines' injectors are periodically taken off and cleaned. On the little engine, the same procedure is followed; and it is only a few minutes' work to unscrew three nuts, take out the cones, wipe off any deposit and poke a wire through, and replace the lot, at fairly long intervals.

Injectors are Quite Reliable

The reliability of injectors has been questioned by "doubting Thomases", also the range of pressure at which they will work. Here, you profit by the fact of my experience of both big and little engines. Being pretty conversant with all the ills and ailments that befall full-size injectors, and being an actual maker of small ones, I have tried to incorporate all my experiences into the making of a small injector that will give no trouble either to make, or install and operate. My old engine *Ayesha* could tell you of the hours we have spent together, testing all sorts of injectors with different sizes of cones and different settings; in fact, I don't suppose the old girl remembers what it is like to get a drink of water through a pump, and forgets what pump water tastes like! All my experimenting has been done with the injectors fitted to a locomotive running on a small railway under service conditions.

The injector which I made and fitted to *Cock-o'-the-North* when rebuilding, has a range from blowing-off right down to about 15 lb. and will start at 20 lb., thus giving a starting range of 100 lb. variation. From 120 lb. down to 80 lb. it requires no water regulation; I don't bother to look at the overflow when running, simply opening the water and steam valves when the water is low in the glass, and shutting them again when it gets near the top. The steam pressure varies but little; if the fire is bright, or when pulling hard, the gauge needle barely moves off the 120 mark. The pump is only operated occasionally to keep it in working order. Below 80 lb. the injector

13

can be operated dribble-free by slightly closing the water valve, right down to knock-off point. The above instances of injector working should reassure anybody who thinks he is going to get a packet of trouble by using an injector instead of a pump to feed the boiler.

How to Make the Injector Body

The injector described below is of the well-known "Vic" pattern, first introduced about 50 years ago in a much larger size, and marketed by Eaton, Bertrand Garside, and other old *Model Engineer* advertisers long forgotten. This type is the simplest for a beginner to make; and with my own improvements in the matter of cone sizes, tapers and spacing, will do all that is needed.

The body is made in two pieces, silver-soldered together; the horizontal part containing the cones, and the vertical valve-box containing the ball valve for releasing the air and steam when starting up. Chuck a piece of $\frac{5}{16}$ in. square brass rod truly in the four-jaw; any kind of brass or gunmetal will do, even screw-rod, as there is no movement and consequently no wear. Face the end, centre, and drill down about 1 in. with No. 23 drill. Turn down about $\frac{3}{16}$ in. of the outside to $\frac{1}{4}$ in. diameter, and screw it $\frac{1}{4}$ in. by 40 with a die in the tailstock holder; then face off the end, so that the screwed part is $\frac{5}{32}$ in. long. Some dies, especially well-used ones, usually spoil the first thread or two; and making the screw long at first, then turning away the first couple of threads or so, ensures good threads on the remaining screwed

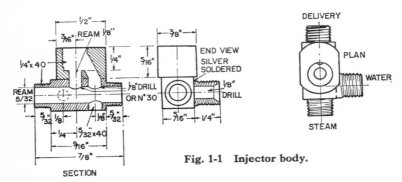

Fig. 1-1   Injector body.

portion. Part off at about $\frac{5}{16}$ in. from the end, and rechuck the piece the other way about. If the metal is truly square, this can be done by slacking Nos. 1 and 2 jaws when removing the stock rod, and tightening the same two when rechucking the parted-off piece; but commercial "square" rod usually isn't, so the best way to ensure accuracy is to rechuck the piece with the screwed end in a tapped bush held in the three-jaw. Anyway, repeat the turning-down-and-screwing operations on the other end, so that when finished, the centre square portion is $\frac{9}{16}$ in. long, with $\frac{5}{32}$ in. of thread projecting at each end, or $\frac{7}{8}$ in. total length. Run a $\frac{5}{32}$ in. parallel reamer through the centre hole.

On the centre-line of one of the facets, make a centre-pop $\frac{1}{4}$ in. from one end, and another $\frac{1}{8}$ in. from the other end. Drill them No. 30; the first one only breaks into the central passageway, but the second goes clean through and comes out the other side. Tap the lower end $\frac{5}{32}$ in. by 40, for the overflow pipe. Next, with the plain side up, and the "thoroughfare" hole to your right, make another pop-mark $\frac{1}{8}$ in. from the left-hand end. Drill this one $\frac{11}{16}$ in. or No. 18, and in it fit a $\frac{1}{4}$ in. by 40 coned union nipple. This gives a side entrance for the water; but the nipple may be fitted underneath if desired.

Valve Box

To make the valve box, chuck a piece of $\frac{1}{2}$ in. brass rod in the three-jaw; face it, and part off a piece a full $\frac{5}{16}$ in. long. The tool mark will clearly indicate the centre; and $\frac{1}{16}$ in. from this make a good deep centre-pop. Next, chuck the piece in the four-jaw with this centre-pop running truly. Drill right through with No. 34 drill; open out about $\frac{3}{16}$ in. depth with $\frac{7}{32}$ in. drill, and bottom the hole with a $\frac{7}{32}$ in. D-bit to a depth of $\frac{1}{4}$ in. exactly. Don't overshoot the platform, or you'll be out the other side! Tap the hole $\frac{1}{4}$ in. by 40, taking care not to let the tap hit the bottom of the hole; slightly countersink the end, and then put a $\frac{1}{8}$ in. parallel reamer through the remnants of the No. 34 hole.

The next operation is where beginners have to watch their step. Stand the fitting upside down on something smooth and solid (I use a square block of iron, truly faced, for a "bench anvil") and at $\frac{3}{16}$ in. from the centre of the reamed hole, make a centre-pop; not too heavy, or you stand a chance of distorting the seating. Run a $\frac{1}{8}$ in. drill into it, slightly on the slant, so that it breaks into the $\frac{1}{4}$ in. tapped hole which forms the ball chamber; see sectional illustration (Fig. 1-1); then clean off any burrs by rubbing the bottom of the fitting on a smooth file laid on the bench.

Assembly

This gadget has now to be silver-soldered to the top of the body. Set it in place so that the two holes line up with the two in the body, as shown in the section, with a light smear of flux between the contact faces; then tie it in place with a bit of thin iron binding wire. Heat the lot to dull red, and touch with a strip of "Easyflo", or ordinary best grade silver-solder, making certain that the molten metal runs right through the joint. This is very important; I recently came across a case of an injector failing through a borax bubble, which formed in the joint. When the injector was first tried, it worked all right, as the borax bubble had formed a seal; but after some little time the combined action of the hot water and the repeated heating and cooling of the injector dispersed the bubble, let the air in, and messed up the works.

The nipple for the water union at the side of the injector body can be silver-soldered at the same heating. When the job has cooled to black, quench out in acid pickle, wash off in water, remove binding wire, clean and polish up.

There is no need to let the sides of the valve box stick out unduly at each side of the body, so they may be filed away almost flush, as shown in the plan view, leaving a bare $\frac{1}{16}$ in. each side of the ball chamber. If preferred, the valve box could be made from a $\frac{5}{16}$ in. length of $\frac{1}{2}$ in. by $\frac{3}{8}$ in. rectangular brass rod, with the ends rounded off before silver-soldering to the body, for the sake of neatness. The piece should be chucked in the four-jaw and machined in exactly the same way as described above. The ball valve and cap are fitted exactly as shown for the check valve in Fig. 1-3.

Vital Points

The two vitally important things to ensure satisfactory working of the injector are (a) the ball seating must be perfect, and (b) the hole through the body of the injector must be accurately reamed, so that the combining cone can be pressed in and made a perfect airtight fit. When the jet of steam meets the water in the combining cone, it condenses, and forms a vacuum in the cone which gives the jet the final kick that sends it across the overflow gap with enough "Sunny Jim" to bump up the clack and enter the boiler. If any air gets in, the jet loses much of its punch, and you get either dribbling at the overflow, or else failure altogether to deliver any water. Simple care in doing the job will well repay the maker by the results obtained. To complete the valve-box part, all you have to do is to fit a $\frac{5}{32}$ in. rustless steel or bronze ball to the seating.

Cone Reamers

If I were one of those awfully learned persons who write instructions in the approved scientific manner, deviating neither to the right nor left, and not daring to "let my face slip" I should now treat you to a dry dissertation on co-efficients, velocities, potential and kinetic energy, angles and degrees of taper, and Uncle Tom Cobleigh and all; and illustrate it with a few rows of cabalistic figures ornamented with various signs, symbols and other hieroglyphics. By the time you had waded through it, presuming your patience held out, you'd be about as wise as you were before, and twice as muddled. However, being one of the world's most unorthodox and unconventional purveyors of instructions, I propose to offer *in lieu*, a few simple do's and don'ts, by following which, you can make a set of injector cones that will squirt enough water into the boiler, to drown all the unpleasant insects mentioned above. I frankly and unashamedly confess that I couldn't read an equation for little toffee-apples; but I have made a lot of injectors—*and they all work*.

First, we need three small reamers, with which to form the tapers in the cones; these are made from $\frac{5}{32}$ in. round silver-steel. Cut off three pieces, each about $2\frac{1}{2}$ in. long. Chuck one in the three-jaw, and with a round-nose tool having a fair top and side rake, turn a taper on it $\frac{3}{4}$ in. long. If your top-slide has a graduated base, set it over to about 6 deg., which will do the necessary; if not, you'll have to set it over correctly by trial and error. When

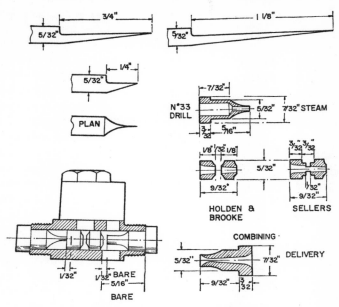

Fig. 1-2 Cone reamers and cones.

O.K., chuck the second piece, and repeat operations, except that the taper this time is $1\frac{1}{8}$ in. long; setting the rest over to 4 deg. should do it. The third piece is tapered very short; merely $\frac{1}{4}$ in., and after getting it to correct length, round it off as shown in the illustration (Fig. 1-2). Judicious wangling of the two slide-rest handles will do it; or the concavity may be formed with a fine file, whilst the lathe is running at a good speed. The exact radius of the curve doesn't matter, as this reamer is only used for belling the mouth of the delivery cone, and putting a small radius on the others where indicated.

Cutting Edges

To make the reamers cut properly and to correct size, exactly half the diameter of the cone must be removed. Too little will cause rubbing, and the reamer will not cut at all; too much will produce a cha'ter-marked and undersized hole. It is very easy to judge the exact amount by careful observation. The easiest way to do the job, is to take off most of the surplus metal with a coarse file, and finish to size with a smooth, or dead smooth one. All three reamers may then be hardened and tempered. I used to do all large reamer hardening by plunging them vertically into a pail of water with a couple of inches of sperm oil floating on top. However, there is no need to go to all that trouble for these weeny gadgets. First heat to medium red, and plunge vertically into clean, cold water; then brighten up the flat part on a piece of fine emerycloth, and—*very* important this—don't let the emery-cloth round off the cutting edges. Lay it on something flat, the lathe bed will do, and very carefully rub the flat part of the taper on it, pressing on the back with your finger; this trick will preserve the edge.

Experienced readers can temper all three at once, but novices and tyros had better do one at a time. Lay the reamer, flat upwards, on a piece of sheet iron or steel, and hold it over a gas flame. The domestic gas stove may be used, the selected burner (smallest) being turned low. Watch the brightened part carefully, and as soon as it changes colour and becomes medium yellow, tip it quickly into cold water again. A vertical plunge isn't essential for tempering, as the metal doesn't become hot enough to crack or distort. Give all three a dose of the same medicine, and then rub the flats on a smooth but fast-cutting oilstone. I keep a brown "India", exclusively for "precision" jobs such as the above. It puts a cutting edge on my little reamers which leaves a perfect surface inside the injector cones; and maybe that is why the jiggers always do the job as per expectation.

Steam Cone

Despite all that has been said and written about the importance of the angle of taper on the entry side of the steam cone, the bald fact remains that I have obtained the best results with a steam cone having no entry taper at all, but merely a plain drilled hole! I always base my "fundamentals" on full-scale practice—this is the reason for the success of my locomotives—and the general reliability and no-trouble starting of the Gresham and Craven injectors on certain classes of the old Brighton engines, led me to adapt some of their features to the small ones. One such feature was the extremely short steam cone with its taper "in reverse"; and to reproduce that in an injector of the "Vic" type, I simply drilled out the inside of the ordinary cone, leaving a little over $\frac{1}{8}$ in. at the end to simulate the Gresham and Craven cone, which was drilled and reamed from the nozzle end. It proved O.K. right away; and since then, as the soap advertisements say, I have used no other.

To make the steam cone, chuck a piece of $\frac{1}{4}$ in. brass rod in the three-jaw; turn down about $\frac{1}{2}$ in. of it to a shade under $\frac{7}{32}$ in. diameter, to fit inside a $\frac{1}{4}$ in. by 40 nut. Face the end, and centre it either with the smallest size centre-drill, or better still, a little stiff arrow-point drill that you could make for yourself from a bit of steel wire. I made several weeny centring drills for injector cone jobs, from broken dental burrs, merely grinding the end flat on both sides like a screwdriver, and then grinding off each side of centre, to form an arrow point. I also made a couple like the cone reamers shown in the illustration (Fig. 1-2), only very small. Drill down about $\frac{1}{4}$ in. depth with No. 64 drill. Turn down $\frac{5}{16}$ in. of the outside to $\frac{5}{32}$ in. diameter, an easy push fit in the injector body; then turn the end to a nozzle shape, as shown. The exact angle of the curves does not matter, but the end should be very nearly parallel; the full diameter part should be about $\frac{5}{32}$ in. long. The diameter of the outside of the nozzle-tip must not be too large; if you own a "mike" make it as near as possible 0.055 in.; if no mike, make it halfway between

$\frac{3}{64}$ in. and $\frac{1}{16}$ in. Now, with the $\frac{3}{4}$ in. taper reamer in the tailstock chuck, slightly enlarge the end of the hole, so that it looks like a piece of very thin tube. Part off the cone to leave a $\frac{3}{32}$ in. flange on the back, as shown in the illustration.

Reverse in chuck, centre, and drill down $\frac{7}{32}$ in. depth· with No. 33 drill; skim off any burrs. Now try a No. 63 drill in the hole; if the "64" has cut correct to size, it shouldn't go through. Enter the point of the $\frac{3}{4}$ in. taper reamer in the hole, and give it one or two twists with your fingers; then try the drill again. If it tries to run through, and jams if twisted with your fingers, you've done enough reaming; put the drill in the tailstock chuck, and poke it through the cone. You then have a proper shaped cone, with a correct-size "63" hole through it, and the weeniest bit of parallel between the two tapers; this is exactly as it should be.

Combining Cone

You can take your choice of two types of combining cone; they are both equally efficient feeders, but the Holden and Brooke is slightly quicker in establishing the jet, or "picking up" as the enginemen call it. To offset that, the Sellers is slightly easier to make and fit. For making either of them chuck the $\frac{1}{4}$ in. brass rod again, and turn down about $\frac{3}{8}$ in. of it to a tight squeeze fit in the injector body. When I say "tight" I mean just that, for the cone must fit absolutely airtight, and not be able to move under the recoil of the jet. With water flying out of the little nozzle with a kick sufficient to bump the clack and get into the boiler against 80 lb. pressure I assure you there is a recoil! I get my proper fit by slightly broaching the steam end of the thorough-fare through the injector body, and turning the cone to suit the slightly enlarged end; the bit of "Sunny Jim" applied by the bush press, soon sends it home to "stay put". Face the end and centre it; then drill down with No. 72 drill for a depth of about $\frac{3}{8}$ in.

I hold the weeny drill in a watchmaker's pin chuck (commercial article which used to cost from 6d. to 1s.) the shank of which is held in the tailstock chuck. If you allow only sufficient amount of drill to project, for the depth of hole required, and work the drill in and out of the hole, so that cuttings cannot choke the flutes, you won't break the drill; and could go full depth of flutes, if required, with confidence. Run the lathe as fast as possible, without rocking the foundations of the house or workshop. After drilling, turn the end to a blunt nose, as shown, and part off at a full $\frac{9}{32}$ in. from the end. If you are making a Sellers cone, before parting off, turn a groove about $\frac{3}{32}$ in. wide and $\frac{1}{32}$ in. deep, with the parting tool, in the middle as shown.

Reverse in chuck; then, with the $\frac{3}{4}$ in. taper reamer in the tailstock chuck, carefully ream out the hole until the extreme point shows beyond the nozzle end of the cone. Now watch your step; put a No. 70 drill in the hole, and see how far it stops short of the end, so you can form some idea of how much more reaming is needed to allow it to pass. I usually pull the belt by hand for the few more turns required, and try the drill in the hole again. When it tries to go through, as before, and jams when turned with your fingers, quit reaming and put the drill through from tailstock chuck, with the lathe running. Finally, chuck the curved taper reamer in the tailstock chuck, and slightly radius out the end to about $\frac{1}{8}$ in. diameter. This gives the water a free run-in, and helps the injector to pick up immediately. Give the end of the cone a final skim off, and bring to dead length. To finish a Sellers type cone, make two $\frac{1}{32}$ in. slots across the bottom of the turned groove, cutting well into the tapered hole; a watchmaker's flat file will do this job well. Clean off any burring inside, by a judicious application of the taper reamer.

To finish a Holden and Brooke cone, chuck it nozzle outwards in the three-jaw with a little over half its length projecting; then with a small hacksaw or a jeweller's piercing saw, cut the cone completely in half, keeping the sawblade against the chuck jaws to ensure a square cut. Slack the chuck jaws slightly, and pull out the half left in them, just sufficiently to allow the saw marks to be skimmed off, and the end of the half-cone backed off to form a very blunt nose as per illustration. Then chuck the other half, sawn end outwards. Beginners can chuck this truly, as easily as eating pie, if they put the little bit of cone on the taper reamer just far enough on so that it does not shake. Put the reamer shank in the tailstock chuck, feed the portion of cone up to the three-jaw, and close same on it when about two-thirds in. Run back the tailstock, and you're all set—literally! Skim off the sawmarks, and back off, as before; then, with the curved reamer in the tailstock chuck, put a very slight radius on the entrance. If you now try both halves together on the taper reamer, there should be a gap of approximately $\frac{1}{32}$ in. between them, when both are just tight enough to prevent shake; this is O.K.

Delivery Cone

Chuck a piece of $\frac{1}{4}$ in. round brass rod, and turn down about $\frac{1}{2}$ in. of it to a bare $\frac{7}{32}$ in. diameter. Face the end, centre, and drill down about $\frac{3}{8}$ in. or so with a No. 76 drill, taking the same precautions and following the same procedure as detailed out above. Turn $\frac{9}{32}$ in. length to $\frac{5}{32}$ in. diameter, a fairly tight push fit in the injector body; then further reduce this for about half length, to the shape shown in the sectional illustration. The diameter at the end should be approximately $\frac{3}{32}$ in. With the curved reamer in the tailstock chuck, bell out the end until only a thin edge is left, as shown; part off at $\frac{3}{8}$ in. from the end. Reverse in chuck, and if the end of the 76 hole is not showing, find it with the smallest size centre drill. Now, with the reamer having the $1\frac{1}{8}$ in. taper, open out the hole, as described above, until a No. 75 drill just "sticks" when pushed in and twisted with your fingers; then put the drill in the pin chuck, hold same in tailstock chuck, and put it through the cone. Finally, bell out the end of the taper hole with the curved reamer, and skim off any burr. The diameter of the hole at the end should be approximately $\frac{1}{8}$ in.

In all the cones, aim for the smoothest possible finish, inside and out. The given "throat" sizes, formed by the 63, 70, and 75 drills, afford sufficient latitude for the injector to operate without cleaning, for fairly long periods, in districts where the water is impure, and scale is deposited. Should you be unlucky in drilling, and your drills "cut large", don't be downhearted and think your work is wasted and will have to be done all over again. Simply make the rest of the cones to match the offender. The following combinations will work equally well, viz., 62-69-74, 61-66-72, or 57-64-71; but the larger the cones, naturally, the fast the feed, and too much water going in at once will make the steam gauge fall back, when feeding on the run. Conversely, experienced workers may care to use a smaller set of cones, with a steadier feed, and no fluctuation of steam pressure when running; 68-72-76, or 70-74-78 will work very well if the feedwater is absolutely clean, but I shouldn't advise anything smaller. I tried an injector with a delivery cone throat drilled only eleven-thousands of an inch, with a home-made arrow-head drill, the combining cone being No. 80. It worked; but on the second run, a tiny fragment of coal dust or grit, small enough to pass promptly "stopped the clock". As I only recommend absolutely reliable gadgets, I shouldn't advise anybody to make an injector with cones that size!

How to Assemble

A part-sectional illustration of the cones in place in the injector body, is given in Fig. 1-2 and there should be no difficulty in assembling them. There is only one fixture, the combining cone; but that must be correctly located, as the amount the steam cone enters it, and the length of the over-flow gap, are both determined by its position. It must also fit absolutely airtight, as the proper working of the injector depends on a perfect vacuum in the combining cone; and any air leak, either between the cone and body, or past the ball valve, will "cattle up the works". Beginners could use a gauge made from a piece of brass rod, an easy fit in the injector bore, and squared off to a bare length of $\frac{5}{16}$ in. This is placed in the delivery end, and the combining cone entered at the steam end, in the slight-broached section. Put the lot between the vice jaws, using a piece of brass rod, countersunk at the end, to press on the end of the combining cone so that it will not be damaged; also use brass or copper clams on the vice jaws.

The Sellers type cone is carefully squeezed in at one go, by turning the handle of the vice until the nozzle of the cone touches the bit of rod used for a gauge; "sight" it through the overflow hole. The Holden and Brooke cone must be squeezed in half at a time; the first half as described above, and the second half in a similar way, except that you can't use the same kind of gauge. Take out the ball valve and put a piece of wire, round or flat, $\frac{1}{32}$ in. in thickness, down the hole, letting it rest against the end of the first half of the combining cone; then press in the other half until it just touches the wire. The other cones can then be pushed in with your fingers, and the spacing should be as shown on the illustration.

Check Valve for Injector

Most injectors fitted to full-sized locomotives have a delivery check-valve placed as close to the injector as possible, in addition to the top or side clack on the boiler. In combination injectors it is usually self-contained. I find on small injectors that the most satisfactory place for the lower clack is on the end of the injector itself, so here is an illustration (Fig. 1-1) of a suitable gadget, and how to make it. Chuck a piece of $\frac{3}{8}$ in. round gunmetal or brass rod in the three-jaw; face the end, centre, and drill down about $\frac{5}{8}$ in. depth with No. 33 drill. Open out about $\frac{1}{4}$ in. depth with $\frac{7}{32}$ in. drill, and bottom the hole to $\frac{3}{8}$ in. depth with $\frac{7}{32}$ in. D-bit. Tap $\frac{1}{4}$ in. by 40 for about $\frac{1}{4}$ in. depth, slightly countersink the hole, and skim off any burr; part off at $\frac{3}{4}$ in. from the end. Make a centre-pop $\frac{3}{16}$ in. from the bottom, and another, diametrically opposite $\frac{5}{32}$ in. from the top; drill out both with $\frac{3}{16}$ in. drill. In the top one, fit a $\frac{1}{4}$ in. by 40 union nipple; the bottom one carries a socket for screwing on the end of the injector, and retaining the delivery cone in place. Chuck the $\frac{3}{8}$ in rod again; face, centre, and drill down about $\frac{7}{16}$ in. with No. 33 drill. Open out to about $\frac{5}{32}$ in. depth with $\frac{7}{32}$ in. drill, and bottom the hole to $\frac{7}{32}$ in. depth with $\frac{7}{32}$ in. D-bit; tap $\frac{1}{4}$ in. by 40. Part-off $\frac{3}{8}$ in. from the end; reverse in chuck, and turn down the other end for about $\frac{3}{32}$ in., to a size that will fit tightly into the hole at the bottom end of the valve body. Squeeze it in, and silver-solder it, and the nipple, at the one heat; clean and polish up.

Put either a $\frac{1}{8}$ in. parallel reamer, or a taper broach of suitable size, down the valve box, enter into the No. 33 hole, and give it a few turns to true up the seating. This is more likely to ensure beginners forming a true ball seat, as the hole is "blind"; if the reamer is applied whilst the piece is in the lathe, it may easily be forced against the bottom of the hole, and spoil its roundness.

If you do it by hand, you can feel if the reamer or broach touches the bottom, and stop turning at once. Then seat a $\frac{5}{32}$ in. ball on the hole, and make a cap for the valve chamber. The ball should have about $\frac{3}{64}$ in. lift, as it does not keep jumping up and down like a pump valve, but stays open all the time the injector is feeding, only closing when the feed ceases.

Screw the completed check valve on to the delivery end of the injector; it should, when right home, stand vertically, in line with the ball chamber on the injector. If it doesn't, don't force it unduly, or put any packing in the recess; merely take out the delivery cone, chuck in three-jaw, flange outwards, and take a slight skim off the flange, which will allow the clack to screw on further. One or two careful shots will do it; the joint must be watertight, but not tight enough to strip the threads.

How to Fit the Injector

The injector may be erected crosswise under the trailing end; and as the whole issue, complete with delivery clack, weighs only an ounce or so, no brackets are needed, the pipes giving all the necessary support. The injector can thus be taken off for cleaning purposes when required, in a matter of seconds, merely by undoing the three union nuts. Its approximate position when erected, is midway between the frames, and a little ahead of the drag-beam, with the top of the clack box a little below frame level, as shown in the illustration (Fig. 1-4). Hold the injector temporarily in position, and with a bit of soft copper or lead wire, make a rough template of the pipe needed

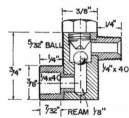

Fig. 1-3
Injector check valve.

between the union on the steam valve on the boiler and the union on the injector, the bends being as easy as possible. Below the footplate, two simple bends will take the pipe to the union on the injector. Straighten out the wire, and use it as a gauge to cut a piece of $\frac{5}{32}$ in. copper tube to length; soften the tube, and fit it with a union nut at each end, plus a cone at the top end, and a plain collar at the bottom, both silver-soldered to the pipe. To make the collar, chuck a bit of $\frac{1}{4}$ in. copper or bronze rod in the three-jaw, turn a $\frac{1}{4}$ in. or so an easy fit in the union nut, face the end, centre, drill about $\frac{1}{8}$ in. down with No. 23 drill, and part-off a slice about $\frac{3}{32}$ in. in thickness. It should be a tight fit on the end of the pipe. Tip to beginners: Silver-solder this first; then if any silver-solder should get on the outside, or on the contact face, you can chuck the pipe in the three-jaw with the collar just projecting beyond the jaws, reface the end, and re-turn to fit the nut. The collar must make an absolutely steam-tight joint against the injector steam cone, without having to tighten up the nut so that there is risk of stripping the threads. Then slip the nuts on, back to back, put on the cone, and silver-solder that very carefully. After dipping the lot in the pickle, washing off, and rubbing up pipe and nuts with a bit of fine steel wool, bend the pipe to shape with your fingers, which will avoid any kinking, and preserve its pristine beauty. I do like to see neat plumbing work on a little locomotive, especially when in full view on the backhead. Couple the collar end of the pipe to the injector, and try the lot in place; adjust pipe bends where necessary, then couple up the top union to the steam valve.

Fitting Pipework

With another bit of copper or lead wire, take the distance from the union on the injector clack, to the clack box on the right-hand side of the boiler. Run the wire down by the side of the ashpan, close to the frames, and then take a sweeping curve upward to the clack box. Straighten out the wire, and use it as a gauge to get the correct length of $\frac{5}{32}$ in. pipe, proceeding exactly as described above, except that a cone is fitted at both ends of the pipe. Be careful not to kink the pipe when making the fairly sharp bend at the injector end.

With a reliable injector, there is really no need for a long overflow pipe, and experienced drivers would find that a bit of $\frac{5}{32}$ in. pipe about $\frac{1}{2}$ in. long, would be quite satisfactory to carry off the overflow when starting; this is simply screwed into the overflow hole on the injector. However, most full-sized engines have the ends of the overflow pipes brought to the outside of the engine, usually under the footsteps, so that the enginemen can see them when operating the injectors; and this can easily be done in the present instance, in the manner shown in the illustration. Bend a bit of $\frac{5}{32}$ in. soft copper pipe into a swan-neck shape as illustrated; put a few $\frac{5}{32}$ in. by 40 threads on the short end, and screw into the overflow hole on the injector. Bend the longer end so that it comes nicely under the step, and secure it with a little clip made from $\frac{1}{32}$ in. sheet brass or copper, fixed with a couple of 10 BA screws.

We now need a bracket to carry the feed-pipe, and the union for the pipe from the hand pump in the tender; this is made from a piece of 16-gauge steel, 1 in. wide and $1\frac{1}{8}$ in. long. Bend at right-angles at $\frac{3}{8}$ in. from one end, then drill two holes at $\frac{1}{2}$ in. centres; one $\frac{5}{32}$ in. clearing (No. 21 drill) and the other $\frac{1}{4}$ in. In the short side, drill two No. 40 holes for the $\frac{3}{32}$ in. or 7 BA screws which hold the bracket to the underside of the drag beam. The bracket is then fixed in the position shown, a simple job needing no detailing-out. A short piece of $\frac{5}{32}$ in. pipe is attached to the water inlet of the injector by a union nut and cone, and passes through the right-hand hole, as shown in the side view; it should project about $\frac{1}{2}$ in., and when the engine and tender are coupled up, a simple bit of rubber pipe is slipped over it and its "mate" on the tender, forming a perfectly satisfactory "feed-bag", as the enginemen call it, needing no additional fastening. The best stuff for feed-bags, is the thick grey corrugated tubing used for automobile windscreen wipers, and similar uses, which just fits nicely over a $\frac{5}{32}$ in. pipe. A very handy place for an injector with the water union at the bottom, is down by the side of the cab, under the running board, as shown in the photograph of *Ayesha*. The steam and water pipes are connected as described; the delivery pipe may either be taken to the left-hand side boiler clack, along the underside of the running-board, or to a separate clack on the side of the firebox wrapper inside the cab, which needs only a very short delivery pipe. *Ayesha* has the latter arrangement.

Injector Water-Valve

Chuck a piece of $\frac{7}{16}$ in. hexagon or round rod in the three-jaw; face the end, centre, and drill down about $1\frac{1}{4}$ in. depth with $\frac{3}{32}$ in. drill. Open out to $\frac{1}{2}$ in. depth with No. 30 drill, and bottom with a D-bit to $\frac{9}{16}$ in. depth. Tap $\frac{5}{32}$ in. by 32 (for quick opening) but don't go down far enough to spoil the seating. Turn down $\frac{9}{16}$ in. of the outside to $\frac{3}{8}$ in. diameter, screw it $\frac{3}{8}$ in. by 40, then turn away the threads for $\frac{7}{16}$ in. length. At the point where the plain part ends, drill a $\frac{1}{8}$ in. cross hole. Part off at about 1 in. from the end; reverse

Fig. 1-4 How to erect a "side-entrance" injector.

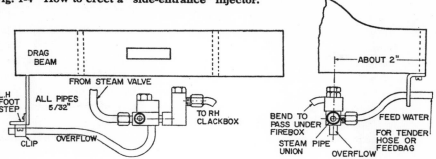

in chuck, taper off the end as shown (Fig. 1-5), open out the hole for about $\frac{3}{16}$ in. depth with No. 23 drill, and skim off any burr.

The valve-pin is made from a $2\frac{1}{2}$ in. length of $\frac{5}{32}$ in. rustless steel or bronze rod. Chuck in three-jaw, and turn a rather blunt cone point on the end, which gives a quicker opening than a long taper. Turn about $\frac{1}{4}$ in. length to $\frac{1}{8}$ in. diameter, then screw a further $\frac{3}{8}$ in. or so to match the tapped hole in the valve body described above. Reverse in chuck, and turn down $\frac{3}{16}$ in. of the other end to $\frac{1}{8}$ in. diameter. Fit a boss $\frac{1}{4}$ in. diameter and $\frac{3}{16}$ in. in thickness on this; it need be only a tight push fit. Drill a No. 43 cross hole through the boss, force in a piece of $\frac{3}{32}$ in. silver-steel with the ends rounded-off, and silver-solder the lot. The gland is merely a bit of $\frac{3}{8}$ in. hexagon rod $\frac{1}{2}$ in. long, with a No. 21 hole through it. One end is turned down to $\frac{1}{4}$ in. diameter for $\frac{1}{8}$ in. length, and the other for $\frac{1}{4}$ in. length, both being screwed $\frac{1}{4}$ in. by 40; the longer end is furnished with a gland nut made from same size rod.

Drill a $\frac{7}{32}$ in. hole in the tender soleplate, $\frac{5}{8}$ in. from the front of the tank, and in line with the injector water-pipe on the engine; that is, about level with the left side of the coal gate. Let the drill go right through the bottom of the coal space. Tap the upper hole $\frac{1}{4}$ in. by 40 for the gland, open up the lower one to $\frac{11}{32}$ in. and tap $\frac{3}{8}$ in. by 40 for valve, screw them in, and solder around both; then screw the valve pin into position, and pack the gland with a few strands of graphited yarn.

General Remarks

An important point to note for successful injector working is that the cones must be *absolutely dead in line*; so watch that your drills and reamers do not "run out" when making them, or the water will follow suit via the overflow, instead of forcing its way past the clack and entering the boiler. During my experiments I found that another generally accepted idea was a myth, namely, that one needs a large delivery pipe or an "outsize" in clack boxes. When fitting a top feed to a $2\frac{1}{2}$ in. gauge Great Western engine, I simply ran a $\frac{5}{32}$ in. thin-walled pipe from the injector (which was fitted in the same position as shown in the photograph of *Ayesha*) to an elbow alongside the safety-valve casing, in two easy bends. The waterway through the elbow was larger than the bore of the pipe, so that the flow of water was not restricted in the slightest; a small bend attached to the elbow inside the boiler threw the incoming water towards the smokebox tubeplate. This arrangement worked perfectly. These small injectors will not start if they get hot, which is the reason for placing them as low as possible so that they may be flooded and rendered perfectly cold by just turning on the water; then if you smack the steam valve wide open they pick up at once.

Simple Clack Box Without Union

The following is a description of how to make a simple clack box, which is quite satisfactory to use with either injector or pump, and is correct in appearance. Chuck a length of $\frac{3}{8}$ in. round gunmetal or bronze rod, leaving 1 in. projecting; centre, and drill 1 in. down with a No. 25 drill. Open out $\frac{3}{8}$ in. deep with $\frac{7}{32}$ in. drill, tap $\frac{1}{4}$ in. by 40 threads for about $\frac{1}{4}$ in. down; square off the bottom of the enlarged hole with a $\frac{7}{32}$ in. D-bit and ream $\frac{5}{32}$ in. to form the seating for the clack ball, which is $\frac{3}{16}$ in. diameter. Take a light cut over the outside to true up, turn to the shape of a big clack box as shown in the drawing (Fig. 1-6), and part off. At $\frac{7}{32}$ in. from the large end, drill a $\frac{3}{16}$ in. hole, and mind you don't run foul of and damage the valve seat. If you do, it can be corrected—only you must chuck by the flange and set to run truly—the $\frac{7}{32}$ in. D-bit being used (in a chuck on the tailstock) to correct the damage.

Next we want the connection to the boiler. Chuck a piece of $\frac{5}{16}$ in. rod, centre and drill down $\frac{3}{32}$ in. or No. 40 for $\frac{5}{8}$ in. in depth; turn down the outside to $\frac{7}{32}$ in. for $\frac{3}{8}$ in. in length, and reduce the end to a tight fit in the $\frac{3}{16}$ in. drilled hole in the body of the clack box. Part off at $\frac{5}{8}$ in., reverse, and turn down the other end for $\frac{3}{16}$ in. length to $\frac{3}{16}$ in. diameter; thread this 40 t.p.i., leaving a $\frac{5}{16}$ in. diameter collar between the thread and the turned part. Tap the branch gently into the clack box body with a piece of wood or something that will not damage the thread, and make certain that they are at right-angles, and silver-solder the joint. From the $\frac{3}{8}$ in. rod make a little cap to fit the top of the box, leaving a piece projecting inside to prevent the ball rising more than $\frac{1}{32}$ in. full, and also leaving a $\frac{1}{8}$ in. projection at the top, which should be filed square to take a small spanner. The boiler connection may be made shorter if desired.

Finishing and Fitting Up

Clean up the outside and brush the scale from the inside; a few minutes in a drop of sulphuric acid "pickle"—one part of acid to fifteen of water— works wonders. Now stand the clack box on a lead block, drop a $\frac{3}{16}$ in. steel ball on the seating; place one end of a $\frac{3}{16}$ in. brass "dolly" on the ball and give the other end a sharp "biff" with the hammer. This is a well-known method of making a true and tight ball seating, but use a little discretion with the bumping part; don't clump it hard enough to drive the clack box right into the lead, but hard enough to take the sharp arris off the ball seat.

Replace the steel ball by a bronze one and screw the cap in. Make a little stepped bush from $\frac{3}{8}$ in. rod, screwed $\frac{5}{16}$ in. outside and $\frac{3}{16}$ in. inside. Screw and sweat it into the boiler shell; screw the clack box in with a smear of plumbers' jointing paste on the threads. Then carefully fit the end of the pump or injector delivery pipe into the lower recess in the clack box and secure with a touch of solder. This is much neater than an unsightly great union nut under a clumsy-looking square or hexagon fitting; true, it needs the application of a hot soldering-bit to disconnect it, but a satisfactory clack box seldom needs removing, so this is no drawback. *Ayesha's* clacks are exactly as described above.

Top Feeds

Where a big engine is fitted with a top feed, fit one also to her little sister. A *working* clack box on a boiler barrel of 3 in. or less diameter, would be too small for satisfactory working; so fit your clack directly to the injector as previously described. Connect a length of $\frac{5}{32}$ in. or $\frac{1}{8}$ in. pipe by the usual union nut and cone, to the top of the clack; this pipe can then be led up to the top of the boiler and attached to a diminutive dummy clack box to preserve the "scale" appearance; the said box having just plain holes drilled in it as large as the fittings will allow. It is silver-soldered to the manhole cover or screwed into the side of a dome, according to the type of engine being built.

There is no need to rig up any device for screwing a "floating" bronze ball down on the seating. This answers all right about three times; then the ball gets marked with rings, and finally looks something like a golf ball on a saw-toothed seating, besides being about as tight as a sieve. You can screw a *coned* valve on its seating if you will, as it always seats in the same place; but not a loose ball, unless it is rustless steel, hard enough to resist marking.

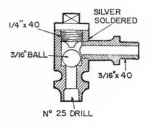

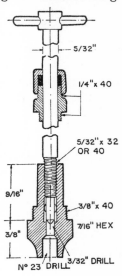

Fig. 1-5
(right) Injector water valve for inside of tender tank.

Fig. 1-6
(top left) Simple clack box or check valve.

Fig. 1-7
(bottom left) Injector steam valve.

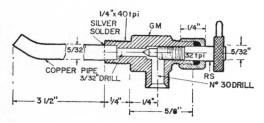

Injector Steam Valve

A suitable steam valve for the injector described can be made from a $\frac{7}{8}$ in. length of $\frac{5}{16}$ in. hexagon bronze or gunmetal rod. Chuck in three-jaw, face the end, centre, and drill right through with No. 42 or $\frac{3}{32}$ in. drill. Open out and bottom to $\frac{1}{2}$ in. depth with No. 30 drill and $\frac{1}{8}$ in. D-bit. Further open out $\frac{1}{8}$ in. depth with No. 21 drill, and tap the No. 30 section either $\frac{5}{32}$ in. by 32, or 40. Turn down $\frac{1}{4}$ in. diameter, and screw $\frac{1}{4}$ in. by 40. Reverse in chuck, open out $\frac{1}{8}$ in. of the other end with No. 23 drill, turn down $\frac{1}{4}$ in. length to $\frac{1}{4}$ in. diamter, and screw $\frac{1}{4}$ in. by 40.

At $\frac{1}{4}$ in. from the shoulder, drill a $\frac{3}{16}$ in. hole in one of the facets; and in it, fit a $\frac{1}{4}$ in. by 40 union nipple. Fit a piece of $\frac{5}{32}$ in. thin-walled copper tube in the plain hole in the end, and silver-solder that and the nipple at the same heat. Pickle, wash off and clean up. The valve pin is a $\frac{7}{8}$ in. length of $\frac{5}{32}$ in. round rustless steel or phosphor bronze. Turn down one end to $\frac{1}{8}$ in. diameter for about $\frac{5}{32}$ in. length, and form a cone point on the end; a quick way of doing this, is to hold a smooth flat file at such an angle that it will form a point about 90 deg., and sweep it across the end of the pin, with the lathe running fairly fast. Screw about $\frac{5}{16}$ in. length of the pin to match the tapped thread in the valve body. File a square on the other end, and fit a little hand-wheel, turned from $\frac{3}{8}$ in. round rod, on the end. If preferred, a peg may be screwed into the rim of this, as shown in Fig. 1-7, to afford a better grip for oily fingers. The gland nut is made exactly the same as a union nut, and packed with a few strands of graphited yarn.

This valve may be screwed into the backhead at any convenient place, if the pipe is bent to come as close to the top of the boiler as possible, so that the injector gets dry steam. It is connected to the injector as described previously.

CHAPTER II

Hand and Axle-Driven Pumps

A BOILER FEED PUMP for a $2\frac{1}{2}$ in. gauge engine can be driven from an eccentric on the driving axle. Failing a cast stay, make it from a piece of $\frac{1}{8}$ in. brass, $1\frac{5}{16}$ in. long, $1\frac{1}{8}$ in. wide, with a piece of $\frac{5}{16}$ in. angle brass riveted to each side, for screwing to the frames as shown in the plan. Put a $\frac{7}{16}$ in. by 32 tapped hole plumb in the middle.

If a casting is available for the pump barrel and valve box, chuck by one end of the latter held in three-jaw, and set the other end to run truly. Face off, centre, drill right through No. 32, open out with a $\frac{7}{32}$ in. drill, and bottom with a $\frac{7}{32}$ in. D-bit to $\frac{3}{8}$ in. depth; slightly countersink the end, tap $\frac{1}{4}$ in. by 40 and skim off any burr. Tip for beginners: to chuck the other way around, for machining the bottom end of the valve box, chuck any odd scrap of rod $\frac{3}{8}$ in. or over, turn a $\frac{1}{4}$ in. pip on the end about $\frac{3}{16}$ in. long and screw it $\frac{1}{4}$ in. by 40. Don't take it out of the chuck, but screw the already-tapped end of the valve box on it; you can then ditto-repeato the above operations, except that the D-bit need not be used. Nick the central waterway as shown in the sectional sketch, and then poke a $\frac{1}{8}$ in. reamer through what is left of the central hole. Next chuck by the tenon, which will be on the casting opposite the barrel, and set the latter to run truly. Face the end, centre, and drill a $\frac{1}{8}$ in. hole right through into the valve box; open it out to $\frac{5}{8}$ in. depth with a $\frac{5}{16}$ in. drill. Turn the outside to $\frac{7}{16}$ in. diameter, and screw it $\frac{7}{16}$ in. by 32 for a bare $\frac{1}{2}$ in. length. Saw off the chucking tenon and clean up the outside.

Failing a casting, use a 1 in. length of $\frac{3}{8}$ in. brass rod for the valve box, and machine it as above, chucking in three-jaw and just turning it end-for-end to drill and tap the second half. The barrel is made from a piece of $\frac{1}{2}$ in. rod, chucked in three-jaw and machined as above. Part-off at $\frac{3}{4}$ in. from the end, then file a half-round groove in the plain end, and silver-solder it to the middle of the valve box. Run the $\frac{5}{16}$ in. drill into the barrel, make a countersink on the valve box, put a $\frac{1}{8}$ in. drill through and you have the counterpart of the casting. Screw it into the stay on the side opposite to the angles, as shown.

The top and bottom connections can be made from tee castings, if you have any. Grip one end of a tee in three-jaw, face, centre deeply, and drill right through $\frac{1}{8}$ in. Turn down $\frac{1}{4}$ in. of the outside to $\frac{1}{4}$ in. diameter and screw $\frac{1}{4}$ in. by 40. Reverse, and chuck in a tapped bush held in three-jaw.

Drop a $\frac{5}{32}$ in. rustless steel ball in the valve box, seat it the usual way, and take the depth from ball to top. Turn the other end of the tee to $\frac{1}{32}$ in. less than the depth, screw $\frac{1}{4}$ in. by 40, and cross nick the end. Chuck by the tenon which will be found on the casting, and turn the stem same as the top, drilling it $\frac{1}{8}$ in.; cut off the tenon, file up and assemble as shown. If no casting is available, make the vertical part of the fitting from an inch of $\frac{3}{8}$ in. round brass rod, and the nipple from $\frac{1}{4}$ in. ditto, drilling a $\frac{3}{16}$ in. hole $\frac{3}{16}$ in. from the shoulder, turning down the plain end of the nipple to fit same tightly, and silver-soldering it in.

The bottom fitting can be made from a similar casting in like manner, except that only half of the tee is used, the other end being cut off flush with the stem.

If you would rather build up, chuck a $\frac{3}{4}$ in. piece of $\frac{3}{8}$ in. brass rod in three-jaw; drop a ball into the valve box, and turn the end of the rod to a length equal to *same distance* from ball to bottom of box. Screw $\frac{1}{4}$ in. by 40. Centre the end, drill No. 32 for $\frac{1}{2}$ in. depth, and ream $\frac{1}{8}$ in.; skim $\frac{1}{32}$ in. off the screwed end, to form a true seating for the ball, and give the necessary clearance. Drill a $\frac{3}{16}$ in. hole $\frac{3}{16}$ in. from the bottom, and silver-solder a $\frac{1}{4}$ in. by 40 nipple into it, same as for the upper fitting. Seat the ball on the faced hole by the usual biff, and assemble as shown in the sectional sketch (Fig. 2-1).

The ram is a piece of $\frac{5}{16}$ in. rustless steel, bronze or nickel rod, $1\frac{5}{16}$ in. overall length, $\frac{3}{16}$ in. of one end being turned down to $\frac{3}{32}$ in. diameter, to form the anti-airlock pin. The other end is slotted in a similar manner to coupling rod knuckles, the slot being $\frac{3}{32}$ in. full wide, and it is cross-drilled No. 43. I have shown the end rounded off, to make it look pretty, but if left square it will pump just the same. The gland nut is made from $\frac{7}{16}$ in. of $\frac{5}{8}$ in. round rod drilled $\frac{5}{16}$ in. in the three-jaw, then opened out and tapped $\frac{7}{16}$ in. by 32 to screw on the barrel. If four slots are made in the nut, it may be turned by aid of a miniature C-spanner, or even a screwdriver; or if you so desire, a hexagon gland nut may be used. The gland is packed with a few strands of graphited yarn.

Clean up the cast eccentric strap with a file, drill the lugs No. 48, then put it in the bench vice and saw across the middle, using vice top as guide. Tap the holes in the larger piece 7 BA, and open the others with No. 41 drill; the pieces may then be screwed together, chucked in four-jaw with the core hole running as truly as possible, and bored to fit on the eccentric. Face one side; the other side can be faced with the strap on a stub mandrel held in the chuck. I use a miniature three-jaw chuck which holds eccentric straps and other small-holed pieces from the inside—anything to save time! File the eccentric rod from a piece of $\frac{1}{2}$ in. by $\frac{3}{32}$ in. steel strip about $\frac{3}{4}$ in. long, to the shape shown, and rivet and solder it into a $\frac{3}{32}$ in. slot milled or filed in the lug provided for same on the eccentric strap.

Set the pump between the frames with the valve box clearing the leading coupled axle by $\frac{1}{8}$ in., and the centre line of the pump barrel $\frac{5}{8}$ in. from bottom of frames; secure it with three 7 BA countersunk screws each side, running through the holes already drilled in the frames, into tapped holes in the angles. Put on the eccentric strap, line up the eccentric (which should be set on front dead centre) with the pump ram, push the latter right home, and put the eccentric rod in the slot. With a bent scriber, scribe a little circle on the rod through the cross hole in the ram. Remove, make a centre-dot $\frac{1}{32}$ in. nearer the strap than indicated by the centre of the little circle; drill it No. 41, replace strap, and squeeze in a wrist-pin made from a bit of $\frac{3}{32}$ in. silver-steel. Don't have the pump gland screwed up so tightly that you nearly wrench a wheel off the axle if you try to turn it; the gland needs to be screwed up just sufficiently to prevent water leaking past, and no more. If the gland is tight in every sense of the word, it puts a needless strain on the working parts of the engine, and mops up power that would otherwise be available at the drawbar.

When a pump is fitted to a small locomotive having top feeds, such as the Great Western engines, a special arrangement is necessary, as there are no clack boxes on the boiler owing to the difficulty of fitting them in a respectable working size. If the pump is fitted with *two* delivery clacks, this gets

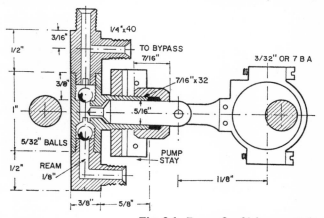

Fig. 2-1 Pump for 2½-in. gauge locomotive.

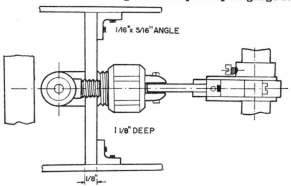

over the trouble, and the by-pass can be easily arranged between them. I might mention here that wherever I can arrange for a top feed I do so. It is just as beneficial to a little engine as it is to a large one, for I have found that squirting the feed water into the steam space seems to "atomise" the lime, chalk, etc., in it; so that if you wash the boiler out with a strong solution of washing soda after about twenty hours' steaming, the deposit comes away in powdery form or else in fine flakes.

Fitting Pump for Top Feeds

There is another advantage of top feed, and that is, in the event of a clack sticking up, you don't lose any water from the boiler. The method I give here practically puts out of court any trouble from furring, and a good strainer in the tender will keep the dirt down to the minimum. Fig. 2-2 shows the different arrangement of the pump delivery clacks and by-pass. Instead of the upper fitting shown in Fig. 2-1, another clack box with a long stem carrying a union for the return pipe is screwed into the top of the valve box on the pump. To make it, chuck a piece of $\frac{3}{8}$ in. round gunmetal rod $\frac{7}{8}$ in. long, centre, and put a No. 34 drill right through it. Open out with a $\frac{7}{32}$ in. or No. 3 drill for a depth of $\frac{11}{32}$ in. and square off the bottom of the hole with a $\frac{7}{32}$ in. D-bit to form the ball seating. Tap $\frac{1}{4}$ in. by 40 threads for $\frac{1}{4}$ in. down, counterbore one thread away to let the cap seat tightly when fitted, and face off the end. True up the ball seat with a $\frac{1}{8}$ in. reamer.

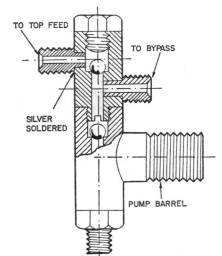

TO TOP FEED

TO BYPASS

SILVER
SOLDERED

PUMP BARREL

**Fig. 2-2
Arrangement of
valves for topfeed.**

Reverse in chuck and turn the other end down, as show in Fig. 2-1, and screw it 40 threads per inch. Remove from chuck and saw or file four nicks in the threaded end. Now screw it into the valve box and see that it seats right home; then at a distance of $\frac{9}{16}$ in. from the top, mark off a place to drill the hole for fitting the union for return pipe. This may either be pointing directly to the rear of the pump or toward either frame, according to where it is most convenient to fit the return pipe on the engine. At $\frac{3}{16}$ in. from the top, another spot is marked off for drilling the hole for delivery pipe union. This fitting should point toward the frame in a forward direction so that the delivery pipe may be led round the boiler barrel with the minimum amount of bending. Remove the clack box from the pump and drill holes at the places marked, using a No. 22 or $\frac{5}{32}$ in. drill. Make up two union fittings from $\frac{1}{4}$ in. round rod, turn them down to fit the holes in the clack box and silver-solder them in. If preferred, the holes in the clack box can be drilled No. 30 and tapped $\frac{5}{32}$ in. by 40 threads, the shanks of the unions screwed to suit, and the joints sweated over.

Next fit a $\frac{5}{32}$ in. rustless steel or bronze ball and a cover to the clack box, making the cover long enough to just allow the ball $\frac{1}{32}$ in. lift when screwed home. Then screw the completed fitting into the valve box on the pump, carefully noting that it does not crush the pump delivery valve hard on its seating. If it does, file a little off the stem, and if the suction valve is taken off the pump *pro tem*, a copper wire poked up through the waterway will serve to gauge the lift of the ball. Finally, assemble with a smear of plumber's jointing on the threads and erect the pump in the frames.

Piping Up

Cut off a length of $\frac{1}{8}$ in. thin-walled tube long enough to reach from the return pipe union to the rear buffer beam; or on a tank engine, to the cab steps. Fit a union collar and nut at one end and a plug cock at the other, and couple up. On a tender engine, arrange the cock under the footplate, fit an extension wire handle to it, and provide a tail-piece to take the hose connection to tender. On a tank engine, fit the cock under the edge of the overhanging footplate so that the handle is unobtrusive and yet get-at-able; and lead the final length of return pipe to the top of the tank and terminate it at the filling hole, so that you can see the water come through when the by-pass cock is opened. A screw-down valve may be used in place of a plug cock, which is an advantage, as the by-pass may be regulated with greater nicety; a suitable valve is described later.

Turning to top-feed delivery pipes, for the Great Western pattern, holes should be drilled in the boiler shell (using No. 21 drill) at either side of the safety-valve bushing. Tap these $\frac{3}{16}$ in. by 40 threads and make two elbow fittings by chucking a length of $\frac{5}{16}$ in. round gunmetal rod, centring and drilling up $\frac{3}{8}$ in. with a No. 40 drill. Turn down $\frac{1}{4}$ in. length to a diameter of $\frac{3}{16}$ in. and screw 40 threads. Part off at $\frac{1}{2}$ in. from the end, and repeat the process. Drill a hole in the side of each plain part to take the end of delivery pipe. Put the boiler in place on the frames, and, using a piece of copper wire for a template in order to get the correct bends, ascertain how long the pipe will be to reach from the pump delivery union to the safety-valve casing. Cut a tube to length; silver-solder a union cone on one end. Slip the union nut on and silver-solder the other end into one of the elbow fittings, softening the pipe at the same time.

Clean up—the pickle bath after silver-soldering will probably be sufficient —and file the elbow fitting carefully to the shape of a G.W. top clack casing. Screw it in to the boiler; the soft pipe will allow this to be done quite easily, and then sweat the joint. The pipe can now be neatly bent round the boiler barrel and the end with the union nut led to the clack box on the pump. A special bent spanner will probably be needed to screw the union up tightly, but this is a plain filing job and any odd piece of $\frac{1}{8}$ in. plate can be utilised. The other elbow fitting on the opposite side of the safety-valve is filed to shape and connected to the injector delivery, or else a long pipe is led from it to a clack under the drag beam for the hand pump connection. Another arrangement of top feed fitting includes a bent pipe silver-soldered into the elbow, to squirt the delivery towards the front end of the barrel. As the elbow could not be screwed into the shell with the bend attached, an oval flange is silver-soldered to it. A clearing hole is drilled in the boiler shell, the elbow with pipe attached then inserted, and the flange secured by two brass screws running into tapped holes in the boiler shell. Flange and screws may be sweated over, as they don't have to be removed any more.

Pump for 3½ in. Gauge "Atlantic"

Figs. 2-3 and 2-4 show a pump suitable for a $3\frac{1}{2}$ in. gauge Atlantic type engine, arranged ahead of the leading coupled axle, which permits a long eccentric rod being used. The construction is similar to the pump already described, except that the pump barrel is set at an angle to the valve box, as shown. The special shape of the stay allows the pump barrel to be set low enough for the ram to clear the front coupled axle.

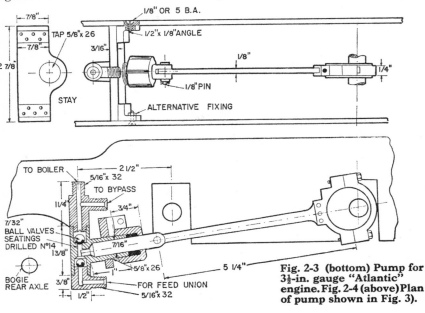

Fig. 2-3 (bottom) Pump for 3½-in. gauge "Atlantic" engine. Fig. 2-4 (above) Plan of pump shown in Fig. 3).

Inside Cylinder Engine Pumps

Anyone wishing to fit a pump of the type last described to an inside cylinder 4-4-0, or single-wheeler, or any other engine where space underneath is limited, can do so by making small alterations as follows: The best place for attaching the pump is underneath the motion plate. Screw the pump barrel into an inverted L-shaped bracket, which can be attached to the underside of the motion plate by suitable screws. Arrange pump and bracket so that a line drawn through centre of barrel cuts centre of driving axle in its running position, and set the valve box to stand exactly vertical. The only point to stress is that the bottom of the motion plate needs filing flat where the bracket is attached, and fairly big screws used for fixing in order to eliminate rock. The delivery pipe passes up between the two sets of slide bars; and, if required for a top feed engine, fit the second clack just above the bars under the boiler barrel.

More Pump Variations

Similar pumps to that shown in Fig. 2-1 can be made to a size suitable for gauge "1" engines. To make a barrel for $\frac{1}{4}$ in. pump ram, part off a length of $\frac{3}{8}$ in. round gunmetal rod $\frac{13}{16}$ in. long. This is for a $\frac{3}{8}$ in. stroke; if a longer stroke is required, cut off a proportionally longer piece. Chuck, centre, and put a No. 40 drill right through; then open out for $\frac{9}{16}$ in. depth with $\frac{1}{4}$ in. drill. Screw the outside with a $\frac{3}{8}$ in. by 32 thread for a length of $\frac{5}{16}$ in.; reverse in chuck, turn the other end to a spigot $\frac{3}{16}$ in. long and $\frac{5}{32}$ in. in diameter for attaching to valve box. Make a gland nut $\frac{5}{16}$ in. long from a piece of $\frac{1}{2}$ in. hexagon stuff or, alternatively, from a piece of $\frac{1}{2}$ in. round rod slotted for C-spanner operation. Now take the cross stay and offer it up on the engine in its ultimate place; then mark off on it a line level with the centre of driving axle in running position. At this level and midway between the brackets for attaching to frames drill an $\frac{11}{32}$ in. hole and tap it $\frac{3}{8}$ in. by 32 threads. After the valve box is silver-soldered to the pump barrel at right-angles to it, the threaded part of the barrel is screwed into the cross stay (Fig. 2-6) and finally secured from turning by a touch of soft solder. On a small-wheeled engine it may be necessary to fit a shaped cross stay, as shown in the sketch (Fig. 2-5), in order to bring the pump barrel level with the axle.

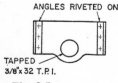

Fig. 2-5
Small pump stay.

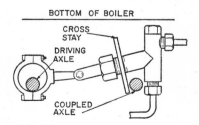

Fig. 2-7
Diagonal pump for gauge "1"
"Atlantic" engine.

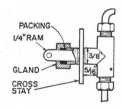

Fig. 2-6
Pump for gauge "1"
engine.

It will be seen that this method of construction and suspension gives an exceedingly short and robust pump, and the ram is well supported at two points. Working to the sizes given, the ram is still a full $\frac{1}{8}$ in. in barrel (allowing for clearances) at the outer end of the stroke; and having the gland to guide it on its return journey into the barrel, *the said gland only being $\frac{5}{16}$ in. or so ahead of the point of suspension*, the pump will be found to work with the minimum of friction, and all endency to rock will be eliminated. The short pump also has another great advantage—it allows bags of room for a fairly decent eccentric rod, sometimes difficult to fit to a gauge "1" engine.

Where Space is Limited

It happens sometimes that you cannot help being tied up for space. Now on a gauge "1" "Atlantic" loco. that I rebuilt, I provided an entirely new pump with a barrel set at an angle with the valve box (Fig. 2-7); and I mounted it on the engine so that the leading coupled axle passed under the angle so formed. This allowed the barrel to line up with the driving axle and prevented undue angularity of the eccentric-rod on either extremity. The clack balls were $\frac{5}{32}$ in. diameter and rested on seatings formed by No. 34 drill reamed $\frac{1}{8}$ in. and D-bitted. I left the original eccentric on (after pinning it to the axle, so that it could not repeat its fancy trick of shifting and upsetting the valve timing—it was in one piece with the stop collar), and as the stroke was a little longer than I should put on for a fast-running pump—$\frac{7}{16}$ in.—I fitted *two* external delivery clacks: one under the running board and one on the side of the boiler. The engine was of the American pattern, so I branched off the return pipe from between the two clacks, led it along underneath the running board and placed the by-pass cock under the cab just in front of the footstep.

Summing up eccentric driven pumps, the points to watch for perfect working are: fairly large bore and short stroke; ample sized ball valves with restricted lift; the minimum clearance in the pump itself, and the water pipes (especially the suction) of sufficient diameter not to throttle the flow of water. Don't forget to put a fine gauze strainer on the end of the suction pipe in the water tank—it will save a lot of heart burning and unparliamentary language.

Tender Hand Pump

The emergency hand pump is just an insurance against the boiler running short of water. You may never have to use it; on my own engines, it is very seldom used after first test, though I always make sure it is in working order by giving a few strokes every time an engine is steamed up. More often than not, among average amateur locomotive-builders, the pump is an insurance against human fallibility, and has saved many a boiler when, in the excitement of running, the driver has clean forgotten that the boiler needs a constant supply of water, and neglected to put the injector on, or regulate the by-pass of the eccentric-driven pump, and the water has disappeared in the bottom nut of the gauge.

No castings are needed at all. The stand is a piece of $\frac{3}{32}$ in. brass or copper, 1 in. wide and a little over 4 in. in length. This is bent to the shape of one of the old G.W.R. broad gauge "bridge" rails, as shown in the sectional drawing. If you have a piece of 1 in. square bar anywhere handy, bend it over that, and you'll find that the job will come out right size. Drill a $\frac{1}{8}$ in. hole in the middle of the top, one at each end of the lugs at the base, and a $\frac{1}{2}$ in. hole at each side, $\frac{1}{2}$ in. from the top; or better still, drill the latter holes $\frac{31}{64}$ in. and put a $\frac{1}{2}$ in. reamer through both of them together, which will ensure the barrel fitting properly.

Treblet Tube

The best thing out of which to make the barrel, is a bit of $\frac{1}{2}$ in. brass treblet tube; but any kind of tube, brass or copper, can be pressed into service, if the inside can be made smooth and round. For beginners' information, treblet tube is thin brass tube which has been through the drawplate three times (hence "treblet") in order to get both inside and outside as true and smooth as possible. The ends of the barrel should be squared off in the lathe to a length of $1\frac{3}{4}$ in., holding the tube in the three-jaw chuck. If you have a reamer that will clean out the inside of the tube, put it through, just as if reaming a steam cylinder; if not, clean out the inside by an improvised lap, a piece of fine emery cloth wrapped around a stick.

Chuck a piece of $\frac{1}{2}$ in. brass rod in the three-jaw, and turn down $\frac{3}{16}$ in. of it to a tight drive fit in the tube; part off at $\frac{1}{2}$ in. from the end. Reverse in chuck, turn down $\frac{3}{16}$ in. of the other end to $\frac{3}{16}$ in. diameter, and screw it $\frac{3}{16}$ in. by 40. Centre, and drill a $\frac{3}{32}$ in. hole right through; then squeeze the piece into the barrel.

The valve box is the next item, a piece of $\frac{3}{8}$ in. brass rod 1 in. long being required. Chuck in three-jaw; face, centre and drill right through with No. 32 drill. Open out with $\frac{3}{32}$ in. drill, and bottom to $\frac{3}{8}$ in. depth with a $\frac{7}{32}$ in. D-bit. Slightly countersink the end of the hole, and tap $\frac{1}{4}$ in. by 40. Reverse in chuck and repeat operation, except that the D-bit need not be used. When tapping the D-bitted end, take care not to run the tap in far enough to damage the seating, which the D-bit has formed for the ball valve.

At $\frac{7}{16}$ in. from the bottom end—that is, the end which was not D-bitted, drill a $\frac{5}{32}$ in. hole in the side of the barrel, and tap it $\frac{3}{16}$ in. by 40. This hole should break into the enlarged part of the power end. Finally, chuck the piece again, and run a $\frac{1}{8}$ in. reamer through the remnants of the No. 32 drilled hole. Screw the fitting on the end of the barrel into the hole in the valve box; insert the barrel into the stand, as shown in the illustration, so that it projects through about $\frac{1}{4}$ in. at the open end, and solder the lot, which will fix the barrel into the stand, and seal the joints.

Ball valves are shown in the drawing, so if you have any $\frac{5}{32}$ in. rustless steel or bronze balls, use them; if not, use cone valves, but don't forget that a bronze ball is not hard enough to form its own seating, and a cycle ball of

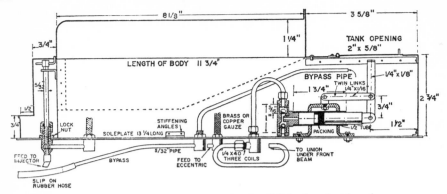

Fig. 2-8   Section of 2½-in. gauge tender for 2-8-0, showing hand pump.

the same size should be used to take the blow from the hammer-and-brass-rod seating operation.

To make the top cap, take the distance from the ball or cone valve to the top of the valve box, with a depth gauge. Chuck a bit of $\frac{3}{8}$ in. hexagon brass rod in the three-jaw, and turn down the end to $\frac{1}{4}$ in. diameter, and $\frac{1}{32}$ in. less than the distance between valve and top of box. Screw it $\frac{1}{4}$ in. by 40 and part-off about $\frac{1}{2}$ in. from the end. Reverse, turn down $\frac{1}{4}$ in. length to $\frac{1}{4}$ in. diameter, screw $\frac{1}{4}$ in. by 40, countersink deeply with a centre drill, and drill right through $\frac{1}{8}$ in. Cross-nick the lower end before screwing home. Turn the lot upside down and repeat operation on the lower end as far as taking depth and turning the fitting is concerned; but the fitting itself is reamed $\frac{1}{8}$ in. and faced off at the end, and the ball or cone seated on it, as shown in Fig. 2-8, the bottom being turned off flush and cross-nicked as shown.

The Ram

The ram is 2 in. long, and turned to a nice sliding fit in the barrel. One end of the ram is slightly reduced in diameter (exact size doesn't matter) drilled either No. 41 or 43, and slotted $\frac{1}{8}$ in. to take the lever. At the other end, turn a groove about $\frac{1}{8}$ in. deep and $\frac{5}{32}$ in. wide, to take a few strands of packing. Either graphited yarn, or the special packing used for hydraulic glands may be used; but don't use the "plumber's friends", hemp and tallow, or you'll have the whole works develop a poisonous green coating.

Lever and Links

The pump lever is a $2\frac{1}{8}$ in. length of $\frac{1}{4}$ in. by $\frac{1}{8}$ in. brass rod, rounded at one end and slightly bevelled at the other. Drill a No. 41 hole at the rounded end, and a similar hole $\frac{3}{4}$ in. above it. The anchor links are two $1\frac{3}{4}$ in. lengths of $\frac{1}{16}$ in. by $\frac{1}{4}$ in. brass strip, with No. 43 holes drilled at $1\frac{1}{2}$ in. centres, the ends being rounded as shown. One of these is placed each side of the upper hole in the lever, and a $\frac{3}{32}$ in. pin of any rustless metal, except aluminium, pressed through the lot; I use hard bronze. Rivet over the ends of the pin if there are any signs of slackness. The anchor lug is a piece of the same kind of material as the lever. Chuck in four-jaw, and turn the end to $\frac{1}{8}$ in. diameter for a full $\frac{3}{16}$ in. length, screwing $\frac{1}{8}$ in. or 5 BA; round off the other end and drill a No. 41 hole in it. Poke the screwed stem through the hole in the top of stand, and secure with a brass nut. Insert ram into barrel, pin the anchor links to the lug, and the lower end of the lever is fitted into the slot in the end of the ram. If the latter is drilled No. 43, squeeze in a pin, but if No. 41, either slightly rivet over the ends of the pin, or use a brass or bronze bolt, made from a bit of $\frac{3}{32}$ in. wire screwed and nutted at each end.

Installing the Pump

The correct location of the pump in the tender is easily ascertained. Set the operating lever vertical; then set the pump centrally in the tender body, with the centre-line of the lever $1\frac{1}{2}$ in. from the back end of the tank, and you have it. Hold it temporarily in position, and mark off on the soleplate the position of one of the holes in the feet, using a scriber point in the hole. Drill a $\frac{1}{8}$ in. or No. 30 hole at the marked spot, and put a $\frac{1}{8}$ in. or 5 BA brass screw through foot and soleplate, with a brass nut underneath. The other three holes can then be drilled, using those in the feet as guide, and the rest of the screws and nuts put in. An inch or so ahead of the pump, drill a $\frac{1}{4}$ in. clearing hole through the soleplate for the connection between the pump and feed pipe, which is made from a piece of $\frac{3}{8}$ in. round or hexagon brass rod about $\frac{7}{8}$ in. long. Chuck in three-jaw and turn down $\frac{3}{8}$ in. of this to $\frac{1}{4}$ in. diameter, and screw $\frac{1}{4}$ in. by 40; centre deeply, and drill about $\frac{3}{4}$ in. down with $\frac{1}{8}$ in. drill. At $\frac{1}{4}$ in. from the "blind" end, drill a $\frac{3}{16}$ in. hole in the side of the fitting, breaking into the centre hole; and in this, silver-solder a screwed nipple made from $\frac{1}{4}$ in. brass rod. Poke this fitting through the hole in the soleplate, and secure it with a lock-nut about $\frac{1}{8}$ in. in thickness, made from $\frac{3}{8}$ in. hexagon brass rod. Now connect the union screw on top of the valve box, and the union end of the fitting, by a swan-neck made either from $\frac{1}{8}$ in. thin-walled pipe, or ordinary $\frac{5}{32}$ in. pipe, furnished with union nuts and cones, the latter being silver-soldered to the pipes.

Tip for beginners: If you use silver-solder in wire form (commercial article) or cut a piece of sheet silver-solder into thin splinters, it won't run all over the contact surface of the cone and cause the union to leak. A pipe of similar material to the swan-neck is taken from the nipple under the soleplate, to the front beam of the tender, where it has a union nut ($\frac{1}{4}$ in. by 26) and nipple for connecting to the hand feed pipe union on the engine. This pipe should have two or three coils in it for flexibility.

The position of the feed and by-pass fittings, shown ahead of the pump for clearness in the illustration, doesn't matter a bean; I usually put them where I can get at the lock-nuts with a small spanner. They are made similar to the hand-pump fitting just described, only instead of screwed nipples, pieces of $\frac{5}{32}$ in. pipe are silver-soldered into them, so as to reach almost to the leading beam. A $\frac{1}{8}$ in. pipe is soldered into the by-pass fitting, and taken to the top of the tender alongside the pump lever, so the by-passed water can be seen through the filler hole. A gauze finger is soldered to the lock-nut of the feed fitting, to prevent any dirt, coal-dust, etc., getting into the valves of the eccentric-driven pump.

Feed Water Strainers

Strainers, I find, are everlastingly getting choked with all kinds of dirt which somehow finds its way into the tank, so builders had better make them removable; here is one way: Turn up a little collar from $\frac{1}{2}$ in. brass rod, similar to a safety-valve bush; drill and tap it $\frac{3}{8}$ in. by 26 or 32, drill a hole in the tank bottom and solder it in. Next make a fitting as shown in the sketch (Fig. 2-9). The lower end is countersunk with a Slocomb, and screwed $\frac{5}{16}$ in. by 32 for the feed-pipe union. The middle is screwed to fit the bush, and the top reduced to $\frac{7}{32}$ in. and left plain. Make a gauze finger by wrapping a piece of fine-mesh copper gauze round a bit of $\frac{7}{32}$ in. rod, securing the seam with a touch of solder; pinch one end up close and solder that also. Then slip the open end over the top of the fitting and make a final application of the "tommy" iron. Screw the complete gadget into the bush, using a jointing washer under the head, and attach a short length of $\frac{3}{16}$ in. tube to the lower end by means of a union nut and collar, as shown in the sketch (Fig. 2-9). When the filter or strainer gets stuffed up, it is only a few seconds' work to disconnect the union and get the whole issue out for cleaning. This fitting is useful for any $1\frac{3}{4}$ in. or $2\frac{1}{2}$ in. gauge tender. The gauze finger may also be attached to a fitting having a circular flange instead of a screw. The strainer is then put through a clearing hole in the bottom of the tank, and

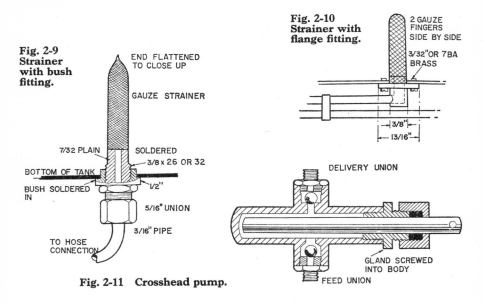

Fig. 2-9 Strainer with bush fitting.

END FLATTENED TO CLOSE UP

GAUZE STRAINER

7/32 PLAIN

SOLDERED

3/8 x 26 OR 32

BOTTOM OF TANK

BUSH SOLDERED IN

1/2"

5/16" UNION

3/16" PIPE

TO HOSE CONNECTION

Fig. 2-10 Strainer with flange fitting.

2 GAUZE FINGERS SIDE BY SIDE

3/32" OR 7BA BRASS

3/8"

13/16"

DELIVERY UNION

GLAND SCREWED INTO BODY

FEED UNION

Fig. 2-11   Crosshead pump.

attached by three or four brass screws through the flange, with a $\frac{1}{32}$ in. "Hallite" or similar joint washer between, as shown in Fig. 2-10.

Stroudley-Type Crosshead Pumps

The immortal "Billy" was very great on pumps, and his were the only type which would pump boiling water. They had six valves altogether. If anybody wants to make a small crosshead pump similar to his design—no need to put *all* the valves in, though, on a small engine—don't use a separate valve box, but make the barrel chamber serve, as sketch (Fig. 2-11). Allow just enough clearance round the tail end of the ram for the water to pass. It is impossible for this pump to become air-locked, as all air will rise to the top clack (highest point) and be blown away. On a $2\frac{1}{2}$ in. gauge engine the bore would be, say $\frac{1}{8}$ in. and the stroke, of course, the same as the cylinder.

"Two Hour" Tender Pump

The stand, or base and barrel support, is a casting. It looks like a switch-stand or point lever (see Figs. 2-12 and 2-13). Clean up with a file; drill a $\frac{1}{2}$ in. hole through the centre of the boss, a No. 40 or $\frac{3}{32}$ in. clearing hole through the anchor lug at top, and four more through the base, one at each corner, for the holding-down bolts. The barrel is a piece of $\frac{1}{2}$ in. treblet tube $1\frac{1}{2}$ in. long. Turn the ends off square and clean the bore out smooth with fine emery cloth or something similar on a round stick.

The end cap is turned from $\frac{1}{2}$ in. brass rod, as shown in the drawing. For the valve box, cut a piece of $\frac{3}{8}$ in. brass rod $\frac{7}{8}$ in. long. Chuck it, centre, put No. 23 drill right through, open out to $\frac{7}{32}$ in. for $\frac{5}{16}$ in. depth, bottom with a D-bit or flat-ended drill, tap $\frac{1}{4}$ in. by 40 threads, slightly countersink, and face off the end. Reverse, and open out the drilled hole in a similar manner, only do not bother to "bottom" the hole. Put a mark on the first end so you can tell it from outside. Drill a $\frac{3}{16}$ in. hole into the passage-way in the centre, and take care to start it a little below the middle of the valve box, so it misses

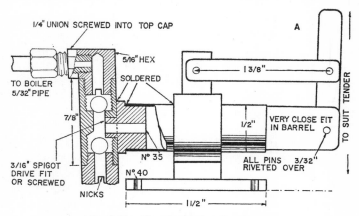

Fig. 2-12 Simple tender hand pump.

the ball seat but breaks through into the lower chamber where the suction-valve lives. Put a $\frac{5}{32}$ in. reamer through the remains of the No. 23 hole.

Valves and Seatings

Drop a $\frac{3}{16}$ in. ball, rustless steel for preference, into the "bottomed" hole and seat it with the usual hammer blow via a bit of $\frac{3}{16}$ in. rod. Chuck a bit of $\frac{5}{16}$ in. hexagon rod, turn one end down to $\frac{1}{4}$ in. diameter, and just long enough to allow the ball $\frac{1}{32}$ in. lift. Screw 40 threads, centre, drill up about $\frac{3}{16}$ in. and part off to leave a hexagon head $\frac{5}{16}$ in. long. Rechuck the cap the other way about and chamfer off, then file a couple of nicks in the screwed part to prevent the ball sealing the outlet when it rises.

The suction-valve seat is also made from $\frac{5}{16}$ in. hexagon rod. Chuck, centre, and drill No. 23 for about $\frac{1}{2}$ in. Turn down to $\frac{1}{4}$ in. for a sufficient length to allow the ball to rise $\frac{1}{32}$ in. This length is easily measured by dropping a ball in the hole and gauging from lip of hole to top of ball with a depth-gauge or a bit of wire, turning the cap a tiny shade under. Face the screwed end, and part off to leave the hexagon section about $\frac{3}{16}$ in. long. Reverse, chamfer off, ream $\frac{5}{32}$ in. and cross slot the hexagon. Put a rustless steel ball on the screwed end and "'it 'im wiv an 'ammer", but not too hard. Incidentally, a small lead hammer is very useful, you can knock things about without damaging them, and it is easily cast in a round cardboard tube or even a piece of brown paper rolled up to required thickness and diameter.

Assembly

Drive the barrel cap in and fit the valve box on the spigot; push barrel through hole in stand; see that valve box is right way up and that it stands vertical; then solder up the lot. Put the valves in and screw the caps home tightly; next make and fit the delivery union. On any one of the facets in the top cap pointing in a forward direction, drill and tap a hole $\frac{3}{16}$ in. by 40, running the drill into the middle hole. Make a $\frac{1}{4}$ in. union with a shank screwed to suit and fix up as sketch (Fig. 2-12). Take the cap out to drill and fit the union after marking off, so as to keep chips out of the valve box. Chuck a piece of rod, turn down $1\frac{3}{4}$ in. of it to a sliding fit in the barrel, fitting it as carefully as you would a steam piston, and part off. No packing will be required, and glands are also not needed. File a slot in one end $\frac{1}{8}$ in. wide and about $\frac{3}{8}$ in. deep for the lever connection, and drill a No. 43 hole across for the lever pin. The rest is just simply plain sailing, as can be seen from Fig. 2-12.

The lever is a plain piece of $\frac{1}{8}$ in. by $\frac{1}{4}$ in. flat brass rod, and the connecting links to the anchor lug on top of the stand are two $\frac{1}{4}$ in. strips of $\frac{1}{16}$ in. plate; or the same sized rod as used for the lever may be worked in if desired. All pins are $\frac{3}{32}$ in. round German silver or rustless steel, slightly burred over at the ends so that they won't come out in the tank when the engine is working.

The pump is fixed by long 7 BA brass screws passed through the tender

Fig. 2-13 Details of simple pump.

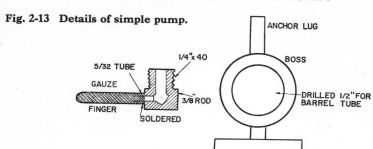

soleplate with heads soldered over underneath, and nuts to hold down the base of the pump, which is located so that the handle comes directly under the filler slot. An extension handle is quickly made from a length of $\frac{1}{8}$ in. by $\frac{1}{4}$ in. brass rod, say, about 3 in. long to give a comfortable leverage against normal boiler pressures. Bend a bit of 16-gauge brass sheet about an inch wide around this to form a socket, and either silver-solder or rivet it to the extension. Carry it on the tender top and slip over the pump lever at *A* when required to operate. Where clean feed water is used, no strainer need be fitted; but it is thought advisable to work on "safety first" lines, the drawing (Fig. 2-13) shows an alternative suction cap with gauze finger.

Pump By-Pass for Fine Regulation

Although a plug cock may be used as a by-pass, some locomotive builders prefer a screw-down valve for giving finer regulation of feed on long non-stop runs. A neat way of arranging a screw-down valve for this purpose is shown in the sketch (Fig. 2-14). Chuck a piece of $\frac{5}{16}$ in. hexagon rod, centre, and drill down $\frac{3}{4}$ in. with No. 48 drill, open out $\frac{1}{2}$ in. with No. 30 drill and $\frac{1}{8}$ in. with No. 21 drill. Tap the centre part $\frac{5}{32}$ in. by 40. Turn down $\frac{1}{4}$ in. of outside to $\frac{1}{4}$ in. diameter and screw 40 t.p.i. Part off at about $1\frac{1}{8}$ in. from end, reverse

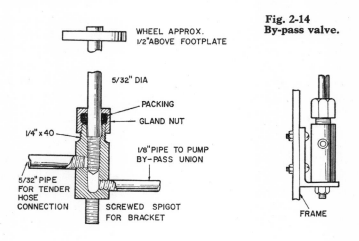

**Fig. 2-14
By-pass valve.**

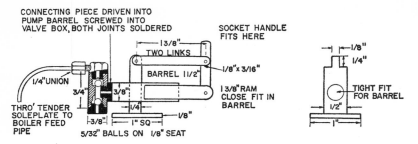

Fig. 2-15 Tender pump for "O" gauge engine.

and turn a spigot about $\frac{5}{16}$ in. long at the end, $\frac{1}{8}$ in. diameter, screwed $\frac{1}{8}$ in. or 5 BA. Drill the pipe holes as shown in Fig. 2-14, make a gland, and fit a rustless steel or German silver needle with wheel. Make the needle long enough to project through the cab deck or footplate, and fix the whole contrivance to the trailing end of frame by a little bracket as shown. Open the valve fully when first starting engine, and as soon as water is seen coming from the end of the by-pass pipe, which should be arranged under the filler lid of tank, close valve and keep an eye on the water gauge on boiler. If the level creeps up, open by-pass valve a little until the level in glass is as near constant as possible.

"O" Gauge Tender Pump

The sketches (Fig. 2-15) give the construction of a simple tender pump for an "O" gauge loco. The stand is made from a bit of $\frac{1}{2}$ in. by $\frac{1}{4}$ in. flat brass, silver-soldered or screwed and sweated to a baseplate and rebated at the top for lever connecting links. The barrel is $\frac{5}{16}$ in. or $\frac{3}{8}$ in. brass tube lapped out with emery cloth wound around a stick. The ram or plunger and valve boxes need no special description, being similar to the $2\frac{1}{2}$ in. gauge hand pump just described. Where a pump is installed, do not solder the top of the tank in, but solder or rivet pieces of angle brass all round, and screw the top plate down by 10 BA roundhead screws. This type of pump is operated by a socket extension lever fitting over the handle and worked through the filling hole, an arrangement made possible by the fulcrum of the pump handle being *above* instead of below the ram; so that the lever, where it passes through the tank top, only needs a small hole instead of the huge slot required by the usual pattern commercial pump.

Pump for "Vanderbilt" Tender

The following notes give details of a suitable hand pump for a "Vanderbilt" tender with circular tank. Dimensions are for a $2\frac{1}{2}$ in. gauge locomotive, but they can be "scaled" up or down in proportion, for other sizes as required. Be generous when "scaling down", as too much water is preferable to too little.

Stand and Barrel

If a casting is used, clean it up with a file, drill a No. 40 hole in each corner of the base, another in the lug at top, and a $\frac{1}{8}$ in. hole through the boss. If you like, you can build up a stand, using a piece of $\frac{1}{8}$ in. plate for the base and silver-soldering (or screwing and sweating) a piece of $\frac{5}{8}$ in. by $\frac{1}{4}$ in. flat brass rod shaped as sketch (Fig. 2-16), to carry the barrel. This is a piece of $\frac{1}{2}$ in. brass tube with turned ends; give the bore a clean out with a piece of fine emery cloth wound around a stick, carefully drive the barrel into the hole in stand and fix with a touch of solder. The ram is a piece of gunmetal or bronze rod, turned a nice sliding fit in the tube and slotted for lever. If desired a packing groove may be turned in one end to contain a few turns of graphited yarn. When the water in the tender gets low, the pump (which is perched on a little platform) has to lift its supply, and the packing will enable a poorly-fitting ram to pick up immediately.

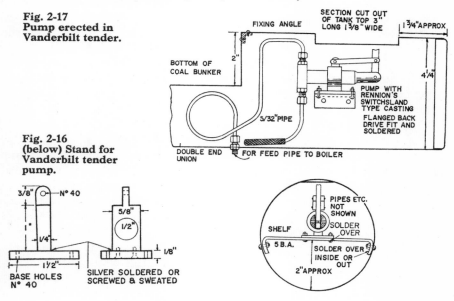

Fig. 2-17 Pump erected in Vanderbilt tender.

Fig. 2-16 (below) Stand for Vanderbilt tender pump.

Valve Box and Valves

The valve box is a piece of $\frac{3}{8}$ in. round gunmetal or brass rod $\frac{7}{8}$ in. long Chuck, centre, drill right through No. 24, open out $\frac{5}{16}$ in. to No. 3 or $\frac{7}{32}$ in., bottom with $\frac{7}{32}$ in. D-bit, tap $\frac{1}{4}$ in. by 40, slightly countersink edge to enable union cap to seat tightly. Reverse and repeat on the other end except that the D-bit is not necessary. Run a $\frac{5}{32}$ in. reamer through. Drill a $\frac{5}{32}$ in. hole into the side of the valve box just low enough to clear the valve seat formed by the D-bit; tap $\frac{3}{16}$ in. by 40 and turn up a little connector, one end screwed to fit valve box and the other a drive fit into pump barrel. Assemble, and solder so that there is no fear of air leaks. The top or delivery valve is a $\frac{3}{16}$ in. rustless steel ball, seated by tapping it down on the sharp edge of the seating left by the D-bit. The cover is a $\frac{1}{4}$ in. union, the stem of which is made just long enough to allow the ball $\frac{1}{32}$ in. lift, and is cross-nicked with a file so that the ball cannot block up the waterway at top position. The bottom or suction valve is another similar ball resting on a seating made from another $\frac{1}{4}$ in. union, the stem of which is drilled down No. 24, reamed $\frac{5}{32}$ in., and faced off to such a length that when screwed home the ball has just over $\frac{1}{32}$ in. lift. A short length of $\frac{5}{32}$ in. pipe is attached to the union, and on the end of this is soldered a gauze strainer (see Fig. 2-17), which lies along the tank bottom when pump is mounted. Before fitting lever and links, try the pump in the domestic sink (safest place!), operate the ram by hand direct and see if it will lift water from a depth of 8 in. or more. If it won't, look for pin-holes, leaky valves or leaky ram, and correct before proceeding further.

Lever, Links and Assembly

Both links and lever are $\frac{1}{8}$ in. by $\frac{1}{4}$ in. flat German silver rod; failing that, use brass. The lever is 2 in. long and the links $1\frac{1}{2}$ in.; the holes for pins, which are $\frac{3}{32}$ in. German silver or brass wire, are No. 43 in links and No. 41 in lever. The drawing (Fig. 2-17) shows the assembly; the lever is pinned in the slot in ram, and the two links connect the centre of it with the lug on the top of the stand, allowing the bottom of the lever to follow a straight line when the pump is being operated.

Having got the pump fixed up O.K. for action, we shall have to put it on a shelf in the tender, as this is rather deep and it would be too much out of the way if bolted direct to the bottom. The shelf is simply a piece of $1\frac{1}{2}$ in. by $\frac{1}{8}$ in. flat *soft* brass, bent over either end to suit contour of tank and secured by 5 BA roundhead brass screws put through from outside and nutted inside, or *vice versa*, as desired. The pump base is bolted down to this by four 7 BA brass screws put through from underneath and nutted on top. Note, although passing through clearing holes in pump base, they are *screwed* through the shelf and may be soldered over the heads to prevent turning. This is in case at any time it should be necessary to take out the pump through the hole in the tank top. A little box-spanner will easily remove the nuts and allow this to be done.

The delivery pipe is coiled, one turn will be sufficient, and both ends are fitted with union nuts. One couples to union on pump and the other to a double-ended union nipple in the centre of the tank bottom. The use of a coiled internal delivery pipe is just a matter of convenience; you can unship the pump if ever needed, and pull it right back so that the union nut is under the manhole and can be easily got at for uncoupling. You couldn't do this with a rigid pipe and it is just "one of the little things that matter". Whilst fixing the double union in the tank bottom, put another in for the mechanical pump by-pass connection, leading a $\frac{1}{8}$ in. pipe from it right up to the filling hole; and also another single union for the mechanical pump feed line. The upper end of this carries a gauze strainer or "strum", similar to that previously described, and illustrated in Fig. 2-9.

CHAPTER III

Duplex Double-Acting Feed Pump

A "DONKEY" PUMP is another good way of feeding the boiler. Here is a design for a duplex double-acting one. We will deal first with the cast cylinder and pump blocks (Fig. 3-1).

The easiest way of machining up the casting will be by mounting in a four-jaw chuck, or, failing that, a little angle-plate bolted to the lathe face-plate. First clean up one end and the back with a file. Mark out the location of the two bores as sketch (Fig. 3-1) and make a good deep centre-pop at each centre. Next chuck the block or mount it on an angle-plate so that one of the centre pops runs truly; and, whatever else you do, make quite certain that if a four-jaw chuck is used the back of the block is pressed well down on one of the chuck jaws (Fig. 3-2) and the casting not tilted in any way, other-wise the drill will go through skew-whiff. Put a $\frac{1}{4}$ in. drill through for $\frac{5}{16}$ in. finished bore; then mount a little boring tool on your slide-rest and carefully *bore* out the drilled hole till the business end of a $\frac{5}{16}$ in. parallel reamer will just enter, after which proceed with the cylinder reaming. Next shift bore No. 2 in position for operating on; with an angle-plate fixture, slack off and move the angle-plate bodily, *not the casting*. When the angle-plate is clamped in its new position the bores must come parallel.

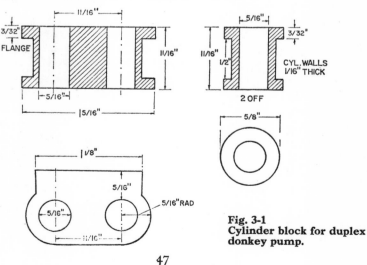

Fig. 3-1
Cylinder block for duplex
donkey pump.

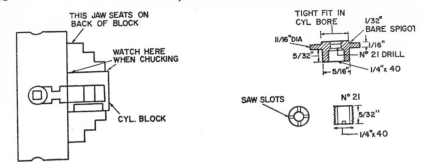

Fig. 3-2
Cylinder casting set up in four-jaw chuck.

Fig. 3-3
Bottom cylinder cover and gland.

If a chuck is used, do not move the jaw against which the back of the casting rests, but leave that for location purposes and reset the casting with the other three. This will also aid in maintaining parallel bores. Drill and ream as before, then take a cut over the flange which should now come nice and square with the bores. The flange at the other end is turned with the cylinder block on a mandrel. Chuck any odd bit of brass rod in the three-jaw and turn down till the cylinder block can be just slipped on by one of the bores. A very tight push fit should be sufficient. I have found no necessity for a drive fit with these tiny cylinders. The length of block over flanges should be $\frac{11}{16}$ in. The flat back, which becomes the port face on the finished job, can be machined on the angle plate by clamping "end-up" with a bolt through one of the bores, and the face can be set true by checking with a scribing-block on the lathe bed or boring-table. The four-jaw chuck may also be used, in which case put a bit of brass or other soft sheet in between the chuck jaws and the finished cylinder flanges. In either case, assuming that the angle-plate or chuck is reasonably true, the port face will automatically come square with the flanges.

How to Build Up the Cylinders

This method entails a little more work, as there is a separate valve block, with ports, to make and fix; but many will prefer it, as the cylinders can be turned and finished in a three-jaw self-centring chuck. Chuck a length of $\frac{11}{16}$ in. or $\frac{5}{8}$ in. bronze or gunmetal rod and leave about an inch projecting from the chuck. Centre and drill down $\frac{3}{4}$ in. deep with a $\frac{1}{4}$ in. drill. Turn away the centre part, face the end, and part off at $\frac{11}{16}$ in. full from the end. Repeat, and then chuck each piece separately by the flanges; bore out, and finally put a $\frac{5}{16}$ in. reamer through with a drop of cutting oil. Turn up a brass mandrel as for the cast block and finish each cylinder on it separately, *taking care that all the flanges are equal.* The bottom cylinder covers, both for built-up cylinders and the cast block, are plain turning jobs, as drawing (Fig. 3-3), and made from $\frac{3}{4}$ in. brass, gunmetal or bronze bar. Turn the spigot at back and drill piston-rod hole first; then reduce with a parting tool to diameter of stuffing-box and part off. Repeat; then reverse and set to run

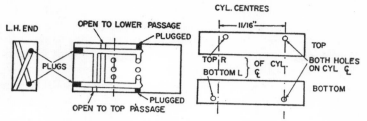

Fig. 3-4 How to drill the crossed passages.

truly in chuck jaws. Don't hold the little covers too tightly or they will buckle or scar. Open out the gland hole with a $\frac{7}{32}$ in. pin-drill and tap $\frac{1}{4}$ in. by 40. The glands are just plain screwed bushes cross-slotted with a fine saw; these headless glands look very neat on a tiny donkey, are easily operated and require the minimum of space, so the cylinders can be set closer together than with the ordinary type.

Port Block for Duplex Pump

Where a casting is used for the donkey pump cylinders, the port block is, of course, cast in one piece with them; but in the case of built-up cylinders the block is separately made, drilled for ports and passages, and sweated in position with plumbers' solder or babbit metal. This construction is plenty strong enough, as there is not a great deal of heat and strain; also, the block, being a drive fit between the cylinder flanges, helps to stiffen up the whole issue. As a matter of fact, a built-up cylinder made by soldering parts together will stand a lot of rough service. Ports and passage-ways being the same on both cast and built-up gadgets, one description will do for both. The block on the built-up one is a piece of $\frac{1}{4}$ in. by $\frac{1}{2}$ in. flat brass rod; even screw-rod will do as there is very little wear. Trim this up with a file until it will just drive between the cylinder flanges without distorting them (see drawing, Fig. 3-5), and then mark out and drill the ports and passage-ways. This is frankly a ticklish job, as some of the holes are deep and you cannot afford to chance the drill running to one side and breaking through into another passage, or else catching up and breaking itself, so watch your step. If you haven't a machine, the best thing to do is to centre-pop the

Fig. 3-5 Built-up cylinders

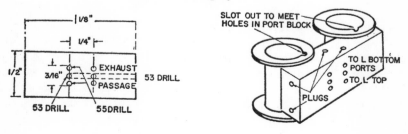

block at opposite sides to the points where the drill enters, and feed up to a drill revolving in the lathe chuck *at high speed*, holding the block tightly against the back centre with left hand and turning the handwheel with the right. Your sense of touch will let you know soon enough if all is not well with the drill inside the block. Withdraw frequently and clear chips. The short holes may be drilled either by hand drill or against a flat drill pad in the tailstock; but a small high-speed drilling machine is the boy for all this work.

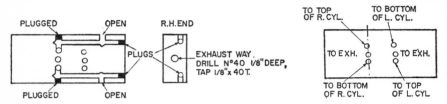

Fig. 3-6　How to drill the straight passages.

The Ports and Passages

Note carefully how the drilled holes run, as per sketches (Figs. 3-4 and 3-6). The two steam ports on each side communicate with the opposite cylinder, and, in addition, one set is crossed top and bottom also. The easiest way of getting over the job is first of all to drill the ports in the face, the left set going nearly through the block and the right set only just entering, except for the exhaust port which should go half-way through. Then drill the exhaust outlet, opening out and tapping the end for the exhaust pipe. Next do the four long passage-ways, taking care to keep them straight and parallel. Next the two communicating holes to the "direct" cylinder, and then the diagonal holes to the "crossed" cylinder. All passage-ways are No. 53 drill (or $\frac{1}{16}$ in.) and the ports No. 55 steam and No. 53 exhaust. Tap the ends of the holes which are to be plugged (Figs. 3-4 and 3-6) with No. 9 BA taper tap, leave the threads on the tight side, screw in pieces of brass wire, and cut off and file flush. The block, when finished, is gently tapped into position between the cylinder flanges and soldered over a gas or spirit flame with Baker's fluid and solder or babbit, using the latter very sparingly. The cast block is drilled in exactly the same way, but should be an easier job, as there is a little more metal in it and, therefore, more room to space the passage-ways.

The Top Covers for Donkey Pump Cylinders

The top cylinder covers (Fig. 3-7) are a plain turning job, but differ from the bottom pair in the glands. These have only the little 16-gauge trip-rod passing through and, therefore, for the sake of neatness, we adopt the plain external type. The covers should be turned from the bar at one setting, which is easily done. Chuck a length of $\frac{3}{4}$ in. brass, gunmetal or bronze rod; face, centre and drill $\frac{1}{2}$ in. or so depth with No. 50 drill. Cut back to form the spigot, using a sharp knife-tool and trying on the cylinder, as the spigots must fit the bore without shake. Then, with a fairly wide parting tool, part down till a slide-gauge set at $\frac{3}{16}$ in. will just slip over the round stock at the bottom of the groove. Note where the cross-slide comes, withdraw tool, shift rest along a little less than width of tool point, feed in again to same depth, and repeat once more if necessary, finally parting off to leave a $\frac{3}{16}$ in. diameter "pip" standing a full $\frac{1}{8}$ in. high off the cover. Reverse and rechuck truly by aid of 16-gauge wire in tailstock chuck; then screw the pip 40 threads per inch, using a die in tailstock die-holder. This ensures truth all ways, as friction on these tiny cylinders *must* be kept to the minimum. The gland nuts are made from $\frac{1}{4}$ in. hexagon screw rod. Note—anyone who desires especially small glands may use $\frac{3}{16}$ in. hexagon screw rod for the nuts and make the "pips" $\frac{5}{32}$ in. diameter, tapping the nuts accordingly. There is still room enough for a few threads of graphited yarn packing. The pips may also be turned and screwed with the cover held in a small stepped bush in the three-jaw.

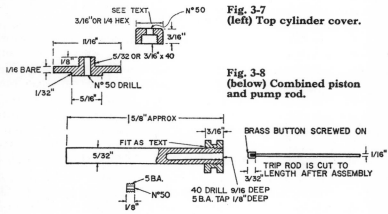

Fig. 3-7
(left) Top cylinder cover.

Fig. 3-8
(below) Combined piston and pump rod.

Pistons, Piston-Rods and Trip-Rods

It would be best, before operating on the pump ends of the piston-rods (Fig. 3-8), to get the steam cylinders to work O.K. first and see how much power you get for pumping; the power will depend on the workmanship. Chuck a piece of $\frac{3}{8}$ in. rod, of a different metal to the cylinders—rustless steel is about the best, but *cast* bronze, German silver or hard brass will do. Rough out two pistons to drawing (Fig. 3-8), leaving about $\frac{1}{64}$ in. over size, and don't forget the centre hole is tapped $\frac{5}{32}$ in. by 40 for half its length and the rest opened out No. 23 ($\frac{5}{32}$ in. drive fit). Cut two lengths of $\frac{5}{32}$ in. phosphor bronze or ground rustless steel rod—the latter is best, but it will give your drill socks when you drill the trip-rod hole unless you have high-speed drills. Put a little bit of true thread on each, using tailstock die-holder. Put a rough piston in chuck on mandrel, and piston-rod in tailstock chuck, gripping the latter tightly; screw piston on truly and tightly by pulling the lathe belt by hand. Chuck piston-rod *truly*, either in a collet, or a bush held in three-jaw and carefully turn down the piston flanges until they just enter the cylinder bore, say, 0.001 in. clearance, or less. Without removing piston-rod from chuck, face the end of piston truly, cutting the rod off flush. Then centre the rod, and drill down $\frac{9}{16}$ in. deep with a No. 40 drill. Tap out the end with about $\frac{1}{8}$ in. full thread, using 5 BA taper tap, leaving the threads on the tight side. The trip-rods (Fig. 3-8) are $\frac{1}{16}$ in. rustless steel, screwed at both ends, but the top end should be left plain till cylinders are assembled. The lower end carries a little brass sleeve or button, the length of which is determined by the travel needed on the valve. With a $\frac{9}{16}$ in. hole and a $\frac{1}{8}$ in. plug in the top, there is $\frac{7}{16}$ in. left for the button or sleeve to travel in. As the stroke of the piston-rod is $\frac{7}{16}$ in., it naturally follows that if the button had no appreciable length it would remain stationary; but if it were, say, $\frac{3}{32}$ in. long, either the plug in the top of the hole or the solid bottom of the hole itself would catch the button $\frac{3}{32}$ in. from the end of the stroke and drag it or push it the remaining distance. Fit the buttons and insert the trip-rods in the piston-rod holes; then turn up two little brass plugs, by chucking a bit of $\frac{1}{8}$ in. rod, centring and drilling No. 50, threading the outside 5 BA, and parting off $\frac{1}{8}$ in. full. Slip one over each trip-rod, screw tightly into hole in piston-rod, and chuck each rod and carefully face off any projection with a knife-tool, being particular to avoid damaging the trip-rod, which will probably flop about whilst this job is in progress. The plugs won't come out any more, but they won't need to! I tried a screwed plate on the piston, similar to that on a big donkey, before adopting this wheeze; but discarded it as being too clumsy, as, indeed, it is if made strong enough in this small size.

Steam-Chest

The steam-chest is made from $\frac{1}{4}$ in. by $\frac{1}{2}$ in. flat brass rod. Cut off a piece as sketch (Fig. 3-9) and mark out for glands and valve cavity. First drill the gland holes. I guess you will be wondering why we want tail-rods and extra glands. Well, the first donkey pump I made had no tail-rods; it worked, but was rather erratic. On investigation, I found that the steam pressure on the ends of the valve spindles began to shift the valves before the trip-rods actuated the rockers. Timing tip: the slack in the valve gear of a slide-valve

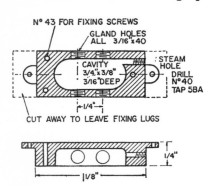

CUT AWAY TO LEAVE FIXING LUGS

Fig. 3-9
(left) Steam-chest for donkey pump.

Fig. 3-10
(below) Steam-chest glands.

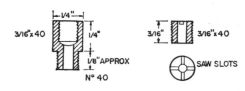

engine with no tail-rods *is always taken up in the same direction irrespective of whether the valve-rod is being pulled or pushed.* Ignorance or non-recognition of that fact causes the syncopated beat so often heard on club and exhibition tracks. Anyway, after drilling the holes right through the block, set it up on the tool-holder of your lathe at right-angles to the bed; this is easy with the usual Willis type clamp, but if you have a new type of lathe, the job must be clamped in whatever way you can wangle. Of course, a vertical slide, or even an angle-plate, affords an easy solution. Mill out the recess with a $\frac{3}{8}$ in. endmill held in the three-jaw chuck, and then file up to outline, leaving a couple of little lugs which will enable the gadget to be bolted to the side of the boiler or a carrying bracket, whichever may be preferred. Tap the gland holes $\frac{3}{16}$ in. by 40.

Steam-Chest Glands

The next step will be the steam-chest glands for the miniature donkey pump (Fig. 3-10). They are turned out of bronze or gunmetal rod. Chuck a length of $\frac{1}{4}$ in. round and turn down $\frac{1}{8}$ in. or so to $\frac{3}{16}$ in. diameter; screw 40 t.p.i. with die in tailstock holder; face off, centre, drill down No. 40 and part off to leave $\frac{1}{4}$ in. plain rod. Repeat four times. Make a little screwed bush to hold in three-jaw chuck. Any old bit of round scrap will do; just face, centre, drill No. 21, slightly countersink, tap $\frac{3}{16}$ in. by 40, and lightly face off the burr. Screw each stuffing-box blank into this; open out to tapping size with a pin-drill and tap $\frac{3}{16}$ in. by 40, supporting tap either in tailstock chuck or by an adapter, or whatever your own pet method happens to be, so long as it ensures the tap going in truly. Screw the little stuffing-boxes tightly into the steam-chest tapped holes. If there is any sign of sloppiness, give them a touch of solder—not with a bit, but heat over a Bunsen or spirit flame, apply a little Baker's fluid, and a bead of solder picked up on the end of a hot copper wire. As the centres of the holes are $\frac{1}{4}$ in. apart, the stuffing-boxes will just touch. The glands are made from $\frac{3}{16}$ in. bronze or gunmetal rod. Chuck a piece of correct size if you can rely on your chuck for accuracy; if not, chuck a piece of $\frac{1}{4}$ in. and turn down. Centre, drill No. 41, screw with die in tailstock holder, and part off four pieces. Don't drill deeper than sufficient for two glands at one time, as the drill may run out of truth. Cross-slot the glands with a fine saw, as previously noted for piston glands. These little glands should fit the stuffing boxes fairly tightly, as it is astonishing what a lot of vibration this little donkey sets up when it begins to "kick" against pressure.

Valves and Valve-Rods

The valves are circular and a plain turning job (Fig. 3-11). In case you have apple-pied the ports and they are slightly varying in size and spacing (if you have, it doesn't matter a button), make the valves to suit. As the steam has to be admitted full piston stroke, no lap nor lead is required. Turn the circular valve from a piece of chucked bronze or gunmetal rod; first turn down a short length, say, $\frac{1}{4}$ in. or so, to a diameter equal to the distance over

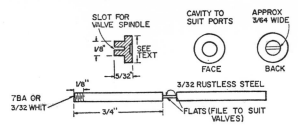

Fig. 3-11　Slide valves and spindle.

extreme edges of ports. Then make a little D-bit, with an edge equal to the distance between *inside* edges of steam ports. Centre and feed in a drill the same diameter as D-bit until it just enters the full width of the cutting edge. Follow with the D-bit until this cuts out the centre-mark and leaves a flat-bottomed hole. Then face off till the cavity is about $\frac{1}{32}$ in. deep only. This is the best method I know for getting a truly concentric flat-bottomed very shallow hole, using an ordinary lathe. With a parting tool, cut back $\frac{1}{16}$ in. behind the face, and reduce the diameter to $\frac{1}{8}$ in., repeating till the valve measures approximately $\frac{5}{32}$ in. from face to back, at which point part completely off. Repeat, and then carefully slot down the bosses with a hacksaw or watchmaker's file. If you are doubtful about holding them without damage, stick them on a bit of bar with shellac; or they may even be soldered, so long as all the solder is melted off afterwards, and the valves given a facing rub on a sheet of fine emery cloth laid on a surface-plate or piece of plate-glass, finishing with a final touch of carborundum powder and oil on the glass itself. Watch the cavities don't get filled up.

The valve-rods are two $1\frac{5}{8}$ in. lengths of $\frac{3}{32}$ in. round rustless steel, with two flats filed in, to enable the rod to drop in the valve slot. File the flats in the lathe chuck. Mark where they are located on the rod; put in chuck with one marking just showing, set No. 1 jaw at top, hold file horizontally, and bearing against chuck jaws, and file the flat to $\frac{1}{8}$ in. so that the valve boss just fits without shake; then slew No. 1 jaw around to bottom position and file the other flat in the same way. Use a safe-edge Swiss-type file. Valves should be free to move up and down, but not endways. The cylinders may now be assembled in the usual way, fixing each cover by four 10 BA round-head screws and the steam-chest by four 8 BA screws. Pack the pistons with a few strands of graphited yarn well rolled in, and thin oiled paper will do for cover and steam-chest joints.

Rockers for Donkey Pump

The cylinders and valves being assembled, we next want the little pillars which support the rockers. These are turned from $\frac{3}{16}$ in. round steel to the size given on sketch (Fig. 3-12), and slotted at the top either by milling or cutting down with a hacksaw and trimming the saw-cut with a watchmaker's file. For slot-milling in the lathe merely mount a small milling cutter on a

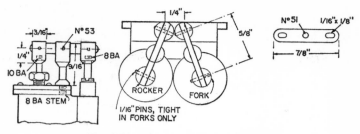

Fig. 3-12   How to assemble rockers.

plain arbor (even a bolt will do in emergency; mount the cutter on the threaded part, clamped tightly between two nuts; saw off the bolt head and hold the stem in your three-jaw chuck) and fix the work on the top-slide at lathe centre height, feeding into cut by the cross-slide, and not forgetting plenty of lubricant. Tip: as the little screwed spigots are very short, turn them to twice the length, and reduce *after the thread is cut*; otherwise the threads at the extreme tip may get spoilt by starting the die, especially if it isn't perfectly clean, or the die not sharp.

The rocking levers (Fig. 3-12) are plain strips of brass or steel, the centre hole being a plain drilled circular one, an easy fit on the pin, and the other holes being slotted, as the ends, of course, describe an arc whilst the little forks move up and down in a straight line. They must not be tight in either forks or pillars. The forks are turned from $\frac{3}{16}$ in. round steel. If milling the slots, cut a couple of lengths of rod about 3 in. long or thereabouts; mill a slot at either end of each while the cutter is in the chuck; then turn all four, after which the ends can be faced off, centred, drilled and tapped in the usual way, chucking the forks in the three-jaw, which will hold the round bodies truly. Draw a line on each cylinder cover cutting through centres of piston trip-rod and valve spindle. On each line, in the cylinder cover and flange, drill and tap a hole for the spigot of rocker pillar, and screw in, making sure that the forks will allow the rockers to line up.

Next screw the ends of the trip-rods and fix all forks, arranging them so that when the valve is in mid-position covering ports, and the trip-rod is in the centre of its travel, the rocker is approximately horizontal. If this is done, the timing will be automatically correct and the donkey will "kick" as soon as steam is applied to it. The setting of the trip-rod is important. A slight variation in *length of travel* does not matter, so long as in "mid-gear", so to speak, the ports are covered by the valve; and the amount of travel should be ascertained by moving the piston-rod up and down by hand, so that the trip-rod is actuated by its button as when under steam, and the extreme positions carefully measured. It can then be set exactly central and coupled up. When packing the glands, get a piece of wire about $\frac{1}{16}$ in. thick and, say 5 in. long. Bend one end into a ring, and flatten the other and file off like a screwdriver blade. Slightly bend the end as sketch (Fig. 3-13). This is called

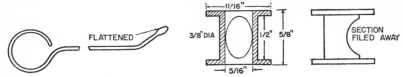

Fig. 3-13 Packing "shover" and distance piece.

a "packing-shover" in big practice, and, by means of a midget packing-shover, the threads of graphited yarn can be well prodded down into the stuffing boxes in a very few minutes. Just push one end in, prod down, and follow around the rod till it all goes in. The job explains itself when you start on it.

Distance-Pieces for Duplex Pump

The chief trouble in donkey pump construction is getting the steam and pump cylinders properly lined up to ensure sweet running and the minimum of friction. In cases such as the Stuart horizontal pump the guide and pump cylinder are cast integral and machined up as a single piece at one setting; this, of course, ensures accuracy, given reasonably good workmanship, but the method cannot be applied to the little locomotive donkey on account of the glands coming between the covers. I tried out several methods and found that a separate turned and bored distance-piece, fitted over spigots on both steam and pump cylinder covers, did the trick all right; and even tyro brothers who are raw amateurs should be able to manage this important part of the business without trouble (Fig. 3-13). Chuck a length of $\frac{3}{4}$ in. round brass rod (any grade will do, there is nothing to wear), turn it down to the same diameter as the cylinder covers, $\frac{11}{16}$ in., for about an inch in length. Face the end, centre, and drill down $\frac{9}{32}$ in. diameter for a depth, of say, $\frac{3}{4}$ in. Take off the bottom covers of the steam cylinders, and carefully *bore* out the drilled hole until the spigot formed by the outside of the stuffing-box is a

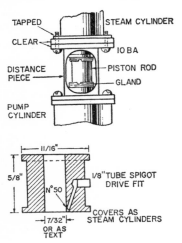

Fig. 3-14
(top left) How to fit distance-piece.

(bottom left) Pump cylinder with separate covers.

(below) Single-acting pump cylinder

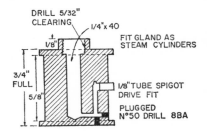

tight push fit. If you haven't a boring tool suitable, a handy weapon for this and many other small boring jobs can be made from $\frac{3}{16}$ in. round silver-steel held in a tool-holder made from a short length of, say, $\frac{1}{2}$ in. square iron bar, or any other size suitable for your slide-rest. Tip: clamp the piece of bar in your tool-holder, centre with a centre-drill held in the chuck, and follow up with a drill (say, No. 12 for $\frac{3}{16}$ in. tight fit) either held in chuck on mandrel, or provided with a taper shank to fit lathe centre hole. An ordinary $\frac{3}{16}$ in. set-screw clamps the tool. You then know that the tool will be on lathe centre-line, and can be adjusted without any packing.

Next turn out the centre part of "bobbin". For quickness sake on a job like this I feed in a parting tool at either end of the section to be removed, calipering one of the grooves as the tool feeds in; then either use an ordinary roughing tool to chaw away the centre part, or else take three or four cuts with the parting tool and traverse it finally along the whole width of the gap to remove any ridges. File out the openings with a half-round file, before finally parting off the distance-piece, as the thin flanges are liable to be squeezed up and distorted if the piece is held in the vice for this operation. If a keen parting tool is used, no further operation will be necessary after parting off; but if a little burr is left, either reverse the job in chuck or mount on a mandrel, and skim up the face of the flange. If this does not bed truly against the cylinder cover, the cylinder and pump will not line up and the piston-rod will bind.

Next drill the screw holes in the flanges of the distance-piece, using the cylinder covers as jigs, as the cover screws pass through the whole issue as sketch (Fig. 3-14). See that you get the openings at the front, a slip is easily made when the covers are off the cylinders. Use No. 50 drill for 10 BA cover screws, which may be round-headed.

Pump Cylinders, "Solid" Pattern

I have tried two kinds of water-pump cylinders on these little donkeys, and both work very well; the first being somewhat after the style of the usual "force-pump" pattern with a solid body and no separate covers, and the second being the regulation Westinghouse or Weir type, either single or double-acting. The first is suitable for the smaller-sized boilers, and has the advantage that no separate pump pistons are required, the $\frac{5}{32}$ in. piston-rods acting as rams which pass through glands similar to those in the bottom covers of the steam cylinders. The valve box on either type is separately made and one pattern does for either. Taking the cylinders first, the "solid" pattern may be turned from brass or bronze rod at one chucking. Turn down the outside to the diameter of the steam cylinder covers, and reduce the centre part as sketch (Fig. 3-14), leaving enough at the end to form the stuffing-box. Face off, centre, and drill down to bottom, as shown with No. 21 drill; open out with $\frac{7}{32}$ in. drill and tap $\frac{1}{4}$ in. by 40; make glands to suit, as for steam cylinders. Next turn down the outside of the stuffing-box until it is a tight push fit in the bottom of the distance-piece, finally parting off. The waterways are shown in the sketch (Fig. 3-14), which gives a section of the pump cylinder. Drill the long hole first, then the bottom connection to the pump bore, finally the upper one which communicates with the valve box. The latter is counterbored and has a little piece of copper tube driven in, which will enter the corresponding hole in the valve box when the contrivance is assembled, and prevent the waterways getting stuffed up when sweating up in position, besides acting as register when assembling.

Pump Cylinders, "Regulation" Pattern

These are made in pretty much the same way as in full size, but have thicker walls in which the waterways may be drilled. The bore may be anything up to $\frac{1}{4}$ in.; but here let me give a warning. "On paper", a $\frac{5}{16}$ in. steam piston, will easily overcome the back thrust of a $\frac{1}{4}$ in. water piston, and such a pump would *feed* perfectly if *made* perfectly; but as there is not a wonderful lot of "spare power" floating around with such small bores, it is not advisable for a novice or one whose work is not fully "up to scratch", to make the pump bores too large. The combined back thrust and friction may "stop the clock", in a manner of speaking, and she won't pump at all. Anyway, I think a $\frac{7}{32}$ in. water piston might be chanced with safety, considering the average amateur's skill. Turn the cylinder barrels from rod, bronze or gunmetal, rough-drilling the bores first, and finally boring and reaming. A boring tool for this small size being fragile, the holes might be drilled, say, $\frac{1}{64}$ in. under size and opened out with a D-bit made from silver-steel, the business end being bevelled off slightly to give a lead. Don't forget to oilstone the cutting edges. Very probably the D-bit will leave a smooth and true bore, and the use of a reamer afterwards would be superfluous. Both the bore and flanges *must* be true and square one with each other or there will be friction and binding when the whole gadget is put together; so you know what to aim for. The waterways may be drilled as shown (Fig. 3-14), or as for the "solid" cylinder, with the exception that there will be no need to plug the bottom aperture; in fact, the waterway is the same, in effect, as an ordinary steam passage, and communication between the long hole and the bottom of the cylinder may be made by a nick filed in the wall. The end of the hole is, of course, closed by the bottom cover, which is merely a plain disc $\frac{11}{16}$ in. diameter turned truly and attached by four 10 BA screws. If the pump is intended for air-brake operation and is required to be double-acting, the top covers of the pump cylinders will be exactly the same as the bottom covers of the steam cylinders, and provided with a gland and stuffing-box, the outside of which is turned a tight push fit in the lower end of the distance-piece. If the pump is wanted for boiler feeding, a double-acting pump is not necessary, and this simplifies matters a great deal, because there will be only four valves and no glands on the top covers. An air port must be drilled in the upper end of the cylinder to release any trapped air or any water which may get past the piston, and a $\frac{1}{16}$ in. bore pipe should be attached to this and led away to the underside of the running-board. The screws securing the top

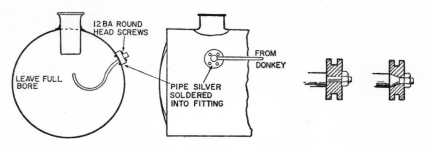

Fig. 3-15 Exhaust pipe for donkey pump.
Alternative pump pistons.

covers must be long enough to pass right through the flange of the distance-piece, the cover itself, and enter well into the flanges of cylinders.

The donkey pump can be supported on the footplate by the water connection fitting, which is amply strong, being made for the job (see Fig. 3-16). The stem of this passes through the running-board and is nutted underneath, after which the water feed pipe is attached as shown in the picture. The lugs on the side of the steam-chest rest against the boiler, to which they are secured by a couple of 8 BA roundhead brass screws driven into the boiler barrel. Studs and nuts may be used if desired, as in real practice; but as the pump very seldom (if ever) needs removing, the screws answer the purpose quite as well. A smear of plumbers' jointing around the threads prevents any leakage.

Pipe Connections

The water delivery from the valve box passes through a short pipe terminating in a union which is attached to one branch of a tee; the stem of this is coupled to the left-hand mechanical pump between the frames, and the other branch of the tee is connected to the feed pipe leading to the clack-box on top of the boiler, so that the feed from the L.H. mechanical pump and the donkey both "go the same way home". Steam is taken from a union on the whistle turret in the cab, by a pipe leading to a wheel-valve fixed to the backhead on the fireman's side of the footplate, thence through the cab front as shown. The pipe should be kept as close to the boiler as possible, so that it keeps hot and you don't have the steam cylinders full of water from condensation every time you want to start the donkey. The exhaust pipe goes from the union screwed into the passage in the port block to a flange fitting on the side of the smokebox, see drawing (Fig. 3-15); and the internal pipe is bent to throw the exhaust steam up the chimney, but is left full bore to avoid back pressure. The steam pipe is $\frac{1}{8}$ in. by 22 gauge copper tube, and the exhaust $\frac{1}{8}$ in. brass treblet with the thinnest walls obtainable, to get a free exhaust passage without a huge unsightly pipe along the side of the boiler. Of course, the exhaust pipe may be turned down and the steam blown away below the running-board, but this spoils the effect and is contrary to full-sized practice.

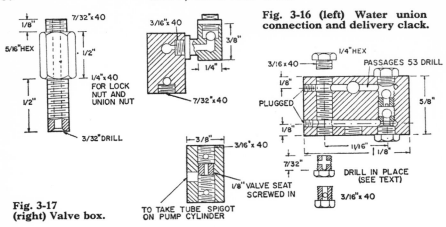

Fig. 3-16 (left) Water union connection and delivery clack.

Fig. 3-17 (right) Valve box.

Pump Pistons

Those who are using "solid" pump cylinders will not need bottom pistons, as the piston-rods will form the pump plungers or rams, and all you need worry about is to see they pass through the glands truly, with the minimum of friction. Users of the regulation Westinghouse-type pistons will have to exercise great care in fitting up, as the pistons cannot very well be turned on their own rods; the two covers—bottom of steam cylinder and top of pump cylinder, which would have to be assembled first—wouldn't leave much room for chucking. If the pistons are turned up truly on a separate rod and then carefully transferred to their own rods, a satisfactory job may be accomplished (Fig. 3-15). Fix them the way you think you can manage best; either the method I gave for the steam pistons, or by a parallel shoulder and nut, or taper and nut. If the nut is used, it will probably need a recess turning out in the bottom cover to allow full stroke. Although a fit as close as a steam piston is not absolutely essential, get them as near as possible, and pack with graphited yarn. Many pump-wallahs of the old school were fond of using tallow-impregnated lamp cotton and suchlike packings; but, although they give very good results in big work, the tallow has a chemical action on brass and gunmetal, resulting in a green, sticky, poisonous deposit, which is liable to choke the valves and passageways of a tiny donkey pump. It will now be necessary to assemble the whole bag of tricks so that the valve box for the pump cylinders may be fitted. When assembled, try under pressure either by tyre-pump or steam, and see that she works freely and does not bind anywhere; it will be a hard job to do any further lining-up once the valve box is on.

Making the Valve Box

The box itself is formed from a piece of $\frac{5}{8}$ in. by $\frac{3}{8}$ in. brass bar, $1\frac{1}{8}$ in. long. Square up the ends—just clamp in chuck and face off; it doesn't matter about setting truly so long as chuck holds work parallel with lathe bed—and mark off for holes as sketch (Fig. 3-17). Drill the two "north to south" holes first and tap them right through their length; 21 drill and $\frac{3}{16}$ in. by 40 tap. Next drill the top hole forming the common delivery passage; and here anyone who wishes may make a digression. If the engine for which the pump is intended has no top feed nor mechanical pumps, the delivery passage can be drilled right through the block, a pipe attached to the end via a union, and the delivery taken direct to a separate clack placed well forward on the side of the barrel.

When feeding into a common delivery pipe, as on my *Fayette*, the outlet should be at the back of the block and a little separate clack attached at this point to prevent any water delivered by the mechanical pumps being forced back into the donkey cylinders. The delivery valve seatings are merely little nipples drilled $\frac{3}{32}$ in. and faced off truly after screwing to fit the holes. Threads should be tight, and a screwdriver nick filed or sawn at the lower end to serve the dual purpose of inserting and preventing the waterway being blocked by the inlet valve rising too high. The valves themselves are $\frac{1}{8}$ in. rustless steel balls. The upper ends of the valve-box passages are closed by $\frac{3}{16}$ in. hexagon-headed plugs, which need no separate description. The lower end caps are combined plugs and valve seatings. Chuck a length of $\frac{1}{4}$ in. hexagon screw-rod, turn and screw outside as shown, centre, drill $\frac{3}{32}$ in. for about $\frac{3}{16}$ in. down, face truly, and part off $\frac{1}{8}$ in. behind the shoulder. Reverse and chamfer. Screw both plugs home tightly in the valve box; then put a drill down the opening of the suction waterway and drill right through both plugs; see drawing (Fig. 3-17).

Scratch a line on the hexagon heads before removing, to show when the plugs are in the right position when replacing at any time. All valve balls are seated by a gentle blow in the usual way. The valve box should fit between the cylinder flanges as the steam-chest did previously, when we made the "upstairs" part. If it does, very carefully mark out on it the position of the two copper tube connecting-pieces we fitted to the pump cylinders; drill a No. 40 hole at these points right through into the valve-box passages or valve chambers, and open out to take the tubes. With the steam and pump cylinders all assembled, the valve box may be fixed in position with some binding wire, and the job sweated up with either ordinary solder (there is no heat to contend with when the pump is forcing cold water) or babbit, whichever you prefer. Don't "use a trowel", and be careful not to block up the connections between pump cylinders and valve box.

The Final Touches

Plug up the ends of the drilled holes where shown, and if the back outlet clack (Fig. 3-16) is being fitted, drill and tap a hole to take the clack stem; this should come midway between the two valve chambers. Underneath the valve box, drill another hole also in the middle and communicating with the inlet passage. This one is $\frac{7}{32}$ in. by 40, and takes the stem of the combined union and support (Fig. 3-16). The latter is like a union with an elongated body, and the part where the nut fits is made long enough to stick through the footplating or running-board and take a clamping-nut. Chuck a length of $\frac{5}{16}$ in. hexagon brass rod, face off, centre, and drill $\frac{3}{32}$ in. for about $1\frac{1}{4}$ in. down. Turn $\frac{1}{2}$ in. of it to $\frac{1}{4}$ in. diameter, and screw 40 threads with die-holder in tailstock. Part off as shown, or longer if you want the donkey to stand higher off the running-board; reverse and turn and screw the other end to fit the tapped hole under the valve box. Make a union nut and lock-nut to suit the $\frac{1}{4}$ in. stem, and then carefully wash any chips out of the valve-box passages and assemble up the valves and caps. To test, mount the complete gadget by the support on anything convenient, and couple a tyre pump to the steam-chest. Slip a piece of rubber tube over the suction union and stand the whole issue in the bath or the domestic sink, with the tube in some water. Pump gently until water starts to come from the delivery hole, then put your finger over the latter and press hard on the tyre pump—you will at once see why it is advisable to test in bath or sink!

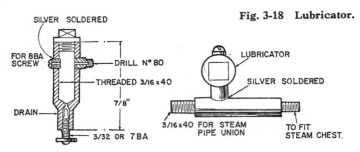

Fig. 3-18   Lubricator.

Lubricator and Delivery Clack

The lubricator is a necessary fitment, and is made from a piece of $\frac{1}{4}$ in. round brass or gunmetal $\frac{7}{8}$ in. long (Fig. 3-18). Chuck, centre and drill No. 21 for $\frac{5}{8}$ in. down; tap the end $\frac{3}{16}$ in. and make a plug, with square pip, to fit. Reverse, centre, drill No. 55 right through into large hole, open out No. 48 for $\frac{3}{16}$ in. and tap 7 BA. Drill drain hole as shown and make a little steel screwed needle (with hand wheel) to fit the tapped hole. The feed nipple and bush for cleaning screw are silver-soldered into plain drilled holes and need no explanation.

The complete lubricator screws into a union fitting, which is attached to the steam-chest, or the union and lubricator can be made integral, as preferred. The clack box or check valve (Fig. 3-16) is also made from $\frac{1}{4}$ in. round rod, and needs no detailed explanation. The drawing gives the sizes. The part which screws into the hole in the valve box is silver-soldered into the side of the clack body, in order to keep the height down and miss the curve of the boiler where the pump is installed. A $\frac{1}{8}$ in. delivery pipe (not shown) is also silver-soldered into the upper part of the clack, and the outer end is provided with a union nut and cone for attaching to the main feed pipe, as mentioned earlier. When the donkey-pump delivery is fed to the boiler through a separate clack, a pet cock will be needed on the pipe between

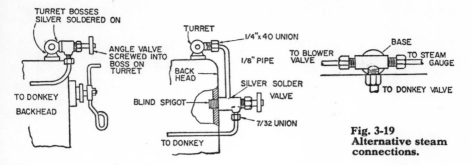

Fig. 3-19
Alternative steam
connections.

donkey and clack to release trapped air and enable the pump to pick up; but where it feeds into a common delivery, trapped air may be let out via the main by-pass on that delivery and no separate cock is needed.

Steam Valve for Donkey Pump

A fine steam regulation is desirable, so that in certain cases the donkey can be set to keep the water in the glass at an approximate level on a non-stop run, as in big practice. Make a wheel valve similar to Fig. 1-5 and turn the point of the needle to a long or "slow" taper; this will give a fine adjustment like our friends the radio fans get on their slow-motion dials. This valve can either be placed direct on a fountain or turret, or else made with a blind spigot, as shown in Fig. 3-19. It is screwed into the backhead and fed with steam from some high point on the boiler shell—the higher the better, as the little donkey uses "wet" steam (the enginemen's term for saturated or non-superheated steam), and if much water goes over with it the clearance spaces are filled up and "the clock stops".

Valve Box for Double-Acting Pump

All that is now required to enable anyone to use the duplex pump for supplying air for brake operation, spray oil burners and suchlike is a valve box with four chambers, each containing a suction and delivery valve for each end of each cylinder. This sounds formidable in such a small size, but is easier than it appears. Instead of the two valve chambers already described, drill four, in two pairs, getting each pair as close as you can without actually breaking into one another—$\frac{1}{32}$ in. between the bores will be quite enough. The top passage connects all four delivery valves, and the bottom connects all four inlets; and take great care when making up the bottom caps, which are drilled crossways as well as longitudinally, to mark the direction of the cross hole on the slotted heads, so they all line up on assembly. Holes are drilled into the space between the valves in each chamber, same as in the two-chamber valve box, and little spigots of tube tapped in. The backs of the pump cylinders must have flats filed in (Fig. 3-20), and holes are drilled to receive the spigots on the valve box. They need not be an exact fit, as their object is only to prevent the solder or babbit blocking up the passageways

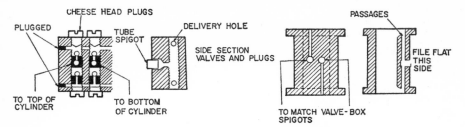

Fig. 3-20   Variation for double-acting pump.

when the whole is sweated up on assembly. Communication between the pump cylinder bores and the spigot-holes is made as shown, in a manner somewhat similar to steam-cylinder practice.

As air pressure for brakes or any other purpose is seldom required at or even near boiler pressure, the pump pistons can be made larger than if used for water, say, $\frac{1}{4}$ in. maximum for $\frac{5}{16}$ in. steam cylinder; a steady back-pressure on a piston this size would enable the pump to kick steadily away with the familiar "ssss-phut!" of its full-sized but equally vigorous relation. For gauge "1" the donkey had better be a little over size; make the steam cylinders $\frac{1}{4}$ in. bore by $\frac{3}{8}$ in. stroke, and do not fit pump pistons at all, but use $\frac{5}{32}$ in. piston-rods acting as direct rams in "solid"-type pump cylinders; $3\frac{1}{4}$ in. and $3\frac{1}{2}$ in. gauge engines use steam cylinders $\frac{1}{2}$ in. bore and $\frac{3}{4}$ in. stroke, with $\frac{11}{32}$ in. bore pumps; $4\frac{3}{4}$ in. and 5 in. gauge engines, steam cylinders $\frac{5}{8}$ in. by 1 in. and pumps $\frac{7}{16}$ in. bore.

Plate 1

Curly's 3½ in. gauge 2-2-2 locomotive and tender
standing by the full-size ex-L.B.S.C.R. signal, presen-
ted to him by old railwaymen

Plate 2

This 3½ in. gauge L.B.S.C.R. single-wheeler was Curly's favourite engine

Plate 3

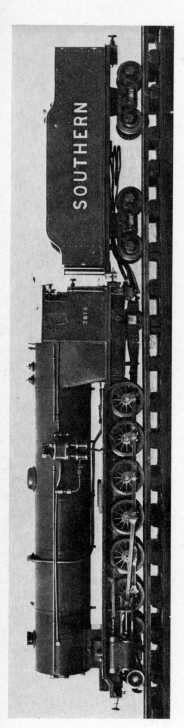

Aptly named Caterpillar L.B.S.C.'s free-lance 2½ in. gauge 4-12-2, with three cylinders and 100 lb. boiler

Below: Tishy was a rebuild from a commercial L.N.E.R. Pacific

Plate 4

Cab view of Curly's 2-2-2 Grosvenor. Note the neat
backhead fittings

Below: 3½ in. gauge Princess Marina built by Mr.
J. T. Brandrick of Birmingham M.E.S.

Plate 5

A Britannia built by Mr. D. H. Jennings of Neath

Below: L.B.S.C.'s own version of Tich is fitted with
outside Stephenson valve gear

Plate 6

Tugboat Annie was the first 2½ in. gauge engine to be fitted with the Holcroft valve gear

Cock o' the North, another Curly rebuild, for 2½ in. gauge

Plate 7

L.B.S.C.'s Flying Horse, a 2-2-2 Eastern Counties engine

Plate 8

The original coal-fired Atlantic, Ayesha, 2½ in.
gauge

5 in. gauge Pannier based on L.B.S.C.'s Pansy and
built by Mr. E. A. Allchin. This engine won the L.B.S.C.
Memorial Cup at the 1968 Exhibition

Below: 5 in. gauge Speedy built by Mr. T. Prime

Plate 9

Mr. W. Fry of Reading with his 3½ in. gauge Doris
Photograph by C. A. Bealing

A 3½ in. gauge Juliet exhibited at a recent M.E.
Exhibition. Alas, the builder is not known to us!

Plate 10

L.B.S.C.'s 3½ in. gauge 0-6-2 tank engine Mona. Photograph by Lorna Minton

Plate 11

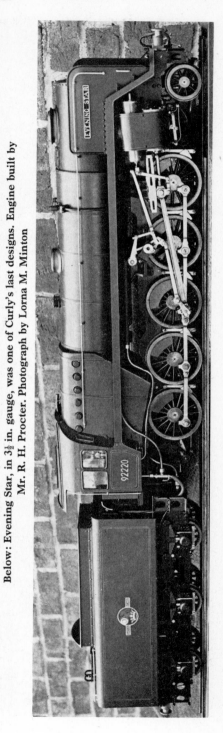

Another view of Tugboat Annie, the 4-cylinder Pacific with Holcroft gear

Below: Evening Star, in 3½ in. gauge, was one of Curly's last designs. Engine built by Mr. R. H. Procter. Photograph by Lorna M. Minton

Plate 12

Some views of L.B.S.C.'s
workshop

Left: The Milnes lathe

Right: Vertical miller,
and some stocks of
materials

Left: Myford Super 7.
Accessories in rear

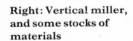

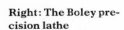

Right: The Boley pre-
cision lathe

Plate 13

The cab fittings of L.B.S.C.'s "single", Rola

Below: This is Betty, based on an imaginary design
for the ex-Southern Railway

Plate 14

Mr. F. Few's 3½ in. gauge Lion is based on L.B.S.C.'s
Titfield Thunderbolt design

Below: Curly's outside-framed G.W.R. 4-4-0 Dilys

Plate 15

Curly's Rola. A free-lance "single" with disc wheels

Plate 16

Another view of Curly's 3½ in. gauge Great Western 4-4-0, based on the Dukedog class

Below: This is Fernanda, a free-lance 2½ in. gauge "Pacific" with piston valves

CHAPTER IV

Water Gauges

A SECTION OF a complete water gauge is shown in Fig. 4-1, and the separate parts in Fig. 4-2. To make it, chuck a length of $\frac{5}{16}$ in. round gunmetal or phosphor-bronze rod; centre, drill No. 12 for $\frac{5}{8}$ in. depth. Turn down $\frac{3}{16}$ in. of outside to $\frac{9}{32}$ in. diameter, screw 40 threads per inch with a die held in tailstock holder and part off $\frac{9}{16}$ in. from the end. Reverse, countersink slightly with No. 2 or $\frac{7}{32}$ in. drill, tap $\frac{7}{32}$ in. by 40 for about $\frac{3}{16}$ in. down, chamfer the edge and face off. This leaves a plain section $\frac{3}{8}$ in. long; centre pop the middle of it, drill right through with $\frac{3}{16}$ in. drill, and scrape off the burrs. Chuck a $\frac{3}{8}$ in. rod, turn $\frac{1}{4}$ in. of it to $\frac{7}{32}$ in. diameter, and put a thread on. Part off at $\frac{5}{8}$ in. from the end. Chuck any odd bit of rod to make a holding gadget for finishing columns; face it, centre, drill No. 12 and tap $\frac{7}{32}$ in., chamfering the hole. Screw the blank in, centre and drill No. 30; turn the

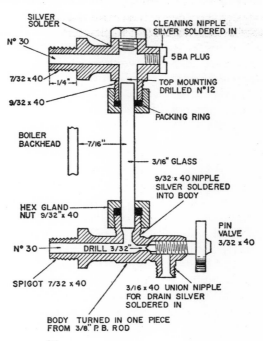

Fig. 4-1 Water gauge.

65

outside to outline shown in Fig. 4-1 and cut back about $\frac{1}{16}$ in. at the extremity so that it is a drive fit in the hole in the middle section. The cleaning plug is a bit of $\frac{1}{4}$ in. round gunmetal rod centred, drilled No. 40 and tapped 5 BA, with a $\frac{1}{16}$ in. spigot as above described.

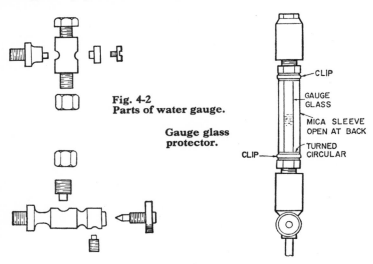

**Fig. 4-2
Parts of water gauge.**

**Gauge glass
protector.**

CLIP

GAUGE
GLASS

MICA SLEEVE
OPEN AT BACK

CLIP

TURNED
CIRCULAR

Bottom Fitting

Chuck the $\frac{3}{8}$ in. rod again, centre, drill about $\frac{3}{4}$ in. down with $\frac{3}{32}$ in. or No. 43 drill. Open out $\frac{5}{16}$ in. with No. 30 drill, tap $\frac{5}{32}$ in. by 40; turn outside to given outline and part off at $1\frac{1}{4}$ in. from end. Reverse, centre, drill No. 30 for $\frac{3}{4}$ in. down; turn down $\frac{1}{4}$ in. of outside to $\frac{7}{16}$ in. and screw 40 threads per inch. At $\frac{11}{16}$ in. from this end drill a $\frac{3}{16}$ in. hole into the body, to carry the nipple and gland which holds the bottom of the glass. The nipple is a bit of rod turned down to $\frac{9}{32}$ in. and screwed 40 threads; drill No. 12 for $\frac{1}{8}$ in. down, continue for another $\frac{1}{4}$ in. or so with No. 40, and part off at $\frac{1}{4}$ in. full. Chuck the screwed piece very lightly and reduce the end with the smaller hole iill it is a drive fit in the $\frac{3}{16}$ in. hole in body, the little spigot being about $\frac{1}{16}$ in. long. Next drill the drain hole $\frac{3}{32}$ in., taking care not to get too close to the pin seat, and make a nipple (as above) to take the $\frac{3}{16}$ in. union nut which secures the drain pipe. The two $\frac{9}{32}$ in. by 40 gland nuts need no special description, neither does the drain union nut. The valve pin is $\frac{5}{32}$ in. rustless steel, turned to a cone point, threaded $\frac{5}{32}$ in. by 40, squared at the outer end and fitted with a little wheel. Tip: whenever you want to square a small rod quickly, put it in the three-jaw chuck with the required amount projecting. Set No. 1 jaw vertically (12 noon), and file a flat with a safe-edged file, holding it horizontally with the safe edge bearing against chuck. Now shift chuck round till No. 1 jaw indicates 3 p.m., and file another flat, still holding file as before. Next shift again to 6 p.m., and file the third flat. Round once more to 9 p.m., and complete the job. You then have a nice square end, all flats same length and width, and angles correct. To assemble the parts (see Fig. 4-2) press the top branch-piece and the cleaning plug into the centre section; press the two nipples into the lower section; apply Boron compo paste, blow up to a bright red (a small gas blowpipe is plenty powerful enough for these small jobs) and apply a strip of No. 1 silver-solder. "Easyflo" silver solder and flux may also be used. Pickle, wash and clean with fine wire brush. Make a couple of plugs for the top column and the job is complete. This gauge is the best I have yet tried where the water is bad and full of impurities, as every bit of it can be cleaned without dismantling; simply remove plugs and valve, and poke a wire through.

Gauge-Glass Protector

To make a protector for any water-gauge, make the two gland nuts a little longer, $\frac{1}{8}$ in. will do, and turn them down as shown (Fig. 4-2). Exact diameter does not matter. Fit the gauge up on the boiler, then obtain a thin piece of mica. The local oil stores sell mica fronts as fitted to Beatrice-type stoves; a piece of this mica split off will be just right, you only want thin stuff. Bend it round the circular part of the gland nuts; if it cracks it is too thick, in which case use two thin layers; leave an open space at the back, and secure top and bottom with a couple of $\frac{1}{8}$ in. strips of hard brass or German silver, each bent to a ring and sprung on. If preferred, the fixing may be by soft clips secured by a 10 BA screw and nut. Personally, I have little use for a protector, the risk of breakage is very remote if the glass if of fairly stout section and the mountings lined up properly; but for those who would rather have one I do not know of any other type which gives a clearer view of the water level.

Water Columns and "Reflex" Gauges

Water columns are found on all modern American boilers, and ensure a correct reading of the water level, as they eliminate the effect of surging, and the water in the glass keeps very steady. On a big boiler the column is usually a casting, with flanges to take two water-gauge fittings and two or three test cocks as well. The bottom of the column is attached to the back-head and communicates with the water-space direct, whilst the top is connected to the steam space by a pipe and union. Valves are provided to isolate the column in the event of a burst gauge or damaged cock, and the whole issue is arranged to stand vertically and clear of the backhead; an advantage when the latter slopes, like many modern types. The sketches (Figs. 4-3 and 4-4) show the little columns I made, and one of them had a "reflex" gauge which can be used direct on the backhead if desired. The columns were made from $\frac{3}{8}$ in. copper tube, with a disc silver-soldered at the top end and fitted with a $\frac{1}{4}$ in. screw plug for cleaning purposes at the bottom. Short pieces of $\frac{1}{4}$ in. copper tube were silver-soldered in at each end, and these were provided with oval flanges for attaching to the backhead by a couple of 8 BA roundhead screws in each. The gauge fittings were silver-soldered to the column in the usual manner, and the result was a very steady and true rendering of the water

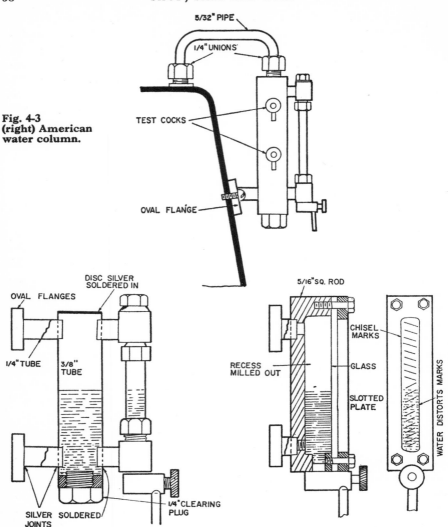

Fig. 4-3
(right) American
water column.

Fig. 4-4   Section of column and reflex type water gauge.

level. The back of the "reflex" gauge was a piece of $\frac{5}{16}$ in. square brass rod, which had a deep slot $\frac{3}{16}$ in. wide end-milled in it. Tubes were attached to top and bottom for connection to the column or boiler, the bottom also had a drain valve, and the front was covered with a flat glass window and retaining plate. At the back of the slot a series of diagonal marks were made with a small chisel, and these appeared distorted when seen through the water, so that the level was easily read. Instead of the plain "window", a corrugated glass, which will give the proper reflex effect—steam space showing silvery and water black, would be an advantage.

CHAPTER V

Whistles

A Single-Note Tube Whistle

OBTAIN A PIECE of $\frac{7}{16}$ in. diameter brass treblet tube about 4 in. long for a deep note. Turn one end off square with the bore—mind how you tighten the chuck; this thin tube is easily distorted—and at a distance of $\frac{5}{8}$ in. from one end, carefully file an opening, as shown (Fig. 5-1), with a small half-round file. This opening is most important; get the edges nice and sharp and free from burrs, and be careful about the shape. Fig. 5-1 shows how the opening should appear when finished, and also shows the way *not* to make it; the latter style, which is commonly found on small whistles, causes them to develop a bad cold under the influence of high-pressure steam. Turn up a disc $\frac{3}{16}$ in. thick and a tight push fit in the whistle tube, and file a segment out as shown, again avoiding a common mistake. Tap this into the tube until the filed part just shows above the squared end of the opening. Now make a temporary adapter for testing by turning up any odd bit of scrap rod to the

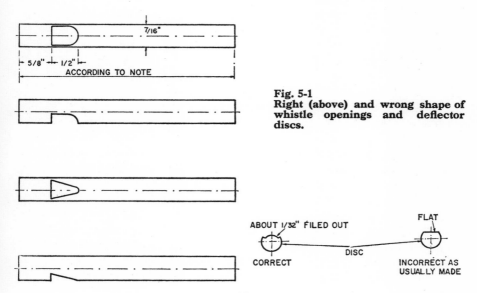

Fig. 5-1
Right (above) and wrong shape of whistle openings and deflector discs.

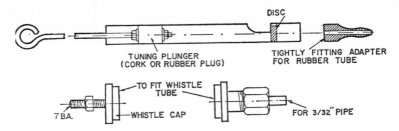

Fig. 5-2 Whistle details.

shape shown in Fig. 5-2; which also shows a gadget for getting the correct note. A bit of $\frac{1}{8}$ in. brass wire is threaded one end for about an inch, the other end being bent into a ring. Put a nut and washer on the thread, then an old medicine bottle cork or a rubber accumulator stopper—anything will do so long as it fits the tube airtight—and secure with another nut and washer. Note, this *must* be airtight, otherwise you will get a false note. Now, borrow a good tyre pump and couple up to the adapter on the whistle with a piece of rubber gas tube.

Tuning Up

First put the sliding plunger about $\frac{1}{4}$ in. down, and give a sharp stroke with the pump. If a clear note results, well and good; but most likely it will sound like the cry of a banshee or the last dying wail of a super-oscillation on an old-fashioned radio set. The clear note is obtained by moving the disc at the bottom of the opening either up or down a fraction at a time and trying with the pump after each adjustment. In theory, there should be a hard and fast fixed distance for the disc to show above the opening, but I don't suppose there is one in a thousand who could file the segment out of the disc dead true. I have machined them before parting off, by using a broad flat tool and pulling the lathe round part of a revolution by hand; but it was hardly worth the trouble. However, having obtained a clear note, the depth of tone is easily adjusted by the sliding plunger. In the position given, the note is like the old Brighton or Midland engines, and as it approaches the opening the note rises until finally you get the old original North London screech or the long-forgotten echoing call of a Metropolitan locomotive at Gower Street in the old steam days. Now there is just one more test after you have obtained the correct note. Squeeze the rubber connecting-tube between finger and thumb, press the pump plunger down as hard as you can—this will give about 70 lb. pressure—and let the tube go. If you get a clear sharp "pop" from the whistle with no huskiness, pass it as O.K. If not, adjust the disc slightly again until the desired result is obtained, after filing a tiny shade more out of the segment. Now note—if you blow into the whistle with your mouth you will probably get only a feeble husky imitation of a whistle; this is as it should be. I have yet to meet the person with 70 lb. lung pressure!

Finishing the Whistle

Mark off the position of the inner end of the tuning plunger before re-moving it, cut the whistle tube short at that point and square it up in the chuck. Make a little cap as shown in Fig. 5-2; this should be a tight push-in fit and is secured with a touch of solder. It carries a 7 BA brass stud and nut, which supports the end of the whistle by the help of a little bracket bolted to the frame of the engine. Next make a union fitting from a short length of $\frac{7}{16}$ in. round gunmetal or screw-rod. The exact size of this does not matter; just turn down $\frac{1}{8}$ in. or so to a push fit in the whistle tube and part off at, say, $\frac{1}{2}$ in. from the end. Re-chuck the short length by the spigot, turn down to $\frac{1}{4}$ in. diameter for about $\frac{5}{16}$ in. and screw 40 threads per inch; centre deeply with a centre-drill and continue through with a $\frac{1}{16}$ in. or No. 52 drill. Make a union nut and a little liner to take a $\frac{3}{32}$ in. diameter pipe. To secure the disc at its proper position in the whistle, put a few drops of killed spirit or Baker's fluid in—*don't* use paste fluxes—and a small bead of solder about the size of a pinhead, no bigger. Hold the whistle (with the opening upwards) over a Bunsen or a spirit flame until the solder melts and secures the disc. Then tap the union fitting in and solder it neatly, and the whistle is complete.

Combined Turret and Whistle Valve

For all built-up fittings, use bronze or gunmetal rod if available; if not, best quality brass can be "made do". To make the above fitting, part off 1 in. of $\frac{5}{16}$ in. round rod; chuck in three-jaw, face, centre, and drill right through with No. 43 drill. Open out to $\frac{3}{8}$ in. depth with $\frac{3}{16}$ in. drill, and bottom to $\frac{1}{2}$ in. depth with $\frac{3}{16}$ in. D-bit. Tap $\frac{7}{32}$ in. by 40 for about $\frac{1}{4}$ in. down, and slightly countersink the end. Reverse in chuck, open out the other end to $\frac{3}{8}$ in. depth with $\frac{3}{16}$ in. drill; tap and countersink as above. Put a $\frac{3}{32}$ in. reamer through the remains of the No. 43 hole. If you haven't one, file off the end of a bit of $\frac{3}{32}$ in. silver-steel to a long angle, like the way a chef would slice a Jerry sausage; harden and temper to dark yellow, rub the flat on an oilstone, and it will ream very well.

At $\frac{1}{4}$ in. from the D-bitted end, drill a $\frac{5}{32}$ in. hole right across. Midway between them, drill another hole of similar size, but just penetrating the passageway; and another similar one at $\frac{1}{4}$ in. from the opposite end. Fit $\frac{1}{4}$ in. by 40 union screws to the two side holes; to make them, just chuck a bit of $\frac{1}{4}$ in. rod in three-jaw. Face, centre deeply with size E centre-drill, drill No. 40 for about $\frac{1}{2}$ in. depth, screw the outside $\frac{1}{4}$ in. by 40 for about $\frac{1}{4}$ in. down, and part off at a bare $\frac{3}{8}$ in. from the end. Reverse in chuck, and turn a $\frac{1}{16}$ in. pip on the end to a tight fit in the hole in the valve body. The hole at the other end is furnished with a similar union screw, but it is smaller, viz., $\frac{7}{32}$ in. by 40. The hole at the bottom is for the boiler connection, which is made exactly like the side connection of the clack-box shown in Fig. 1-3; it may be shorter, if the cab roof comes low down on top of the boiler. Silver-solder the whole lot at one heat; pickle, wash, and clean up. Seat a $\frac{1}{8}$ in.

rustless steel ball on the hole in the D-bitted end. Turn up a little cap from
¼ in. hexagon rod, screw to fit the tapped hole, and drill No. 30 to take the
spring, which is wound up from thin bronze wire, say about 30 gauge.

A similar cap is needed for the opposite end, but this one should be made
from ⅜ in. hexagon rod, and drilled right through with No. 48 drill. Screw
it right home, then file away the top and bottom corners, leaving it rectangular.
Cut a ¹⁄₁₆ in. slot right across, either by milling, planing, or filing. File up a
little lever, like a weeny reversing lever, to fit the slot, and pivot it in same by
drilling a No. 56 hole through the lot, as shown in the plan section, Fig. 5-3.

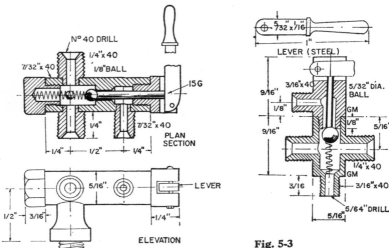

Fig. 5-3
Horizontal and vertical
whistle turrets.

Slightly enlarge the hole in the lever, then replace it, and drive a piece of
domestic blanket pin, or a piece of wire of similar thickness, through the
fitting and the lever. The latter must be perfectly free on the pin. The pushrod
is a bit of 15-gauge or ⁵⁄₆₄ in. bronze, brass, or rustless steel wire, of such a length
that when the lever is pushed home, the ball is forced off its seating, and
steam is allowed to pass it and get to the union to which the whistle pipe is
attached. This fitting is screwed into a ¼ in. by 40 tapped hole on top of the
wrapper sheet of the firebox, or into a bush silver-soldered into same, if the
metal is too thin to take a thread. Put a smear of plumbers' jointing (Boss
White, or any similar preparation) on the threads, to ensure a steam-tight
joint. The right-hand union is connected to the blower valve, and the pipe
leading to steam gauge is coupled to the left-hand union; the whistle pipe
cannot, of course, be connected until the boiler is erected.

A similar turret arranged vertically, for low-pitched boilers, is also shown
in Fig. 5-3. It is made in much the same way, but no end cap is needed, the
end being threaded to suit the tapped hole or bush in the boiler. The section
carrying the lever is made longer, and the union fitting for the whistle con-

nection is silver-soldered into it, instead of in the valve body itself. This permits of a little shorter fitting, and is suitable for a tank engine.

A Two-Note Chime Whistle

Two notes are easier than three for a start, so get a piece of $\frac{7}{16}$ in. brass treblet tube about 4 in. long, and at $\frac{3}{4}$ in. or so from one end file two arch-shaped openings, diametrically opposite, as shown in the sketch (Fig. 5-4). Next divide the whistle tube into two parts by a partition-piece reaching from the bottom of the opening to a point about $\frac{3}{4}$ in. from the end of the tube. Cut this piece from soft brass sheet about 20 gauge and bend over $\frac{1}{4}$ in. at one end of the strip, filing the projecting angle to a curve which will fit the inside of the whistle tube. Clean the inside of the latter and insert the division-piece; then put a little Baker's fluid inside along with a blob or two of solder, and hold the lot over the gas or a spirit lamp. If the tube be tilted about when the solder melts, and a little more fluid dropped in with a brush, the solder will run and seal up the joints without any trouble.

Next turn a brass disc, say, $\frac{1}{8}$ in. thick, to a tight driving fit in the tube, and file a little of the edge away at each side to let the steam blow across the openings. Tap this into place and then make a union fitting for the bottom of the tube, as described earlier in this chapter. Next put a cork or piece of rubber in the top end, and couple a tyre pump to the union; or a better way would be to arrange an air reservoir so that you can pump it up and get a longer blast. Something more substantial than an old oil drum is needed. As a matter of fact, I use my five-pint blowlamp as a whistle-testing device—don't laugh, but it works. The lamp has a big hefty pump, a shut-off valve on the oil pipe to the burner, and a pressure gauge to 100 lb. An adapter, which carries a whistle valve and union, fits in place of the filling plug; and to test a whistle (or anything else needing a few puffs of compressed air) all that is needed is to turn the oil out of the tank, screw the adapter on, pump up to any desired pressure, couple up the whistle or other gadget, and there you are. Not a "constant supply", true, but enough for the purpose.

Tuning Up the Whistle

Give her some air and see what sort of a row you get. No good blowing with your mouth, because if the whistle is all right for high-pressure steam you will only get a husky wheeze with the pressure of your lungs. First try each side of the whistle separately for clarity of note, by stopping up the other opening with your finger. If she sounds husky, the opening is too long, or there is too big a gap for the steam to come out. If she screeches and has umpteen overtones, the opening is too short. When either side of the whistle gives a clear note at 60 lb. or so, seal the joint between division-piece and disc by heating up again with a very tiny bit of solder and a smear of fluid; then try both sides blowing together. You will probably get a discord; if so, then adjust the cork or rubber stopper in or out of the tube until the two notes harmonise. Then measure up to the inner end of the cork, cut off the tube to requisite length and fit a turned brass plug. When mounting the whistle on the engine, arrange the openings at the sides, and tilt the whistle slightly so as to allow all water to drain out of it, otherwise it will do everything except produce chime notes.

Three Notes

If anybody wants to go one better and make a three-note chime, Fig. 5-4 also shows how the internal divisions may be arranged for ease of construction. If the division-pieces are made as shown, they will "stay put" while being soldered up. Care is necessary when filing out the three sound openings, and also when sealing the steam disc in, otherwise the solder will run where you don't want it to go, and very probably block up the steam ways. Tune up the reverse way to a two-note. After having got all three sections to blow clear notes at the required pressure, permanently seal up one of them at the full length of the tube. Then put a triangular-shaped piece of cork into No. 2 division to slightly raise the note and harmonise with No. 1. When the right note is found, seal with a soldered-in metal piece in place of the cork; then harmonise No. 2 with No. 3 in the same way, then try all three together; finally covering the end of the tube with a little turned ornamental cap.

The three-note chime is especially suited to small electric locomotives and motor-coach units, as it can be arranged to blow at low pressure if required

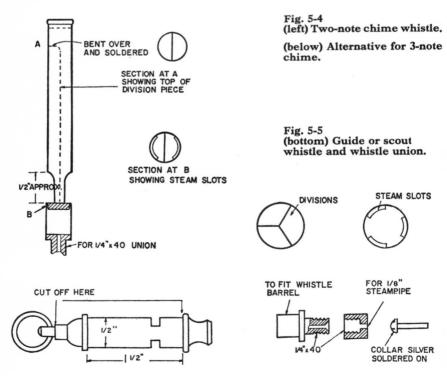

Fig. 5-4
(left) Two-note chime whistle.

(below) Alternative for 3-note chime.

Fig. 5-5
(bottom) Guide or scout whistle and whistle union.

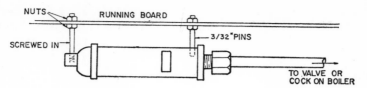

Fig. 5-6   How to erect whistle.

by varying the size of steam slots and sound openings. A little reservoir holding sufficient air for a couple of "blows" could be arranged under the locomotive or coach and kept charged by an eccentric-driven pump. No release valve or other device would be necessary, as the pump can be arranged to deliver not more than a predetermined pressure by leaving a clearance space behind the ram, as on certain types of automobile pressure pumps.

A Cheap Chime Whistle

Chime whistles are common on American engines, and their musical toot is also familiar to passengers on the electric suburban lines. Although I have described the making throughout of a chime whistle, maybe some readers would be glad to know that a satisfactory one can be fitted to their engine in a matter of twenty minutes. Purchase a "girl guide" or "boy scout" whistle (Fig. 5-5)—the notes are the same, only the girls' whistles are nickelled and the boys' oxidised. Cut off the mouthpiece and the ring. (Incidentally, the mouthpiece makes a fine gauge "O" safety-valve cover.) Turn up a union fitting as shown and make the nut to suit a $\frac{1}{8}$ in. steampipe. Drive the fitting into the whistle, and either secure by a touch of solder or screw one of the support pins through the whistle barrel into the union block. The whistle may be mounted under the running board by the two pins shown (Fig. 5-6), one in the pip which held the ring and the other as shown. No alteration of the slots will be necessary. The makers of these whistles evidently reckon on guides and scouts having good healthy lungs, and a $\frac{1}{8}$ in. steam pipe will pass just the right amount of steam to give clear notes at 70 lb. pressure or thereabouts. A louder whistle, with deeper notes, can be obtained by using one of the same pattern but much larger whistles, as supplied to football referees, and to air raid wardens, etc., during the war years. It is adapted for locomotive use, in exactly the same way.

Extra Deep-Tone Whistle

Here is a description of a simple way of giving a little L.M.S. locomotive a voice that resembles that of her full-size relations. It is possible to get the exact note and timbre by means of a mouth-organ reed in a suitable tube, arranged in a manner somewhat similar to the old motor bulb-horn reeds; but it needs careful manufacture and adjustment, whereas the veriest Billy Muggins can easily make up the gadget shown. L.M.S. engines used to come

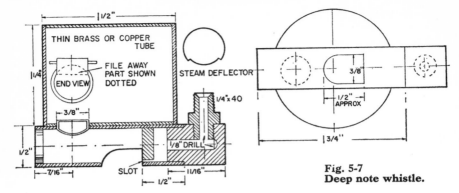

Fig. 5-7
Deep note whistle.

past my home every day, on the through run to Three Bridges, so I tuned up my experimental one to resemble their note.

There is nothing new in the use of a resonator-box to obtain a deep note on a small whistle; Carson's used them on their $3\frac{1}{2}$ in. and 5 in. gauge engines 40 years ago. But there is one difference, which makes all the difference, in a manner of speaking; the Carson whistles were arranged vertically, with the box right on the end of a short tube whistle of the usual pattern. When steam was turned on, any water that went over, or any produced by condensation of the steam in a cold pipe, was blown up into the box, and kept there by the rush of steam, producing a "bobbling" sound. The whistle gave a clear note only when hot, and supplied with dry steam. One was fitted to the 5 in. gauge Carson "Precursor" which I did up for Mr. R. C. Hammett; this had the above characteristics. To get a clear note, you have to keep the water out of the "sound-box"; and the easiest way of doing this, is to use a short horizontal whistle with the sound-box on top of it. There is a simpler way still, and that is to put a short tube in the bottom of the sound-box, and blow a jet of steam straight across the end of it, by means of a "mouthpiece" having a very fine steam slot in it; but while this is certainly simpler "on paper", in actual practice it isn't, as the mouthpiece with the steam slot is rather ticklish to make and adjust. I tried one before making the gadget shown, and it took far longer, with more "messing about", and no better result. Incidentally, the first of this type I made, was for my L.B. & S.C.R. engine *Grosvenor*; and by using a sound-box $1\frac{1}{4}$ in. diameter and $1\frac{1}{8}$ in. long, the little engine had the voice of her big sister.

How to Make the Whistle

The sound-box is a piece of $1\frac{1}{2}$ in. diameter brass or copper tube squared off in the lathe to a length of $1\frac{1}{4}$ in. The gauge of tube doesn't matter within reason, but the thinner it is, the better. If a piece of tube this size isn't available, roll up a piece of sheet brass or copper, of about 22-gauge, and solder the joint. It need not be silver-soldered, or even riveted, as there is no heat or pressure to withstand. The two ends are discs of 22-gauge sheet brass or copper, cut to fit tightly, and soldered. At $\frac{3}{8}$ in. from the edge, on one of the ends, drill a $\frac{3}{8}$ in. hole.

The part that makes the noise is made from a piece of $\frac{1}{2}$ in. thin brass or copper tube, the ends being squared off in the lathe, to a length of $1\frac{3}{4}$ in. At $\frac{1}{4}$ in. from one end, file the arch-shaped hole to the dimensions shown. The length of the opening need not be made to "mike" measurements, but the width of it should not be greater than shown; it must be less than the diameter of the tube, to give the best results. Chuck a bit of $\frac{1}{2}$ in. brass rod in the three-jaw, and turn down about $\frac{1}{2}$ in. of it to a drive fit in the tube; part off two $\frac{1}{8}$ in. slices. One is driven into the end of the tube to plug it; and the other has a tiny segment filed away, to the length of the "sound-hole" and a depth of about $\frac{1}{32}$ in., so that when it is driven into the tube, with the filed-away portion level with the "sound-hole" (see Fig. 5-7) steam issuing from the curved slot between disc and tube, passes right across the hole.

Chuck the $\frac{1}{2}$ in. rod again, and turn down $\frac{3}{16}$ in. of the end, to a drive-fit in the tube. Centre, and drill down to $\frac{5}{8}$ in. depth with $\frac{1}{8}$ in. or No. 32 drill. Part off at $\frac{11}{16}$ in. from the end; reverse in chuck, face off the pip if any, and slightly chamfer the edge. At $\frac{1}{4}$ in. from the blank end, drill a $\frac{7}{32}$ in. hole right through into the blind hole, and tap it $\frac{1}{4}$ in. by 40. In this, fit a union screw, as described for pumps and boiler fittings; this is screwed $\frac{1}{4}$ in. by 40 at both ends.

At about $\frac{7}{16}$ in. from the plugged end of the whistle tube, drill a $\frac{3}{8}$ in. hole, diametrically opposite to the arch-shaped hole. In this, fit a short piece of $\frac{3}{8}$ in. tube, same as used for boiler tubes, or a bit of thin brass treblet tube would do. File off the end, with a round file, so that the tube doesn't project into the whistle tube, and cause obstruction. The other end of the tube is fitted into the hole in one end of the sound-box, the whistle tube fitting tightly against the cover or end plate. All the joints can then be soft-soldered. Note, there must not be any air leaks, especially around the short bit of tube connecting the whistle tube to the sound-box. Now, if you blow into the open end of the whistle tube, you should get a faint, rather husky, low note. If the whistle blows easily by lung pressure, it is not suitable for high steam pressure. Push in the spigot of the union fitting, then connect a tyre-pump to the union screw. Press on the handle of the pump, bending any part of the connecting hose almost double, to prevent air passing; then suddenly release it when the gauge of the pump indicates 60 lb. or so. The whistle should then give a clear note. If it doesn't, either there is a leak in the soldered joints, or else the disc at the arch-shaped hole needs adjusting. If O.K. the whistle should blow the very deep L.M.S. note, quite clearly, at 60 lb. pressure. It will not be very loud, as the laws of acoustics (I believe that is the "scientific" term!) won't permit a little whistle to give the same volume of sound, at the same pitch, as a big one. If you want the sound of the whistle to carry a long way, a small whistle must be made to give a shrill tone. I have seen it stated that the proper way to make the opening is to cut it straight across, and not in the form of an arch at all; all I can say to that, is that the great majority of tube whistles, including the American chime whistles, have arch-shaped openings, and I have found this shape very satisfactory on my own engines.

How to Erect the Whistle

It took about 15 minutes to erect the whistle on my *Grosvenor*. The sound-box was located about half-way between the backhead and drag-beam with the pipe union pointing to the left. I then took the distance between the union on the whistle and the union on the turret, with a bit of lead fuse wire; cut my pipe, made the two nuts and cones, and silver-soldered the latter to the pipe, softening it at the same time. After pickling, washing off, and rubbing up with a bit of fine steel wool, the pipe was bent to the right contour by finger pressure, and the unions connected up. The pipe held the whistle in place *pro tem*. The piece of footplate between frames, backhead and drag-beam had been temporarily removed, naturally, before locating the whistle; and on this I marked a spot corresponding with the approximate centre of the sound-box, drilled it No. 40 and countersunk it. The footplate was then put in position, and a mark scribed on the top of the sound-box through the hole. The sound-box was then removed, the marked spot drilled No. 48 and tapped 7 BA; replaced, union tightened up, footplate replaced "for keeps", and a 7 BA countersunk brass screw, with a smear of plumbers' jointing on the thread, put through the hole in the footplate, into the tapped hole in the top of the sound-box.

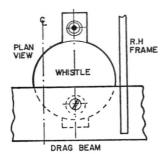

Fig. 5-8
How to erect the deep note whistle.

Should the space under the footplate be occupied by a brake cylinder the whistle may be erected as shown in Fig. 5-8. The sound-box can go partly under the top angle of the drag-beam, and the fixing screw can pass through a hole drilled in same; there is no need for the screw to be exactly in the middle of the sound-box. It has very little weight to support; the steam pipe does the lion's share of the holding up. If thin plate is used for the top and bottom of the sound-box, solder a little disc of brass about $\frac{1}{16}$ in. thick and about $\frac{3}{8}$ in. diameter, at the place where the screwhole is drilled and tapped; otherwise there won't be sufficient hold for the thread. Use $\frac{1}{8}$ in. pipe, to connect the whistle union to the one on the turret.

CHAPTER VI

Safety-Valves, Relief-Valves and Snifting Valves

IF YOU MAKE a "pop" valve of the usual type to work with a decent pop action on a $2\frac{1}{2}$ in. gauge engine, it usually has a fault often found with full-size valves—away goes your water when she pops off. The only way to check this is by increasing the clearance between the upper part of the valve and the recess it operates in, and then it is, in the majority of cases, good-bye to the pop action altogether. One good dodge is to use a ball valve in a "pop" recess. This gets over all the trouble. The pop action is not nearly so violent as with the coned valve, and, while it relieves the steam pressure at once, it does not "relieve" the boiler of any water at all. A section is shown in Fig. 6-1. Chuck a length of $\frac{1}{2}$ in. hexagon bronze or gunmetal rod in three-jaw; turn down $\frac{5}{16}$ in. length to $\frac{5}{16}$ in. diameter, screw $\frac{5}{16}$ in. by 32, and part off $\frac{5}{8}$ in. from the shoulder. Reverse, and rechuck in a tapped bush held in three-jaw, centre, and drill right through with No. 16 drill. Open out to $\frac{1}{2}$ in. depth with $\frac{9}{32}$ in. drill and D-bit; tap the end $\frac{5}{16}$ in. by 32 for the nipple, form the recess with a $\frac{15}{64}$ in. pin drill, and ream the small hole at the bottom with a $\frac{3}{16}$ in. reamer, or true the seat with a taper broach.

Chuck a $\frac{7}{32}$ in. bronze ball in three-jaw (hold it carefully!) centre, and drill nearly through with No. 48 drill. Tap 7 BA, and fit a spindle made from

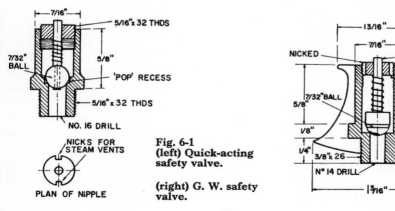

Fig. 6-1
(left) Quick-acting safety valve.

(right) G. W. safety valve.

79

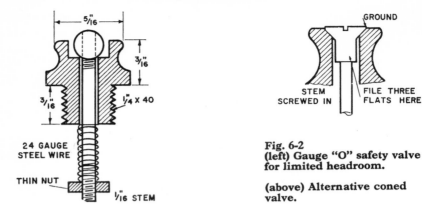

Fig. 6-2
(left) Gauge "O" safety valve for limited headroom.

(above) Alternative coned valve.

$\frac{3}{32}$ in. bronze or hard brass rod. Assemble as shown. It you graduate an inch of your tailstock barrel with $\frac{1}{16}$ in. divisions, you will find it mighty handy for this and many similar jobs. The spring is coiled up from 22-gauge steel music wire. Keep a few spare springs handy, and change them as soon as they begin to rust thin.

Safety-Valve and Casing

Pop-valves are not used on Great Western engines, one reason being that they usually run with a high water-level, and the safety-valves, being on the taper barrel and, therefore, close to the water, would tend to lift it every time the engine blew off. A plain valve is made from a bit of $\frac{1}{2}$ in. hexagon rod, 1 in. long; $\frac{5}{8}$ in. of this is reduced to $\frac{7}{16}$ in. diameter, drilled right through No. 14, and opened out, bottomed to $\frac{11}{16}$ in. depth, and tapped $\frac{5}{16}$ in. by 32. True up the ball seating with a $\frac{3}{16}$ in. reamer or a taper broach. Reverse in chuck, turn down and screw to fit safety-valve bush on barrel. The ball is a press fit in the cup, the edge being spun over, and the spring is 22-gauge tinned steel wire. The cap is merely a slice of $\frac{5}{16}$ in. rod, screwed as shown, and nicked to let the steam out.

The casing may be turned from a casting, or from a piece of $1\frac{1}{4}$ in. thick-walled tube, or even from the solid. Two slots will have to be filed to clear the top elbows, but these are done after the latter are fitted.

Safety Valves for Gauge "O" Locomotives

Chuck a length of $\frac{3}{8}$ in. hexagon gunmetal rod, turn down $\frac{3}{16}$ in. of the projecting end to $\frac{1}{4}$ in. diameter, and screw it 40 threads per inch; then part off $\frac{3}{8}$ in. total length. Ditto repeato twice, in case you spoil one; even if you don't it is as well to have a spare valve. Chuck any odd bit of scrap brass rod, face off, drill and tap $\frac{1}{4}$ in. by 40, to use as a tapped bush for finishing valves. Screw each blank into this, drill right through No. 34, follow with No. 22 till the point just enters fully, then bottom this shallow recess with a D-bit and ream the hole $\frac{1}{8}$ in. Form a valve-seating with a $\frac{5}{32}$ in. steel ball as described for clack and pump valves; then drill and tap a $\frac{5}{32}$ in. bronze ball for each valve (10 BA) and fit stems of $\frac{1}{16}$ in. brass or German silver wire. Thread the lower ends of the stems 10 BA and assemble with nut and spring as shown in Fig. 6-2. An alternative way is also given for those who prefer a coned valve ground to its seating. In the latter case, do not bottom the large hole, but turn the valve to the same angle as drill point. The springs being inside the boiler are no drawback to pressure adjustment, for if an adapter be made to fit in one of the bushes (which are turned from $\frac{3}{8}$ in. rod and screwed and sweated into the boiler shell), a tyre pump can be coupled to this, a valve screwed into the other bush, and a few strokes will soon show what she blows off at. About 70 lb. will enable the engine to pull all you are likely to need.

Automatic Cocks or Relief-Valves

The simplest form of what the enginemen call "automatic cocks" is, of course, the plain spring-loaded cover relief-valves as used on the G.W.R. engines and many other types. When we get down to $\frac{3}{4}$ in. bore cylinders we are faced with the alternatives of a small valve, neat, but uncertain in its action; a big valve, which works well, but is unsightly; or a fresh arrangement altogether. I think the latter is best, so give my version herewith. It will be seen from the sketch (Fig. 6-3) that the water outlets are really small safety valves formed in the body of the cylinder casting itself. They are nicely out of the way; can be made large enough for satisfactory operation; and if required, the discharge steam and water can be led away to any desired place by means of a pipe connected by a union to each outlet. The drawings show the arrangement for outside cylinders. For inside cylinders I should combine the relief-valves with the fixing arrangements (Fig. 6-4) and "kill two birds with one stone" in a simple yet effective manner.

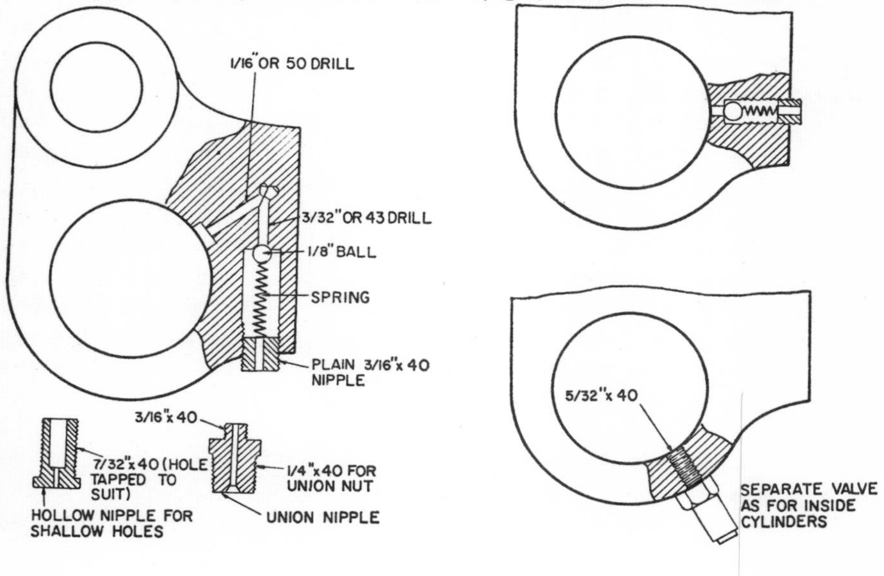

Fig. 6-3   (below) Water relief valve.   (right) Alternative relief valves.

1/16" OR 50 DRILL

3/32" OR 43 DRILL

1/8" BALL

SPRING

PLAIN 3/16"x 40 NIPPLE

3/16"x 40

7/32"x 40 (HOLE TAPPED TO SUIT)

1/4"x 40 FOR UNION NUT

HOLLOW NIPPLE FOR SHALLOW HOLES

UNION NIPPLE

5/32"x 40

SEPARATE VALVE AS FOR INSIDE CYLINDERS

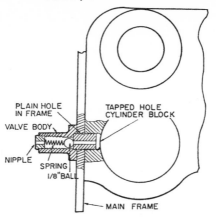

PLAIN HOLE
IN FRAME

TAPPED HOLE
CYLINDER BLOCK

VALVE BODY

NIPPLE

SPRING

1/8" BALL

MAIN FRAME

Fig. 6-4
Relief valve for
inside cylinders.

Waterways and Valve Holes

File a $\frac{1}{8}$ in. notch with a watchmaker's square file in the edge of the cylinder bore; make a centre pop in the notch and carefully drill the $\frac{1}{16}$ in. waterway towards the bolting face, bearing slightly inward. Repeat at the other end. If preferred, the holes can be drilled from the bolting face and the ends plugged; but it is a tricky job to get the drill to emerge into the bore exactly where you want it. Now turn the cylinder block upside down and carefully drill down to meet the waterways using either $\frac{3}{32}$ in. or No. 43 drill. Next make a pin drill, $\frac{5}{32}$ in. across the cutting edges, with a pilot which will enter the $\frac{3}{32}$ in. holes an easy fit; with this, open out these holes to $\frac{7}{16}$ in. or $\frac{1}{2}$ in. in depth, and tap $\frac{3}{16}$ in. by 40 threads. Form a valve seat with a $\frac{1}{8}$ in. steel ball at the bottom of each hole. (See Fig. 6-3).

Fitting Up and Adjusting

Make a couple of nipples from $\frac{3}{16}$ in. round brass-rod. These can be about $\frac{3}{16}$ in. long, with a $\frac{3}{32}$ in. hole in the centre, and a screwdriver slot so they can be easily adjusted. If the casting only admits of a shallow hole, use the long nipple shown. Wind a length of 22-gauge tinned steel "music" wire around a piece of 15-gauge spoke wire to form the springs. Drop a $\frac{1}{8}$ in. phosphor bronze ball into each valve hole; cut off a sufficient length of spring to reach from the ball to the top of the hole, insert it and screw a nipple in. That completes the arrangement; any water trapped between the piston and cylinder cover is forced down the waterway and pushes the ball off the seat, escaping through the nipple. The valves should be set to lift a few pounds above the normal working pressure of the boiler. If anyone wants to fit waste pipes instead of plain nipples, replace the latter by small unions having a $\frac{3}{16}$ in. tailpiece, as shown in the detail sketch (Fig. 6-3).

A "Wangle" for Inside Cylinders

The following simple way of arranging automatic cocks (Fig. 6-4) is available for use on any engine where the leading wheels do not reach as high as the cylinders, e.g., all 4-4-0 and 4-6-0 inside cylinder types; but, of course, not suitable for engines with coupled wheels leading, as Stroudley "Gladstones", Drummond bogie tanks, etc. Simply drill holes (using No. 30 drill) right through the frame plates and into the cylinder bores close as possible to the flanges, with the cylinders located in their correct position. Then remove them, tap the holes $\frac{5}{32}$ in. by 40 threads, carefully scrape all burrs from the cylinder bores and smooth off the bolting faces. Open out the holes in the frame $\frac{5}{32}$ in. clearing (No. 21 drill). Next make four miniature "safety valves" from $\frac{1}{4}$ in. hexagon brass-rod, using $\frac{1}{8}$ in. phosphor bronze balls for valves. The sizes are, "through" hole $\frac{1}{16}$ in., opened with $\frac{5}{32}$ in. pin drill and tapped $\frac{3}{16}$ in. by 40 threads. Spring and nipple as just described for valves formed in casting. Turn the body of the valve circular, but leave a $\frac{1}{16}$ in. hexagon collar at the shoulder. To assemble, locate the cylinders in the frame and screw the "safety valves" in with a smear of plumbers' jointing on the threads, and a turn or two of cotton under the shoulder. They not only do their own job of saving the cylinder covers from "going west", but also form very effective cylinder securing-bolts. As additional support an extra $\frac{1}{8}$ in. steel screw may be put through the frame and into the cylinder block on either side; but don't run *that* one into the bore. I usually put mine up higher, about $\frac{3}{8}$ in. or so above the cylinder centreline on a $2\frac{1}{2}$ in. gauge engine.

Cylinder Drain Cocks

Whilst some full-sized engines have ordinary plug-cocks, others have small poppet-valve gadgets operated by a push-rod, whilst others have cocks with parallel sliding plugs working like a piston-valve. The plug has a groove in it, and when this lines up with the steamways through the cock body, it allows the steam and water to blow past to the outlet pipe. When the solid part of the plug is slid between the steamways, naturally it closes the "entrance to the way out". Whilst these cocks are easy to make, and need only a fraction of an inch lateral movement to open and close them, it is a fiddling job to get the weeny parts steam- and water-tight, yet perfectly free to operate. The also-weeny poppet-valves are very fond of performing the sticking-up antic, as it only needs a speck of dirt on the seating, to cause a blow. Either type, in a size to be workable and absolutely reliable, would be far larger than "scale". The taper plug cock can't play the usual stick-or-leak tricks, as the plugs get plenty of lubrication from the cylinders, and the cocks can be made small enough to avoid being unsightly.

Connecting the cocks to the operating lever in the cab is another trouble, on account of the length of rodding involved. If connected as on the big engines, the rod would have to be in several sections with a hanger at each joint, otherwise it would simply buckle on the "push" movement; and a long continuous rod would need intermediate bearings or bridles. However, Sir H. N. Gresley got over the same trouble in full size by using a Bowden wire; and what was good enough for that much-lamented eminent engineer, is good enough for me, so we can fix a cross-shaft underneath the cylinders, and connect the operating arm on it by a Bowden wire with the bottom of the lever in the cab. There is no need to use the Bowden casing, which is much too clumsy for our purpose; just get a bit of the wire itself from your local cycle-dealer, and run it through a piece of brass tube.

How to Make the Cocks

The novice's trouble is to turn a taper plug that will fit the hole in the body of the plug-cock and work easily, yet be perfectly steam- and water-tight. I solved that problem many years ago, when I had my first $3\frac{1}{2}$ in. Drummond lathe. The specification said that the headstock was made to set over, so that (for example) small taper cock-plugs could be turned, and the holes bored exactly to the same taper. Well, I tried it, but somehow it didn't work out that way! The cock bodies wanted some setting up for cross boring; and the sort of boring-tool used for holes $\frac{3}{32}$ in. diameter at the small end, was only suitable for use in a watchmaker's high-speed lathe. On a light cut it chattered; if fed quickly or deep enough to avoid chattering, it broke. Also, unless the boring and turning tools were set "to mike measurements" in a manner of speaking, with a surface gauge, the internal and external tapers came out at different angles, and wouldn't fit. Anyway, I wasted no more time, but went to work as follows. I chucked a bit of round silver-steel a little bigger than the largest diameter of the cock-plugs, turned a taper on it, filed away half the diameter of the tapered part, and hardened and tempered it to dark straw, finally giving the flat face a rub on the oilstone. Then I turned up about a couple of dozen bits of brass rod, same diameter as the largest end of the cock-plugs, to a taper at the end, *without altering the lathe setting, nor the tool, in any way whatever*. As both reamer and plugs were turned with the same tool, and same setting of the lathe, it stands to reason that the plugs would be a perfect fit in holes made with the reamer, and so it proved. I have always made cock-plugs that way. If I need more than I have turned after making the reamer, the slide is reset to the degree I used for that job.

For the reamer (Fig. 6-6), chuck a bit of $\frac{5}{32}$ in. round silver steel, and turn a cone point on it 1 in. long. Serve it as stated above. To temper: rub the flat part on a piece of fine emery cloth or similar abrasive—don't spoil the cutting edges—then hold a bit of sheet-iron over the domestic gas stove, with the reamer on top. As soon as it turns yellow, tip it off into some clean cold water. Rub on the oilstone, and you're all set. Turn a taper on the ends of half-a-dozen pieces of $\frac{5}{32}$ in. bronze or gunmetal rod about $\frac{3}{4}$ in. long. Don't turn to a point, leave the end about $\frac{1}{16}$ in. wide; and whatever you do, don't alter the setting of the slide-rest.

Turn the cock-bodies from $\frac{1}{4}$ in. round bronze or gunmetal rod. Chuck in three-jaw and turn $\frac{3}{16}$ in. length to $\frac{3}{16}$ in. diameter; screw $\frac{3}{16}$ in. by 40, then face off until the screwed part is $\frac{1}{8}$ in. long. This ensures full threads to the end. Make half-a-dozen whilst you are at it, parting each off $\frac{7}{16}$ in. from the shoulder. Then chuck a short bit of rod about $\frac{3}{8}$ in. diameter; face, centre,

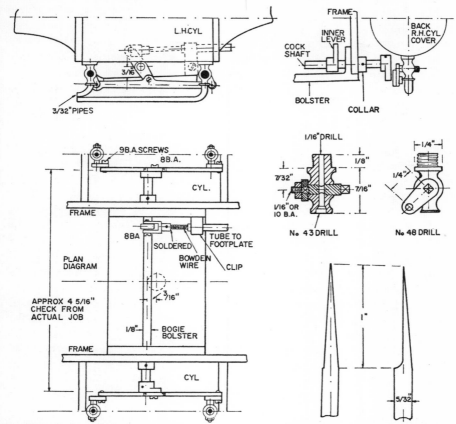

Fig. 6-5 Cylinder drain cocks and details.   Fig. 6-6 (above) Reamer for cock plugs.

drill $\frac{5}{32}$ in. or No. 22, countersink the end slightly, tap $\frac{3}{16}$ in. by 40, and skim off any burrs. Screw each blank into this, and turn the outside as shown in the illustration. Centre the end, drill through with $\frac{1}{16}$ in. or No. 53 drill, and counterbore the end slightly with No. 43 drill, to take a bit of $\frac{3}{32}$ in. pipe. (Fig. 6-6.)

Cross-drill the bulge in the middle with $\frac{5}{64}$ in. or No. 48 drill, and be sure the hole goes right across the "equatorial line" and doesn't wander sideways towards the tropics of Cancer and Capricorn. When drilling on the machine, I use a bit of rod with a $\frac{3}{16}$ in. tapped hole in the end, for a handle, and rest the cock-body in a dint made by a $\frac{1}{4}$ in. cycle-ball in a bit of hard wood; mighty simple, but very effective. Put a tap-wrench on the end of the reamer, and ream out the cross hole until one of your plugs will enter, and project about $\frac{5}{32}$ in. the other side.

Chuck the plug by the parallel part, and turn the end to $\frac{1}{16}$ in. diameter for $\frac{3}{32}$ in. length; screw $\frac{1}{16}$ in. or 10 BA. Directly after this, file a square on the plug, just long enough to enter the cock-body about $\frac{1}{32}$ in. when the plug is right home. This allows for grinding-in. Part off the plug so as to leave $\frac{5}{32}$ in. projecting at the large end; then file a $\frac{3}{32}$ in. square on that end, to accommodate the handle. To hold the taper plug whilst filing this square, chuck a bit of brass rod $\frac{3}{16}$ in. diameter or larger; face, centre, drill down a little way with $\frac{3}{32}$ in. drill, then ream it taper with the cock reamer in the tailstock chuck. Push each plug tightly into the taper hole, and it will hold quite tight enough to allow the square to be filed.

The handles are filed up from $\frac{1}{16}$ in. by $\frac{1}{16}$ in. steel strip, and need no detailing; fit each to a square on the plug, and two or three taps with a hammer will burr the edge of the square sufficiently to prevent the handle coming off. Put each plug in place with a commercial nut and a $\frac{1}{16}$ in. washer (file the hole in this square, naturally, to fit the square on the plug) then screw the cocks temporarily into the holes in the cylinder flanges, marking which is which, on the cock handles. Then set the handles back 45 deg. as shown in Fig. 6-5. Take the cocks out without shifting the handles; put the tapped bush in three-jaw, screw each cock into it, and run the $\frac{1}{16}$ in. drill up the bore, right through the plug. Take out the plugs, silver-solder a bit of $\frac{3}{32}$ in. pipe into each cock (get the length from the actual engine) but don't bend it yet. Grind the cock-plugs in with a scraping off your oilstone; just a few turns back and forth should be all that is needed. Clean the plugs well with a spot of paraffin, and poke out the steamway in both plug and cock body; then replace plugs, smearing a taste of cylinder oil, or a little graphite (off a soft blacklead pencil will do), leaving the nuts so that the plugs work easily. Finally, screw them into the cylinders with a weeny bit of plumbers' jointing on the threads, then bend the pipes as shown in the illustration.

Operating Gear

The cocks may, of course, be merely connected by a oooo-gauge coupling-rod between the two handles, and operated "at ground level" as desired; for footplate control, proceed as follows. Make up the little connecting-rods from a bit of steel strip, to the dimensions shown (Fig. 6-7); a simple filing and drilling job. A cross-shaft will be needed underneath the cylinders, so drill a No. 30 hole in the position indicated, through the frame at each side; if these holes pierce the flanges of the bogie bolster, it doesn't matter. Note: this location—$\frac{3}{16}$ in. ahead of the centre-line of the bolster, and $\frac{3}{16}$ in. from the bottom of frame—won't do for anybody who has used a built-up bolster, as there will be a big nut in the middle, right in the way of the shaft. In that case, drill the holes a little farther forward, between the next pair of bolster screw-holes, and alter the position of the lugs on the rods connecting the cock handles, to a like amount. That will put things O.K. and the working will not be affected.

The shaft is a piece of $\frac{1}{8}$ in. round silver-steel; get the length of this from the actual engine by putting the connecting-rods temporarily on the cocks, and measuring the distance between them. This shaft carries three arms or levers; two for operating the cock-rods and one for connection to the lever

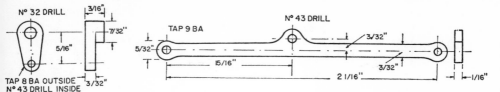

Fig. 6-7 Opening arm.   **Connecting-rod for cock levers.**

in the cab. One lever is just a plain flat doings filed up from $\frac{3}{32}$ in. by $\frac{1}{4}$ in. flat steel, and drilled as shown; press this on to one end of the shaft, and braze it in place. The other two have bosses which are formed by brazing on a small solid boss and then drilling through the lot with the boss held in the three-jaw. The small end of the inside arm is drilled No. 43 to accommodate an 8 BA screw in the fork operating it. Two small collars are also needed, to prevent any side movement of the shaft when erected; see Fig. 6-5. These should be drilled a tight fit for the shaft, say No. 31.

To erect the shaft, just remove the connecting-rods from the cock handles; put a collar on the shaft, and poke the end through the hole in the frame on one side. Put on the lever with the plain drilled end, push the other end of the shaft through the other hole in frame, put on the other collar, and finally the other lever. Line all three levers up, so that the end holes are both in line and the middle directly opposite; push the collars against the frame at each side, so that the shaft cannot move endwise, then pin the collars and the levers to the shaft. I use bits of blanket pins for jobs like these; a No. 57 drill is just right for a nice drive fit. Big pins are not needed; and, anyway, if you drilled a hole for a $\frac{1}{16}$ in. pin in a $\frac{1}{8}$ in. shaft, it would soon break at the hole.

You will probably have to make the screws, as they should have a plain section under the heads, for the cock handles to take a bearing on; this is dead easy, as it only means chucking a bit of $\frac{1}{8}$ in. round steel in three-jaw, turning down the end for about $\frac{5}{32}$ in. length, and putting a few threads on with a die in the tailstock holder. The threads should be a tight fit, and when screwed right home, the cock handles should be quite free to move. Couple up the connecting-rods to the cock handles, then put an 8 BA screw through the middle hole each side, into the lever on the end of the cross-shaft. Note again—as the cross-shaft levers are longer, from centre to centre, than the cock handles, the hole in the middle of the connecting-rod must be filed slightly oval, to allow for the difference in the radial movement. All four cocks should move perfectly freely, when the inner lever is operated with your fingers. Don't screw up the nuts on the cock-plugs so tight that they will be hard to turn, or scoring will result, and you'll get the old stick-and-blow trouble.

Cab Lever

The cocks are "remotely controlled" by a lever in the cab, connected as previously mentioned, by a Bowden wire, to the inside lever on the cross-shaft. The lever is a plain filing job, the handle being either turned solid with it, or turned up separately from $\frac{1}{8}$ in. round steel, and brazed on to the flat part. Drill a No. 41 hole at the bottom, and a $\frac{5}{32}$ in. hole 1 in. above it. Turn up a hexagon-headed screw from a bit of $\frac{1}{4}$ in. hexagon steel rod, leaving a full $\frac{1}{8}$ in. of "plain" under the head, turned to a working fit in the $\frac{5}{32}$ in. hole in the lever. The end is turned down to a $\frac{1}{8}$ in. diameter, and screwed $\frac{1}{8}$ in. or 5 BA (Fig. 6-8).

At any convenient point ahead of the drag-beam, drill a hole in the frame with No. 40 drill, tap to match the screw and file off any burr. Attach the lever to the inside of the frame as shown; when the screw is tight home, the lever should move without any side-to-side movement. Make up two little forks or clevises from $\frac{7}{32}$ in. or $\frac{1}{4}$ in. rod, drilling the stems $\frac{1}{16}$ in. Measure the distance by the nearest route, between the bottom of the lever and the end of the middle arm on the cross-shaft, both being vertical. By "nearest route" I don't mean a straight line, but the nearest way that misses the location of the bottom of the firebox, and any other obstruction. Cut the Bowden wire about $\frac{1}{2}$ in. shorter than this, grease it well, and thread it through a piece of $\frac{3}{32}$ in. brass treblet tube, or any other thin-walled tube that it will fit easily. The tube should be about 1 in. shorter than the wire. Fix the two forks at either end of the wire; solder the wire into the stems, and if desired, you can put a set-screw in as well. Couple up the forks to the arm of the cross-shaft and the lever, by screws as shown; these should have a plain part where they pass through the levers, one side of the fork being clearing size, and the other tapped for the screw. Then set the tube so that it clears all obstructions, and secure it at each end by two little clips made from about 18-gauge sheet brass. If the clips tend to move or slip on the tube when the lever is operated, teach them good manners with a touch of solder. The location of the clips is shown in the illustrations. The cocks should now work freely by moving the lever back and forth, the lever staying wherever it is placed, merely by friction alone. No stops are required—you'd be puzzled to miss the "on" and "off" positions!

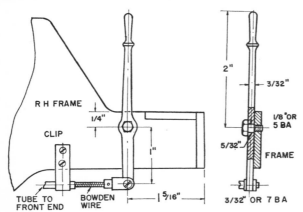

Fig. 6-8
Cab lever for working drain cocks.

Snifting-Valves

Every engine with cylinders over $\frac{5}{8}$ in. bore, and having piston valves or overhead flat side-valves, should be fitted with snifting-valves. Reason No. 1 is that when you shut off and coast, the engine—if the pistons and valves are fitted as they should be—runs as dead as ditch-water without them, and sucks ashes and dirt down the blastpipe to the detriment of the cylinder bores and valve faces. Reason No. 2 is avoidance of oil waste.

All who use displacement lubricators, both large and small, know that the pressure in the steam-chests and the lubricator is practically equal when the engine is taking steam; but as soon as you shut off, down flops the steam-chest pressure to zero and the pressure remaining in the lubricator forces out an extra dose of oil and flushes the cylinders, provided the lubricator is working properly. Now this in big practice is very beneficial, and all large Roscoes have a central tube which makes this action certain. On the small engine, however, the job is usually overdone; for the pumping action of the cylinders naturally creates a vacuum and does its best to get the "last drop from the oil pot". Signs of oil around the chimney cap of a little engine are an indication that all's well in the regions below. To get the desirable flush-out without excessive flooding, it is only necessary to destroy the vacuum, and the solution is the little working snifting valve, or vacuum relief valve, to give it the "scientific" title.

Where to Put the Valves

I think the best place to fit snifting-valves is on top of the smokebox, so that they are out of the way of all ballast dust, etc., and feed clean air into the top header of the superheater. It is good practice to draw the air in through the superheater, because if you happen to run the return bend of the element a bit close to the firebox it minimises any chance of overheating and burning the tube. The admission of hot air to the cylinders also tends to reduce the condensation trouble by maintaining the temperature of the cylinder walls.

Construction

Here are a few notes on making snifters for $2\frac{1}{2}$ in. gauge engines; dimensions can be increased or decreased to suit other sizes. The valve body is of the usual mushroom-head type and is arranged to screw into the top fitting of a single element superheater, or into the header of a multiple ditto (Fig. 6-9). Chuck a piece of $\frac{3}{8}$ in. round gunmetal or phosphor bronze rod, centre and drill down about $\frac{1}{2}$ in. with a $\frac{1}{16}$ in. or No. 52 drill. Open out to a depth of $\frac{3}{16}$ in. with a No. 21 drill; tap $\frac{3}{16}$ in. by 40 threads, then carefully bottom the hole with a $\frac{5}{32}$ in. D-bit, as described for clack box and other valve seatings. The hole should now be $\frac{1}{4}$ in. deep. Face off the end and counterbore the first thread away so that this part, which forms the head of the valve body, will seat steam-tight upon the stem. Turn down the end to $\frac{1}{4}$ in. diameter for a distance of $\frac{3}{16}$ in. and part off from the rod at $\frac{5}{16}$ in. from the end. Form a valve seat at the bottom of the hole with a $\frac{1}{8}$ in. rustless steel

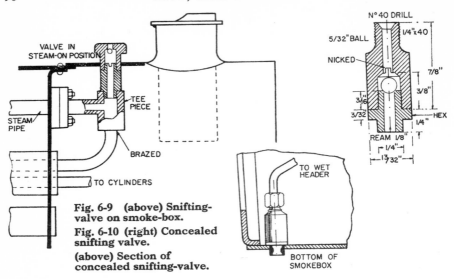

Fig. 6-9 (above) Snifting-valve on smoke-box.

Fig. 6-10 (right) Concealed snifting valve.

(above) Section of concealed snifting-valve.

ball. Now either turn the rod down to $\frac{1}{4}$ in. diameter for $\frac{3}{4}$ in. length and part off, or else chuck a fresh bit of $\frac{1}{4}$ in. rod $\frac{3}{4}$ in. long. Centre and drill right through with $\frac{3}{32}$ in. or No. 43 drill. Turn down $\frac{1}{8}$ in. of either end to $\frac{3}{16}$ in. diameter and screw $\frac{3}{16}$ in. by 40 threads. Remove from chuck and carefully file a couple of little slots across one end, to prevent the valve ball seating itself on and blocking up the airway. Drop a $\frac{1}{8}$ in. rustless steel ball into the hole in the valve head, and screw the slotted end of the stem in tightly with a smear of plumbers' jointing on the threads. Don't get any in the valve hole if you can avoid it, needless to say. Now chuck the complete valve by the stem and turn down the head part to the well-known shape of the snifting-valve on a full-sized engine. The job is then complete.

Fitting Up

Instead of the usual flanged elbow which connects the top superheater pipe to the boiler steam pipe, or "dry pipe", as our transatlantic friends call it, make up a flanged tee-piece with the flange on the stem of the tee. Drill the head of the tee right through with a No. 21 drill, and tap one arm $\frac{3}{16}$ in. by 40 threads. Open out the other arm to take the superheater pipe $\frac{3}{16}$ in. or $\frac{7}{32}$ in., as the case may be, and braze the pipe in, afterwards cleaning up the face of the flange and seeing that no dirt or burnt brazing compound has got into the threads; of course, the tapping may be carried out *after* the brazing, if preferred. Assemble in the usual manner, and bolt the superheater flange to the steam-pipe flange so that the screwed arm of the tee stands exactly vertical. Now put the smokebox temporarily in position, mark out a point exactly above the tee and drill a $\frac{1}{4}$ in. hole to take the stem of the valve a tight fit. When the engine is finally assembled, the snifting-valve is passed down through this hole and screwed tightly into the threaded arm of the tee-piece. On opening the regulator, steam flies along the pipe and "plonks" the ball up against the seating formed in the valve head. The characteristic "click" and little wisp of steam as the snifter ball seats home is "the big girl's little sister" to the life. On shutting off, the ball drops down on to the stem, but the end of this being slotted as described, the air passes around the ball and proceeds via the superheater to the cylinders; and the engine, if properly made and fitted, will coast along as freely as a bicycle. Where the snifting valves on a full-sized engine are invisible, or if the "button" on the smokebox is not wanted, the valve can be placed upside down, with the head projecting through a hole drilled to suit, in or near the bottom of the smoke-box. This arrangement is shown in Fig. 6-10.

Maunsell Snifting Valve

Many Southern engines originally had the well-known and familiar Maunsell "snails' horns" on either side of the smokebox, just behind the chimney. They were later removed, the holes being covered with patch plates; an anti-carbonising device was substituted. This procedure became a debatable point in full-sized locomotive circles; but whether the "ayes" or "noes" have it, there isn't the slightest doubt about the necessity for relieving the vacuum caused by the pumping action in the cylinders of a little engine, which takes place as soon as the regulator is shut. Unless some other means of admitting air is provided, it will go down the blastpipe, and take a certain percentage of the contents of the smokebox with it; and it doesn't need a Sherlock Holmes to deduce that the ash and grit are going to do what the kiddies call "a bit of no good" to the valves, port faces, and cylinder bores. A mixture of smokebox ash, grit, and cylinder oil forms an excellent grinding paste! This can be avoided, as has been done in full-size, by admitting air to the superheater header via an automatic valve—an air clack, if you like— and the "snifting" action of this when running with steam shut off, gave it its nickname of snifting-valve. Air could, of course, be admitted direct to the steam chests (which has also been done in full-size) but this would tend to cool the cylinders, and cause the engine to throw drops of water from the chimney when opening up again. By snifting the air through the superheater, the cylinders are not only kept warm, but overheating and burning of the superheater elements are prevented.

How to Make the Maunsell Type

The valves shown in the illustrations are externally correct for a 5-in. gauge engine. However, the internals are considerably simplified without sacrificing any efficiency, as the section will show. The valve is made from bronze or gunmetal rod, for preference, though brass will do if nothing better is available. Chuck a bit of $\frac{7}{16}$ in. round rod in three-jaw, and turn down about 1 in. of it to $\frac{13}{32}$ in. diameter. Further reduce $\frac{5}{16}$ in. length to $\frac{1}{4}$ in. diameter with a round-nose tool, and screw $\frac{1}{4}$ in. by 40 for a bare $\frac{1}{4}$ in. length. Face the end, centre deeply with size "E" centre-drill, then drill down about

1 in. depth with No. 40 drill. Part off $\frac{7}{8}$ in. from the end. Reverse in chuck, open out the other end to $\frac{3}{8}$ in. depth with $\frac{7}{32}$ in. drill, and tap $\frac{1}{4}$ in. by 40. Nick the bottom of the hole with a little chisel made from $\frac{1}{8}$ in. silver-steel, so that air can pass the ball freely when it is resting on the bottom of the hole, its position when coasting. Slightly countersink the end of the tapped hole, and skim it up truly.

Chuck a piece of $\frac{1}{2}$ in. rod, and turn down a full $\frac{3}{16}$ in. length to $\frac{1}{4}$ in. diameter, using a knife-tool this time, to form the shoulder. Screw $\frac{1}{4}$ in. by 40. Centre, and drill down with No. 34 drill, to a depth of $\frac{7}{16}$ in. then follow up with a $\frac{1}{8}$ in. parallel reamer, putting same in as far as it will go. Take a skim off the end, to form a true seating for the ball. Part off at $\frac{13}{32}$ in. from the shoulder; this gives "scale" height. Re-chuck in a tapped bush held in three-jaw; any odd bit of round rod over $\frac{3}{8}$ in. diameter will do for this. Just face, centre, drill $\frac{7}{32}$ in. and tap $\frac{1}{4}$ in. by 40, slightly countersink the end, and skim it off truly. Screw the top of the snifting valve into it tightly; form the recess with a $\frac{3}{32}$ in. parting-tool, the diameter at the bottom of the recess being $\frac{5}{16}$ in. The outline of the ornamental top can be formed by careful manipulation of both slide-rest handles, or by using a hand-tool, of the shape shown in Fig. 6-11. This is made from a bit of $\frac{3}{8}$ in. square tool-steel; odd lengths of high-speed stuff which have become too short to use in the slide-rest, make nobby hand-tools if brazed to a bit of mild-steel of same section from 9 in. to 12 in. long, fixed in an ordinary file handle. No special hand-rest is needed; I just put a tool in the slide-rest tool-holder with the shank end projecting, run same up to the job, and use the shank to rest the hand-tool on, whilst in use.

At $1\frac{1}{4}$ in. from the rear end of the smokebox, and $1\frac{5}{8}$ in. off top centre, drill a $\frac{3}{8}$ in. hole each side of the smokebox. If you have a $\frac{13}{32}$ in. parallel reamer, put a tap-wrench on the shank, insert into the hole, and as you turn it, bring it up vertical. If you haven't a reamer, use a drill same size; hold it in a carpenter's brace for preference, and bring the drill to vertical position as you open out the hole. Carefully file off all burrs, and slightly countersink the holes with a small half-round file. Now drill two $\frac{3}{8}$ in. holes in a piece of 18-gauge sheet brass or copper, bend this to the radius of the smokebox, and give both holes a dose of the same medicine; after which, cut around the holes,

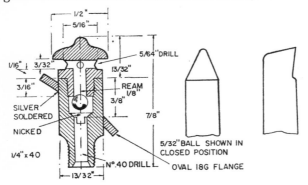

Fig. 6-11
Maunsell-type
snifting-valve and
hand turning tool.

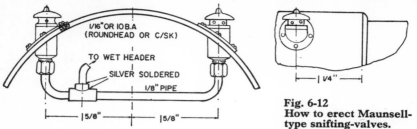

Fig. 6-12
How to erect Maunsell-type snifting-valves.

so as to leave a couple of slightly oval washers a full $\frac{1}{8}$ in. wide. Screw the ornamental tops of the snifting-valves in the bodies (don't put the balls in yet) and put on the washers or flanges as shown in the illustration. Then try the snifting-valves in position, adjusting the flanges so that the valves fit exactly as shown; bodies vertical, and the cap or top almost flush with the flange on the side nearest to top of boiler. Remove valves, being careful not to upset the position of the flanges; remove the tops, and silver-solder the flanges to the valve bodies. Pickle, wash off and clean up.

Seat a couple of rustless steel balls, $\frac{5}{32}$ in. diameter, on the faced ends of the caps. Drill two cross-holes, with $\frac{5}{64}$ in. or No. 48 drill, at right-angles across the bottom of the recess; these holes will cut into the central passage. Drop the balls into the pockets, screw home the caps with a touch of plumbers' jointing on the threads—keep it off the ball seats!—then drill four No. 51 holes around the flange, put the valves in place on the smokebox, and attach them by four 10 BA brass screws, roundheads or countersunk, whichever you prefer.

These little snifting-valves are well worth the trouble of making and fitting, especially by those good folk who love a touch of realism in details. Apart from their usefulness, their personal appearance, the tiny puff of steam and the audible click as the balls smack against the seats when the regulator is opened, reproduce some of the characteristics of a full-sized Maunsell-designed locomotive on the old Southern Railway.

How to Connect Up

The pipe connections are simplicity itself, and the illustration, Fig. 6-12, hardly needs explaining. All that is needed, is a piece of $\frac{1}{8}$ in. copper tube with a union cone and $\frac{1}{4}$ in. by 40 union nut on each end, long enough to connect the two unions under the snifting-valves. A tee is provided anywhere in the pipe, and a $\frac{1}{8}$ in. pipe attached to the wet header, is silver-soldered into the stem of the tee. Regular bends and a straight pipe are shown in the drawing (easier to draw, that way!) but actually it doesn't matter how or where the pipes are run inside the smokebox, as long as they are out of the way of the other pipes. The essentials are, that they start and finish at the right places, so that when steam is shut off, the balls drop, and admit air via the pipes to the wet header, whence it is drawn through the superheater into the cylinders and blown out through the blastpipe, thus preventing any grit or ashes going down.

CHAPTER VII

Motion Work

VALVE GEAR IS the *pons asinorum* of beginners, and even after experience has been gained, many folk are chary of tackling its construction. It should not be so. Admittedly, a couple of bobbins mounted on a spindle and sliding to and fro in a slotted tube, or a block of gunmetal with a cavity in it, "rowing the boat" over three slots on a flat face, are capable of causing enough trouble to turn a locomotive engineer's hair grey, but all things have a reason which can be found and dealt with, so that in time one may tackle any trouble with equanimity. The loose eccentric offers an easy method of obtaining an excellent steam distribution at both ends of each cylinder in either direction. True, it cannot be notched up, and the engine has to be pushed to reverse it; but we have to make certain sacrifices to obtain certain advantages.

The notching-up business can be partially overcome by setting to cut-off to 65 or even 60 per cent and driving on the throttle. A 50 per cent cut-off would be ample for all usual purposes, but the engine would be a bad starter, for if one crank were on dead centre and the other exactly half-stroke no steam would be admitted to the latter, as she would be on the cut-off point, and the "lead" steam in the dead centre side would, of course, have no effect on the crank. Now as to fitting up. With an inside-cylinder loose-eccentric engine I have fitted the gear in three ways, viz., solid eccentrics between outer crank webs and axleboxes; solid eccentrics on a built-up crank axle (tricky job, that), and split eccentrics on a solid axle.

The Three Methods

The first case is one in which the cylinders are set with their centres fairly close, say, ¾ in. on a 2½ in. gauge engine; and by keeping the outer crank cheeks fairly thin, an eccentric $\frac{5}{32}$ in. wide can be got in between the cheek and the axlebox. No stop collars are needed, as the drive is copied from the old Webb compounds on the L.N.W.R.—a slotted eccentric with a pin fixed in the crank web and engaging in the slot which is curved to the radius struck by the pin. There is just one little snag here, and I know one or two who have fallen over it. The slot must needs be cut *in the wide part* of the eccentric, and, if the pin be placed between the main crankpin and the axle, the eccentric will *follow* the crank instead of *leading* it, and this will, of course, be all wrong for an ordinary outside-admission valve. This does not matter a button where the valves are either on top or underneath the cylinders and the direction of motion is reversed by the rocking levers usually fitted to transmit the line of motion to the "first floor or the basement". But if anybody tries to fit up this arrangement with direct-coupled rods there will sure be some fur flying. If direct coupling is desired, use the slotted sheaves just the same, but fit a balanced crankshaft; that is, one in which the webs are extended on the opposite side to the crankpins. If the stop pins are fixed in the balances, the eccentrics will lead the cranks and the rods may be direct-coupled to the valve spindle forks. Timing is very easy. Make the curved slot short to start, and if you find the ports open too soon, lengthen it. The second method of fitting solid eccentrics to a built-up axle is a more serious test of merit, but is applicable to engines having the cylinder centres wide enough apart to allow the sheaves to be placed between the crank webs.

Build up the two cranks complete, and fit the middle part of the axle to one of them; make the two eccentrics, drill and file the slots, and fit pins to crank webs. Then assemble the side with the centre part of axle in it, slip on one eccentric and temporaily couple up. The correct length of slot can now be ascertained by turning the crank in either direction and watching the valve, proceeding to lengthen the slot as before if found necessary. When this side is O.K., cut the slot in the second eccentric to exactly the same length, assemble on centre part of axle, and finally put on the other crank, taking care that the crankpins are at right-angles. All crankshaft joints should be pinned and brazed with the exception of the last one, which is a tight drive fit and pinned only. The final adjustment of the valves can be made on the valve spindle forks, and the laps of the valves filed a tiny shade should it be found necessary. The third method, split eccentrics on a solid shaft (Fig. 7-1), is the one I used on *Caterpillar*'s inside motion, also on other engines. The sheaves had to be made in halves, as the cranks and axle were turned from the solid. They were $\frac{5}{32}$ in. wide; could not allow any more owing to big cylinder bores limiting crank centres, and the *modus operandi* was to part off

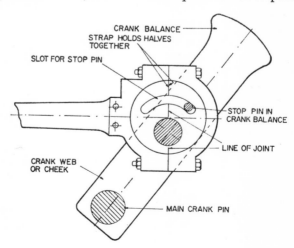

Fig. 7-1
Split eccentrics on a
crank axle.

two discs from a piece of 1 in. steel bar, mark off and drill axle holes a full $\frac{1}{8}$ in. out of centre, cut across with a fine saw, trim up the halves, clamp in three-jaw chuck and carefully ream out the axle holes, and then solder the whole to a brass mandrel. This was held in a four-jaw chuck, and the jaws carefully set to give the desired amount of wobble to the mandrel. The outsides were then carefully turned to fit the straps, after which the solder was melted off and the sheaves freed.

They were cleaned up, the reamer passed through axle holes again, slots marked out and filed (half slot in each half eccentric) and then the whole assembled. The two halves of each eccentric "float" in the strap and require no fixing. They cannot shift sideways and fall out because of the crank webs, which are wide and of the balanced pattern; and, of course, the straps prevent the halves falling apart. On *Caterpillar* the valves of the inside cylinders are underneath, so the eccentric rods are slightly curved and pass under the first coupled axle. Since this engine has been in service no trouble has developed anywhere. She pulls better than ever, although she has been running since 1926 without any repairs.

The Baker Valve Gear

The Baker valve gear was invented by Mr. Abner D. Baker, of Swanton, Ohio. Mr. Baker designed his first gear in 1903 for traction engine use, and adapted it for locomotives in 1908. It was first tried in that year on a locomotive of the Toledo, St. Louis and Western Railroad, and worked experimentally for some two years or so, during which it underwent many alterations and improvements. The gear was finally perfected in 1911, and the improved form as we now know it was used on some twenty thousand locomotives in America, and became adopted as standard by many railroad companies. It was fitted to the huge 4-8-4 Canadian National locomotives, which were among the biggest passenger engines in the British Empire.

The Gear Assembly

The action of the Baker valve gear is in some respects similar to a Walschaerts inasmuch as it derives its primary motion from a return crank and eccentric rod; and the lap and lead action is attended to by a combination lever worked off the crosshead in the usual manner. The slotted rocking link and die-block is, however, dispensed with, and a simple swinging radius bar takes its place. The pivot or bearing of this bar can be shifted to change the direction of the arc in which the lower end of the bar swings, and the action of this will be seen when we come to the diagram. The gear itself is mounted on a frame, which in full-size practice is made in two forms, according to the type of locomotive it is intended for; a bracket pattern for attaching to the upper part of the guide-bar yoke, and a girder pattern, similar to that often used for carrying Walschaerts links.

On this frame is mounted a reverse yoke pivoted at the bottom, and connected at the top to the reverse gear in the cab, or the power reverser, by means of the usual rods. The upper part of the reverse yoke carries a pin on which is hung the radius bar already mentioned; so by throwing over the reverse yoke the position of this pin is set either forward or back of the centre line of the reverse yoke bearing. The lower end of the radius bar carries another pin, on which is mounted, by its centre hole, a bar called the gear connecting-rod; the lower end of this is coupled to the eccentric rod; the upper to one arm of a bell-crank which works on a bearing in the gear frame. The other arm of the bell-crank is connected to the combination lever by a simple valve rod. To ensure stability and strength the reverse yoke and radius bars are double, and made to a special shape and section, but, in order to explain the action of the gear and show it in diagram form, we will assume that the various rods are just plain bits of metal like the little pocket gadget which has enabled me to easily demonstrate the simple action of the Baker gear to many enthusiasts.

How the Gear Operates

If you cut out and drill strips of metal—bits of $\frac{1}{16}$ in. by $\frac{3}{16}$ in. flat brass rod will do—to the shape of the parts, and rivet them lightly together to form a working gadget like the one I made, you will learn more about the Baker gear in five minutes than you could gather from a description occupying the whole of this book. However, first look at the diagram (Fig. 7-2). I have lettered and numbered the various parts, so you can see how they go together. (See also Fig. 7-4.) F is the gear frame, side plate only. RY is the reverse yoke, the top of which is connected to the reach-rod from the cab or power reverse. The bottom hole of RY is pivoted to No. 1 point on the gear frame and the yoke can be swung over on that fulcrum as before-mentioned. RB is the radius bar; this is the little arab which does all the damage, and its No. 2 hole is pivoted to a pin in No. 2 hole in the reverse yoke, so that it is free to oscillate on it. No. 3 hole carries a pin on which works No. 3 hole in the gear connecting-rod which oscillates also on this pin as it is pushed back and forth by the eccentric-rod coupled to the bottom hole. The top hole No. 4 is connected to the horizontal arm of the bell-crank BC, which, in turn, works on a stud passing through No. 5 hole and fixed in No. 5 hole in the gear frame.

On the actual locomotive, in $1\frac{3}{4}$ in. gauge and upwards, this bell-crank is mounted on a bush. On the simple demonstration gadget, all you need do is to fix a pin in the gear frame and pack out the bell-crank to the requisite

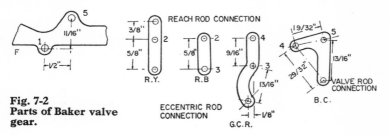

Fig. 7-2
Parts of Baker valve gear.

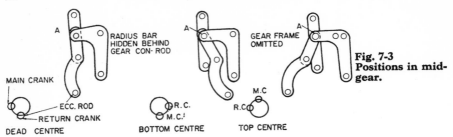

Fig. 7-3
Positions in mid-
gear.

distance with a few washers or a couple of nuts. Having become acquainted with the parts and their assembly, we can now easily follow the action.

Neutral and Forward Positions

Put the reverse yoke in midgear (Fig. 7-3), that is, in such a position that No. 4 hole in the gear connecting-rod and bell-crank are exactly over the centre-line of the yoke. Now, if the bottom end of the gear connecting-rod be wigwagged to and fro it will just swing pendulum-like and carry the radius bar with it. The bell-crank (and the valve-rod connected to it on the actual engine) remains stationary, as the connecting point coincides with the radius bar pivot which does not move in this position, but acts like the die-block in a Walschaerts link when in midgear; this does not move when the link is oscillated. Now hold the gear connecting-rod in the centre of its travel and shift the reverse yoke back and forth. There will still be no movement of the bell-crank, as the bottom pivot of the radius bar and the centre hole of the gear connecting-rod are line and line. This corresponds to reversing a Walschaerts gear with the slotted link exactly vertical, so that the die-block goes from top to bottom without moving the valve-rod. Now shift the reverse yoke forward and see what happens when the gear connecting-rod is moved. The radius bar swings off centre and describes an arc at the point where the gear connecting-rod is coupled to it, and naturally the latter follows this arc and carries the end of the bell-crank along with it, as they are all coupled together. In forward gear the lowest point of the arc is *ahead* of the reverse yoke bearing (Fig. 7-4); the gear connecting-rod at this point has pulled the horizontal arm of the bell-crank right down, and the vertical arm has moved forward, travelling in the same direction as the end of the gear connecting-rod. On the back swing, the gear connecting-rod moves upward as it follows the arc of the radius bar, and pushes up the bell-crank arm, bringing the vertical arm back again. It will thus be seen that in forward gear, the end of the gear connecting-rod and the vertical arm of the bell-crank move in unison; therefore, the eccentric-rod and valve-rod go the same way, hence the direction of motion of the engine.

The Gear in Reverse

To reverse the gear, the reverse yoke is pulled back so that the pivot on which the radius bar oscillates is behind the reverse yoke fulcrum (Fig. 7-5).

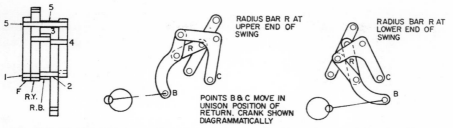

Fig. 7-4 **Demonstration Baker gear assembled and positions in forward gear.**

The arc is now described in the opposite direction; whereas before, the lowest point was *ahead* of the reverse yoke fulcrum, it is now *behind* it. As the gear connecting-rod is pushed forward, the swing of the radius bar carries it *upward*, pushing the horizontal arm of the bell-crank up and bringing the vertical arm back towards the gear connecting-rod. When the latter is pulled back it moves downward as it follows the line of the arc, pulling the horizontal arm of the bell-crank with it, and the vertical arm moves away again. As the latter movement is now opposite to that of the gear connecting-rod, it will be apparent that the valve-rod and the eccentric-rod also move in opposite directions and the engine is reversed. Now I am afraid it seems a joyful mix-up when explained (more or less) by words and diagrams; but if you will just cut out and tack together the four components (illustrated in Fig. 7-2), and fix them on any bit of metal for a gear frame, I guess you will say you never saw anything so simple in all your life. The size of rods given and distances between the pivot holes were worked out for a $2\frac{1}{2}$ in. gauge engine. The sizes mentioned can be fractioned up to suit any gauge engine, and need no alteration in proportions.

Baker Gear for $3\frac{1}{2}$ in. Gauge

Here is the how-to-do-it for the Baker valve gear. As you can see from the illustrations, the layout is simple, and the whole doings easily made and erected. The chief advantage over the Walschaerts gear is that there are no slotted links to make and erect, and no die-blocks to worry about; die slip is eliminated, as there are no dies to slip, and the complete sets of gear are built up in simple frames, off the engine, and then erected by aid of two simple brackets which can be made from bar and sheet metal, no complicated

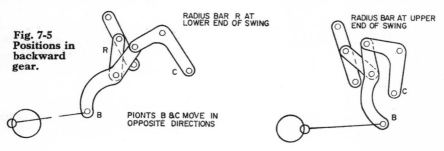

Fig. 7-5 Positions in backward gear.

castings being needed. The gear is applicable to either slide or piston-valve cylinders without any alteration whatever to the gear itself. For slide-valve cylinders, the connections are as shown on the general arrangement given here; for piston-valve cylinders, the return crank follows the main crank instead of leading it, and the valve-rod is connected to the top hole in the combination lever, the lever itself being pinned to the valve crosshead through the lower hole.

The Baker gear is not suitable for inside cylinders, although the gear, as I have arranged it, could be erected inside the frames quite easily, and would miss the bottom of the boiler barrel; the trouble would be the drive. The Baker gear needs a much bigger throw of the return crank than a Walschaerts gear, as the bottom of the grear connecting-rod needs to swing from three to four times the required valve travel, according to the amount of movement the reverse yoke can be given between full forward and backward positions. To get the full-gear movement, the return cranks need to describe a circle 1⅜ in. diameter, which is nearly as much as the swing of the main cranks. That would mean, of course, that we should have to use an eccentric on the crank-axle to give a similar movement; and as this joker would be about the size of the bogie wheels, it is completely out of court. The easiest way to drive the inside valve of a three-cylinder engine is to extend the outside valve spindles through the front bosses of the steam-chests, through glands similar to those on the back bosses. The extended spindles carry plain forks, in which work short links coupled to a simple two-to-one conjugated gear, as used on all the Gresley Pacifics. This consists of two levers only, and is erected on a simple bracket across the frames between the inside and outside cylinders.

The steam distribution will be all right when the three cylinders are all in the same plane, and the cranks set at 120 deg. The trouble with the "two-to-one" usually arises when the cylinders are out of line, and the inside crank has to be arranged to suit the gear; any wear or slight inaccuracy soon upsets the valve setting and causes syncopation in the beats of the exhaust.

The first job is to make the gear frames and brackets. The frames are of the girder type, of the standard pattern used for full-sized Baker-fitted engines in the U.S.A. and elsewhere.

Gear Frames

Although one left-hand and one right-hand gear assembly is needed with the ordinary kinds of valve gear, both sets of Baker gear are exactly similar. One is erected with its right-hand side nearest the main frames, and the other with its left; so you don't have to stop and consider which bits have to be turned around to be erected properly. Four side-frame plates are needed; these are cut from ⅛ in. mild-steel plate, any odd bits left over from main frames being just right if of suitable size. The dimensions are given in the drawing. As the gear has to be properly proportioned to give correct valve movements, the vertical distance between the centres of the upper and lower

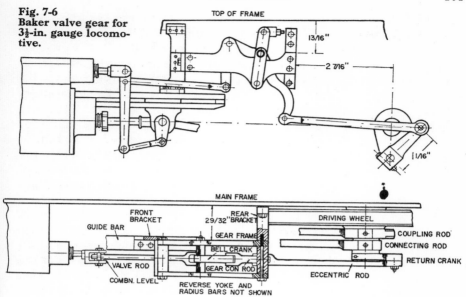

Fig. 7-6
Baker valve gear for
3½-in. gauge locomotive.

holes is $\frac{31}{32}$ in. Note, whilst all the holes in the lower lugs on the frames are reamed $\frac{5}{32}$ in., the holes in the upper lugs are not the same size. Those on the inner sides of the frames, when same are erected, should be drilled $\frac{1}{8}$ in. or No. 30, and those on the outer sides are $\frac{5}{32}$ in. The best way to avoid forgetting which side is which, is to drill all the top holes No. 30, and open out the outside ones when the brackets have been made, and the gear frames temporarily erected.

The end-pieces, or spacers, are made from $\frac{1}{2}$ in. by $\frac{1}{4}$ in. bar; it doesn't matter whether steel or brass is used, as there is no movement and no wear. As the ends must be dead-square, to ensure correct alignment of the gear frames all ways, chuck the piece of bar truly in the four-jaw, and part off four lengths a tiny shade over $\frac{3}{4}$ in. long. To ensure that they are all alike, beginners should part off to about $\frac{1}{32}$ in. over length, then chuck each separately, and face the ends, so that when checked with slide gauge or calipers, each piece fits exactly between the jaws. Drill the four No. 41 screw-holes in one of the gear frames, and use that as a jig to drill the others; the holes are $\frac{1}{8}$ in. from the ends, and $\frac{1}{8}$ in. from top and bottom, the exact positions being of no moment as long as all four frames are drilled alike. Now assemble a pair of frames with a spacer at each end, holding the lot together with a toolmaker's clamp, and poke the No. 41 drill in each ditto hole in the frames, making countersinks on the ends of the spacers. Mark which end is which, and which is top and bottom of each spacer; then take them apart. Drill the holes in the front spacer No. 48, and tap them 7 BA. Drill the holes in the back one No. 41, and take them clean through; the best way is to drill about halfway through from one side, using either drilling machine or lathe, then turn the piece end for end, and drill again until the drill breaks through into the first half of the holes. Be careful with your feed as it does break through, or you'll have a break of another kind, to remedy which will cause a slight fluctuation in the firm's finances. The frames can then be temporarily erected, using any odd suitable screws at the front end (one each side will do) and a bit of screwed wire with a nut on each end at the back, just to hold them together.

The spindles for the bell-cranks can now be made and fitted. These are simple enough, being merely pieces of $\frac{5}{32}$ in. round silver-steel a full $1\frac{1}{8}$ in. long. Chuck each one truly in the three-jaw, and turn down a full $\frac{1}{4}$ in. of one end to $\frac{1}{8}$ in. diameter, screwing $\frac{1}{8}$ in. or 5 BA. Open out the hole in the outer frame plate to $\frac{5}{32}$ in.; push the spindle through, so that the screwed end goes through the $\frac{1}{8}$ in. holes in the inner plate, and secure with an ordinary commercial nut.

Front Bracket

The front bracket can be cut from a piece of $\frac{3}{32}$ in. mild-steel sheet, and have the angles riveted on; or it may be cut out and bent to shape. For the former process, you need a bit of $\frac{5}{8}$ in. by $\frac{3}{32}$ in. steel strip, $2\frac{3}{16}$ in. long. File to shape, as shown in Fig. 7-7. At the upper end, rivet a bit of angle; you can bend this up from any suitable scrap of sheet steel about 13-gauge, the upper part being $\frac{3}{8}$ in. wide. The lower end is bent over at right-angles for $\frac{3}{8}$ in. to form the lug which is screwed to the top of the guide-bar. The angle for attachment of the gear frame is bent up from $\frac{1}{2}$ in. by $\frac{3}{32}$ in. steel strip, and is riveted to the bracket at $\frac{9}{16}$ in. from the bottom; see Fig. 7-7 for shape, size and assembly. Don't forget that you'll need one of these brackets right-handed and one left-handed.

To make a one-piece bent-up bracket, a piece of soft ductile sheet steel of 13-gauge is required. Mark out as shown in the alternative sketch, then carefully bend on the dotted lines. The same marking-out does for both right and left-hand brackets; simply bend one lot of "tags" toward you, and the other away from you. Yet another way would be to bend the top and

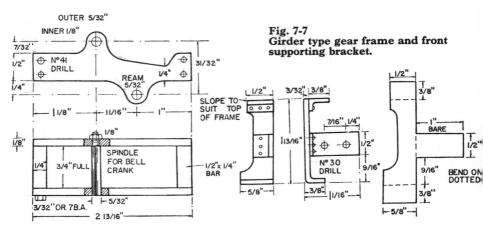

Fig. 7-7
Girder type gear frame and front supporting bracket.

bottom angles, and attach the side one separately by using an oxy-acetylene blowpipe and a touch of Sifbronze, which would form a fillet in the angle, and add to the strength of the bracket. Drill two No. 30 holes in the side angle as shown; place the bracket against the end of the gear frame, the side angle being in line all ways with the spacer, hold in position with a tool-maker's clamp, and drill and tap the holes in the spacer, using those in the angle as guide, for two $\frac{1}{8}$ in. or 5 BA screws; see elevation of complete assembly. Two No. 30 holes can be drilled in the foot of the bracket, for attachment to the guide-bar when the whole gear is finally erected.

Rear Bracket

This is very simple, and may be made from a casting, built up, or cut from solid, just as you please. If a casting is used, it will only need cleaning up and drilling; but in order to ensure the back and face being parallel, it would be advisable to chuck it in the four-jaw and face the back; drill the screw holes, and screw it to a truly-faced bit of wood or metal, which in turn is attached to the faceplate. The contact face for attaching to the gear frame can then be machined off to the exact dimension required, viz $\frac{29}{32}$ in., and it will be parallel with the back. If a milling machine is available, or a planer or shaper, the job is, of course, just a cakewalk.

The complete bracket could be cut from a $1\frac{1}{2}$ in. length of 1 in. by $\frac{1}{4}$ in. bar, the unwanted portions being sawn away and the piece finished to shape with a file. The holes should be drilled, and the contact face machined-off as described above. The bracket is also built up very easily; the back is formed from a piece of $\frac{1}{8}$ in. by $\frac{1}{4}$ in. rod (steel or brass will do) $1\frac{1}{2}$ in. long. The projection for attachment to the gear frame is a piece of $\frac{1}{2}$ in. by $\frac{1}{4}$ in. bar, parted-off in the four-jaw to a dead length of $\frac{25}{32}$ in., and brazed or silver-soldered to the back part in the position shown in the illustration No further machining of either back or contact face would be necessary.

Erection

Put the rear bracket against the rear end of the gear frame, the temporary bolt being removed, and hold it in position with a toolmaker's clamp. Poke the No. 41 drill right through spacer and both frames, making countersinks on contact face of bracket, then remove clamp, drill the countersinks No. 48, and tap 7 BA. The frame is secured to the bracket by two bolts made from pieces of $\frac{3}{32}$ in. silver-steel about $1\frac{1}{4}$ in. long, with $\frac{1}{4}$ in. thread on one end, and just enough to take a nut on the other; see plan view of assembled gear, bottom of Fig. 7-6.

Now put the gear frame in place, as shown in the elevation; the top of the rear end of the gear frame should be $1\frac{3}{4}$ in. above centre-line of motion, and $2\frac{7}{16}$ in. ahead of the centre of the driving axle. The foot of the front bracket should rest on the top of the guide-bar. Poke the drill through holes in bracket and foot, make countersinks on frame and guide-bar, then drill No. 40 and tap for $\frac{1}{8}$ in. or 5 BA screws. You can drill the frame No. 30, and use bolts if you so desire; bolts are used on full-sized engines. File off any portions of screw projecting below the guide-bar, so that they won't be able to foul the crosshead. That settles the gear frames and their erection; the next job will be to make the rods and levers, and put them in the frames, which is easier than making curved slotted links.

In order to keep the reach-rod below the running-board, as in some types of Walschaerts gear, the reversing connection is made direct to the stay-bar between the reverse-yokes, instead of having a separate connection above the bar. Otherwise, the gear is pretty much the same as applicable to any normal type engine. The dimensions and pin centres of the rods and levers are exactly proportionate to the full-size gear, as given in the manufacturing company's drawings; so there is no question about the accuracy of the various parts, and the steam distribution will be O.K. A glance at the accompanying illustrations will soon convince any doubting beginner that the Baker parts are far easier to make and erect than any arrangement embodying slotted curved links.

Reverse-Yokes

The full-sized Baker gears originally had single reverse yokes on the inside of the gear frame; and on the first Baker-fitted engine in this country, *Fayette*, which I built in 1926, I used single yokes. Soon after that, the double yoke was introduced, on account of breakages occurring on full-sized Baker-fitted engines in the U.S.A., where they haul *really* heavy loads; and naturally, I wasn't going to be left out in the cold, wherever any improvements were concerned. Apart from the extra strength of the double yoke, there is another great advantage, viz., that the width of each radius bar bearing is also doubled, thereby prolonging the life of the gear, and retaining its accuracy. Drop stampings and castings are used for the component parts of the full-sized gears; but all parts of the small ones are easily made from steel strip, saving a lot of trouble. The minimum of detailed instruction is needed, all dimensions being given on the drawings; and I guess that by this time, everybody who has read this far knows how to use a file, drill holes accurately, and do a bit of plain turning!

Whilst on the job of making components, you might as well make both sets together, as they are the same on both sides of the locomotive; so cut eight $1\frac{3}{4}$ in. lengths of $\frac{5}{16}$ in. by $\frac{3}{32}$ in., drill one, and use it as a jig to drill the rest. Use a Wilmot filing jig, or button, to guide the file when rounding off the ends. Turn the bushes from a bit of $\frac{5}{16}$ in. bronze rod held in the three-jaw; face, centre, drill No. 23 for about $\frac{1}{2}$ in. depth, turn $\frac{1}{8}$ in. of the end to a squeeze fit in the $\frac{3}{32}$ in. hole in the yoke-plate, part off at $\frac{3}{8}$ in. from the end, reverse in chuck, and turn down the other end for $\frac{1}{8}$ in. length to a squeeze fit as before, leaving a full $\frac{1}{8}$ in. of full-size between shoulders. Squeeze a yoke-plate on to each spigot, putting a bit of rod, or a drill shank, through the top and bottom holes, to keep the lot in line whilst applying the "Sunny Jim". File off the spigots flush with the yoke at each side; then very carefully poke a $\frac{3}{32}$ in. parallel reamer through each bush.

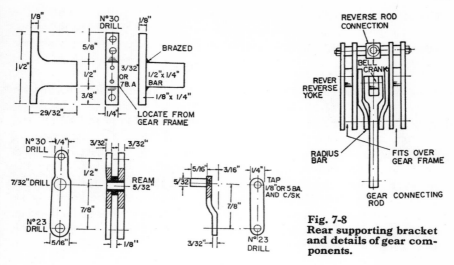

Fig. 7-8
Rear supporting bracket
and details of gear com-
ponents.

Radius-Bars

These can be filed up from $\frac{3}{32}$ in. by $\frac{1}{4}$ in. steel strip and bent to shape, as shown in Fig. 7-8. Don't forget the bars want to measure $\frac{7}{8}$ in. between the centres of trunnion-pin and bottom hole, *after bending*. The trunnion-pin is made from a bit of $\frac{5}{32}$ in. silver-steel held in three-jaw. Turn a pip on the end $\frac{1}{8}$ in. long and $\frac{1}{8}$ in. diameter, screwing it $\frac{1}{8}$ in. or 5 BA; then screw it into the end of the bar, hammer the end into the countersink, and file flush. That will prevent the trunnions ever coming loose in the bars.

Gear Connecting-Rod

This is nicknamed the "sickle" on account of its shape (Fig. 7-9), and can either be made from $\frac{3}{8}$ in. by $\frac{1}{4}$ in. steel rod, and bent to shape, or it may be cut from the solid, just as preferred. I've never had any trouble in getting a true bend; but some would rather mark out the whole doings on a hunk of steel, and carve it to finished outline, and if you like to take the trouble, well, it's your pigeon! Whichever way you do the job, note the offset at the bottom. Benders who are slotting the forks on the lathe should use a bit of steel long enough for both rods, which is easier to clamp under the slide-rest

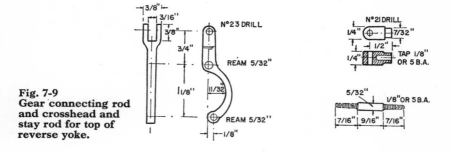

Fig. 7-9
Gear connecting rod
and crosshead and
stay rod for top of
reverse yoke.

tool holder. After forming the fork in one end, reverse the metal and do the other; then mill, plane or file either side until the rod is correct thickness. It can then be sawn apart, and each half drilled and bent to shape as shown.

Bell-Crank

A bit of $\frac{3}{16}$ in. steel plate about $1\frac{5}{8}$ in. long and $1\frac{1}{4}$ in. wide is needed for each bell crank. Here is a marking-out tip for beginners; draw two lines $\frac{1}{16}$ in. apart near one side of the plate, dot the site of the bush hole on one, at the top, and the hole for the valve-rod pin on the other, at the bottom, $1\frac{1}{8}$ in. below the top one. Set your divider points $\frac{13}{16}$ in. apart, and strike an arc from the upper dot; then alter them to $1\frac{1}{4}$ in. apart, and strike another arc from the bottom dot, cutting the first one. At the "level crossing", make your dot to locate hole No. 3. The useful bit of serrated wire known as an "Abrafile" will make short work of cutting out the superfluous metal between the two arms of the bell crank. Drill the two holes in the extremities No. 23, and ream $\frac{5}{32}$ in.; the hole in the knee is drilled $\frac{15}{64}$ in. or letter "C", and reamed $\frac{1}{4}$ in. The bush is simply a bit of $\frac{5}{32}$ in. round bronze $\frac{3}{4}$ in. long chucked truly in a three-jaw, centred, drilled No. 23 and reamed $\frac{5}{32}$ in., squeeze it into the hole in the knee of the bell crank, and silver-solder it in position for the sake of "safety-first" (Fig. 7-10).

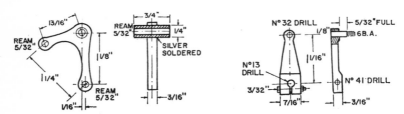

Fig. 7-10 Bell crank and return crank.

For a long-wearing and trouble-free gear, all the holes that have pins working in them—the reamed ones—should be case-hardened. The gears on the full-sized engines are furnished with easily-renewable bushes; the holes in the small edition could also be bronze-bushed, the only disadvantage being that you would either have to use smaller pins, or else make the ends of the various parts of larger radius, so as to have enough metal around the outside of the bush, to provide for requisite strength. Not much sense in bushing, if the housing splits and the bush drops out when the engine is doing a bit of record-breaking, either for speed, haulage, or both!

How to Erect the Gears

Cut off two pieces of $\frac{5}{32}$ in. silver-steel each $1\frac{7}{16}$ in. long, for the stay bars for the reverse yoke assemblies. Chuck each in three-jaw, turn down $\frac{7}{16}$ in. of each end to $\frac{1}{8}$ in. diameter, and screw $\frac{1}{8}$ in. or 5 BA. Each assembly needs four distance-pieces or spacers; two are $\frac{3}{16}$ in. diameter, $\frac{1}{8}$ in. long and drilled No. 30; they go between the two plates forming each side of the reverse-yoke. The other two may be $\frac{7}{32}$ in. diameter, $\frac{5}{32}$ in. long, and drilled No. 21, and are used to keep the reverse-rod connection in the middle of the bar; see Fig. 7-8. Any metal will do, but steel looks best. The connection for the reverse-rod looks like a fork which some absent-minded locomotive builder forgot to slot. It is simply a small piece of $\frac{1}{4}$ in. square steel rod, cross-drilled No. 21 ($\frac{5}{32}$ in. clearing) and rounded off at one end; the other is turned circular, and drilled and tapped to take a $\frac{1}{8}$ in. rod; see Fig. 7-9. The latter job is easily done in the four-jaw.

To assemble, proceed as follows: Put the shorter arm of the bell-crank between the jaws of the fork on the gear connecting-rod, concave sides facing, squeeze a piece of $\frac{5}{32}$ in. silver-steel through the lot, and file flush each side of the fork. Put a radius-bar each side of the gear connecting-rod, bottom holes level with centre hole in the "sickle"; squeeze a $\frac{5}{32}$ in. silver-steel pin through the lot as before, and file off flush. Put a $\frac{1}{8}$ in. spacer between the two plates at the top of one of the reverse-yokes; poke one end of the stay-bar through, and secure with a nut. Put a $\frac{5}{32}$ in. spacer on the bar, then the reverse-rod connection, and then another spacer; then—mind the bits don't fall off whilst you do this!—enter one of the trunnion pins of the radius bar, into the bush in the reverse yoke. Next, put another $\frac{1}{8}$ in. spacer between the tops of the plates on reverse-yoke No. 2, and place it in position, the other radius-bar trunnion entering the bush, and the end of the stay-bar going through the holes and spacer at the top. Put on a nut to keep the bits together, and the "movies" are complete (Fig. 7-8).

It only remains to erect the gear in the frame. Take the bell-crank spindle out of the frame, and drop in the whole lot of rods from the top, so that the bell-crank bush lines up with the holes where the spindle goes through, and the bottom holes in the reverse yoke line up with the bottom holes in the gear-frame. Replace the bell-crank spindle, poking it, screwed end first, through the long bush, and put a nut on where it projects beyond the gear frame. Squeeze short $\frac{5}{32}$ in. silver-steel pins through the bottom holes in the reverse yokes and the holes in the frames, and file off flush each side. The erection is then complete, and the gear-frames, with all the blobs and gadgets attached, can be replaced on the engine in the location already described. The next stage will be to connect up to reversing wheel and combination levers, which is easier, if anything, than coupling up a Walschaerts gear.

The Baker gear is coupled up in pretty much the same manner as Walschaerts, the eccentric-rod and return-crank being of identical pattern, and a simple forked rod connecting the combination-lever with the lower end of the vertical-arm of the bell-crank. The only difference between the Baker and Walschaerts return-cranks, is that the former is longer between centres, viz., $1\frac{1}{16}$ in.; it is made and fitted in exactly the same way (Fig. 7-10). Same applies to the eccentric-rod; the procedure for setting the return-crank correctly, and at the same time obtaining the correct length of the eccentric-rod between centres, is as follows. First, set the return crank as near as you

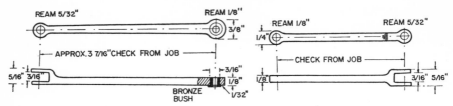

Fig. 7-11   Eccentric rod and valve rod.

can, "by eye", at right-angles to the main crank; leading it, for slide-valve cylinders, and following it for piston-valve cylinders. Next, set the gear connecting-rod in such a position that you can swing the reverse-yoke back and forth for its full movement, without moving the bell-crank, and temporarily fix it there.

Put the main crank on front dead centre, and take the distance between the centres of the hole in the end of the gear connecting-rod, and the return crank-pin, with a pair of dividers. Shift the main crank to back dead centre, and check the same points without shifting the setting of the dividers. If they do not tally, shift the return crank-pin half the difference, and have another shot. When the distance between centres of the gear connecting-rod tail hole, and the centre of the return crank-pin, tally on both front and back dead centres, the return-crank is correctly set, and the distance between the divider points is the exact length to which your eccentric-rod should be made between centres of pin-holes; so you can then go ahead and make it, coupling the forked end to the gear connecting-rod with a little silver-steel bolt (Fig. 7-11).

The length of the valve rod is determined as follows: Put the reverse yoke in mid gear; that is, in such a position that the bell-crank does not move when the wheels are turned, and temporarily fix it there. Set the piston at half-stroke, so that the combination-lever is vertical, and the valve in mid position; then take the distance from the centre of the hole in the hanging arm of the bell-crank, to the centre of the appropriate hole at the top of the combination-lever—upper for piston-valve cylinders, lower for slide valves—using a pair of dividers. The distance between the divider points is the centre-to-centre measurement of your valve rod. This is made to the shape shown in the illustration, a simple filing and slotting job.

The eye of the valve rod is secured to the combination-lever by a squeezed-in $\frac{1}{8}$ in. silver-steel pin; the bell-crank and forked end are fixed by a little bolt made from $\frac{5}{32}$ in. silver-steel, shouldered down to $\frac{7}{64}$ in. at both ends and furnished with ordinary commercial 6 BA nuts.

Reverse Shaft

As each side of the engine has a separate independent set of valve gear, a separate reverse-shaft is needed to operate them in unison, and this is situated between the driving wheels and the trailing coupled wheels, as shown in the illustration. Mark off on the frame at each side, a point exactly mid-way between the coupled wheels, and high enough to clear the coupling rods; make centre-pops, and drill a No. 30 pilot hole at each point. Put a piece of $\frac{1}{8}$ in. round silver-steel through both holes, and see if it is square and level with the frames; if not, correct with a rat-tail file. When O.K. open out both holes with a $\frac{3}{8}$ in. drill, and turn up two bronze or gunmetal bushes from $\frac{1}{2}$ in. round rod. The flanges of the bushes should be $\frac{1}{8}$ in. wide, and the turned-down part a squeeze-fit in the $\frac{3}{8}$ in. holes in the frames. Drill them either with letter "C" or $\frac{15}{64}$ in. drill, and ream them $\frac{1}{4}$ in. after they are pressed home, which will ensure accuracy.

The shaft itself (Fig. 7-13) is a piece of $\frac{1}{4}$ in. round steel $6\frac{1}{8}$ in. long; silver-steel is best, but ordinary drawn stuff will do if nothing better is available. Both ends should be squared-off in the lathe, for sake of appearance, as they show through the reverse-arms. The latter are filed up from $\frac{1}{8}$ in. by $\frac{3}{8}$ in. mild-steel strip, to the shape shown in Fig. 7-13, and the holes are drilled at $1\frac{5}{16}$ in. centres, those in the small ends being reamed $\frac{1}{8}$ in. One of the arms is brazed direct to the shaft, the hole in the large end being drilled with letter "D" drill, or the nearest you have below $\frac{1}{4}$ in., then opened out until a drive-fit on the shaft. Alternatively, you can drill it $\frac{7}{32}$ in., and turn down $\frac{5}{32}$ in. of the end of the shaft to a drive-fit in the hole, applying a spot of silver-solder on the inner side of the arm around the shaft. The other arm has a boss fitted to it; and two collars, with set-screws, are also made to fit on the shaft as shown.

To erect, poke the shaft through the left-hand bush, put on the two collars between the frames, then insert through right-hand bush and put on the other arm, setting the centres of the arms $5\frac{15}{16}$ in. apart, each projecting from the frames an equal amount. Set the arms as near as you can, parallel with each other, and run the collars up to the bush flanges, tightening the set-screws so that they cannot shift; but don't pin the loose arm to the shaft yet.

Two short reach-rods are needed, to connect each reverse-arm to the reverse yokes in the gear frames (Fig. 7-14). These merely consist of a simple fork, made exactly as described for valve-spindle and other forks, coupled to the connection on the stay-bar of the reverse yoke by a piece of $\frac{1}{8}$ in. round silver-steel screwed at both ends. Check the distance from the

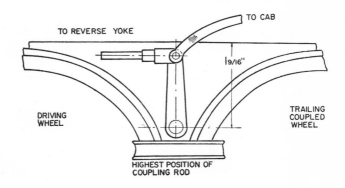

Fig. 7-12
Location of
reverse shaft

TO CAB

TO REVERSE YOKE

|9/16"

DRIVING
WHEEL

TRAILING
COUPLED
WHEEL

HIGHEST POSITION OF
COUPLING ROD

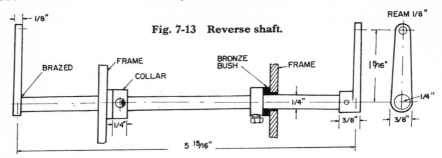

Fig. 7-13   Reverse shaft.

engine itself. Put the left-hand reverse yoke in mid-gear, so that the bell-crank doesn't move when the wheels are turned by hand; set the brazed-on arm exactly vertical, and take the distance between the centre of the hole at the top of the arm, and the centre of the reverse yoke stay bar.

Make both of the short reach-rods the same length, and couple up both sides; then adjust so that both gears operate in unison. You can put a proper bolt in the right-hand arm (the adjustable one) but just poke a bit of $\frac{1}{8}$ in. silver-steel through the left-hand one for the time being. Put the left-hand reverse yoke in mid-gear again, and temporarily fix it there; then see if the right-hand one is in mid-gear also. If it isn't, carefully adjust the reverse-arm on the shaft until it is; then drill a No. 43 hole clean through the boss of the reverse-arm and the shaft, and squeeze in a pin made from $\frac{3}{32}$ in. silver-steel. Both gears should then reverse or notch-up exactly in unison.

The long reach-rod is made with a boss brazed on one end, and a little block on the other, which is formed into a fork or clevis; but the jaws of the latter are made $\frac{1}{4}$ in. wide, to embrace the top of the smaller fork on the left-hand short reach-rod; see Fig. 7-15. The rod is also directly connected to the nut on the reversing-screw, and slopes downward towards the gear, above the running board, after the fashion of the reach-rods on the Maunsell 2-6-0's, terminating in an easy bend to connect to the top of the reverse-arm. When making the reversing nut, screw in a shouldered pin, as shown in Fig. 7-15. Drill the side of the nut No. 30, and tap it $\frac{5}{32}$ in. by 40. Make the pin from a bit of $\frac{5}{32}$ in. silver-steel, with a few threads of $\frac{5}{32}$ in. by 40 on one end, and turn the other down to $\frac{1}{8}$ in. for about $\frac{3}{16}$ in. length, screwing it 5 BA. When the pin is screwed home in the nut, there should be just enough plain part projecting, to let the 5 BA nut be screwed home against the shoulder, without jamming the boss on the reach-rod. A similar arrange-

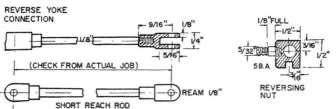

Fig. 7-14
Short reach rods.

ment was used on many of the Brighton engines, a fork joint not being found necessary.

Before making the reach-rod, get the exact length required from the actual job. Put the nut on the reversing-screw in the middle of its travel, and the arm on the reverse shaft exactly vertical. Take the distance between the centre of the temporary pin in the fork on the short reach-rod, and the centre of the pin in the reversing-nut, which gives the exact length of the long reach-rod, between pinhole centres, *after bending the curve at the forked end*. The permanent connection to the reverse shaft is made by a $\frac{1}{8}$ in. silver-steel bolt through the lot—reach-rod forks (long and short) and the top of the reverse-arm, as shown in Fig. 7-15.

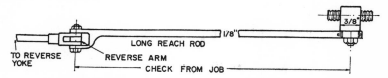

Fig. 7-15   **Reversing rod, or long reach rod.**

The Holcroft Valve Gear

Most four-cylinder engines have the cranks opposed, the inner cranks being set diametrically opposite to the outer cranks; thus it is easy to operate the valves of both cylinders on one side, by a single valve gear plus a plain rocker. However, this cannot be done if the cranks are set at 135 deg., giving eight impulses per turn of the wheels, similar to the "Lord Nelson" class on the old Southern Railway; and in these engines, a separate set of valve gear was employed for each cylinder. My $2\frac{1}{2}$ in. gauge experimental Pacific engine *Tugboat Annie* has the same crank arrangement; but she only has two sets of valve gear, actuating the valves of the outside cylinders. The inside valves are operated by a special arrangement of conjugated levers, especially designed for her by Mr. H. Holcroft, who was chief technical adviser to the C.M.E. of the S.R. previous to his retirement.

Although *Tugboat Annie* was the first engine, big or little, in the wide world, to be fitted with this type of conjugated valve gear, the idea is now many years old; for back in 1920, Mr. H. Holcroft read a paper on "Four-cylinder Locomotives" before the Institution of Locomotive Engineers, in which he described all the types then in existence, or which had been tried out, and gave details of his own devices. He dealt with various Continental, Colonial and American four-cylinder drives—Vauclain compounds, French and Belgian Pacifics, the G.W.R. 4-6-0s and so on, describing the various forms of vertical and horizontal rocking shafts, and the different connections to the inside and outside valve spindles, explaining the action as follows. I quote his own words from his paper:

"In a four-cylinder engine with cranks at 180 deg. the rocking levers can be represented geometrically as in Fig. 1. A circle is drawn with centre O

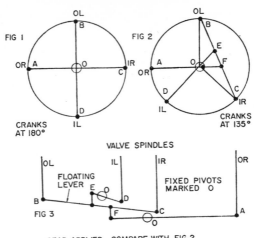

Fig. 7-16 Valve gear diagrams.

to indicate the valve travel, and four points are taken on the circumference 90 deg. apart at *A*, *B*, *C*, and *D*. The motion of the valve-gear can be replaced by an equivalent crank, so that the four points represent four valve motions, outside right, outside left, inside right and inside left respectively. Join *A C* and *B D*; then *A O C* and *B O D* are two rocking levers pivoting on the engine frame at fixed points. If either the two inside or two outside valves are driven by ordinary valve gears, the remaining two can be operated through simple rocking levers attached to them.

"Now in Fig. 2, one pair of cranks are moved around through an angle of 45 deg. so as to give eight impulses per revolution, the same lettering as in Fig. 1 being used. In order to form one system of levers, join *B C*, draw *A O F* cutting *B C* at *F*, and *D O E* cutting *B C* at *E*. The mechanism will therefore consist of a rocking lever, *A O F*, attached to the outside right valve at *A*, pivoted to the frame at *O*, and attached to a floating lever, *B E F C*, at *F*. The latter is attached to the outside left valve at *B*, and to the inside right valve at *C*. In order to operate the fourth valve; the rocking lever *D O E* is attached to the inside left valve at *D*, pivots on the frame at *O*, and connects with the floating lever at *E*. The proportions of the various levers are shown by the diagram, but may be made of any proportionate length. The corresponding mechanism is set out diagrammatically in Fig. 3, and it will be seen that by the addition of one lever only, the two valve-gears may be made to operate four valves when the main cranks are set at 135 deg. instead of 180, there being three levers in place of two."

Mr. Holcroft then went on to say that there was another way of getting a similar result, by using a separate combination to operate each inside valve-spindle, and superimposing the two combinations on one another; and it is the latter type of gear that is fitted to *Tugboat Annie*. When he first saw may *Caterpillar* goods engine, which has four cylinders and 135-deg. cranks, he said that a simple arrangement of lever as described above could be applied to it. However, the nigger in the woodpile was that the inside cylinders are "upside down", as the kiddies would call it, and the original arrangement of Holcroft gear called for all valve-spindles in the same plane. I therefore abandoned the idea of fitting the gear to that engine, and decided to fit one to the next four-cylinder job, arranging the valve-spindles all in line.

One of my pet fads, fancies, notions or whatever you like to call it for an ideal four-cylinder locomotive, is that both inside and outside "works" should be as nearly as possible similar; that is to say, same length of cylinder blocks, guide bars, connecting rods and so on; especially with regard to moving parts, as this simplifies the balancing very considerably. Therefore, when I built my "answer to the driver's prayer" (in the "flesh" mind you; not on paper, or by proxy) I followed out this system; and as the drive is divided, the cylinders were arranged *a la* Great Western practice, the outside pair being set over the rear bogie wheels to drive the middle coupled axle, and the inside pair set ahead to drive the leading coupled axle. The valve gear for the outside cylinders worked in very nicely, the Baker sets being adaptable to any type of engine, as either a girder or bracket frame can be used as is found most convenient. I used the girder frame, bracketing the rear end direct to the frame behind the coupled wheel, and fixing up a support ahead of the wheel which served both for the valve-gear frame and the guide-bar yoke. This arrangement, however, was not suitable for the original Holcroft assembly; and the only way to arrange the drive for the inside valves was by rigging up the conjugation to work in the same space usually occupied by plain rocking levers, as seen on the G.W. and L.M.S. four-cylinder engines. When I showed the chassis with the cylinders assembled to Mr. Holcroft he said it was certainly going to be a tight squeeze, but he would get out something that would fit in; so I gave him a photograph of the chassis showing the cylinders in place, also a plan view of it, and he got busy.

I had every confidence that Mr. Holcroft would solve the problem, and he certainly did (Fig. 7-17). I am going to say right here, and without fear of contradiction, that in your humble servant's estimation *and* that of a good

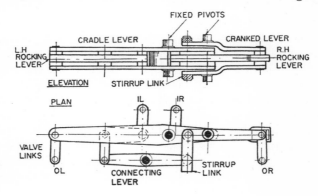

Fig. 7-17
Holcroft valve gear assembled.

many others, there is not another locomotive engineer in the whole world who can hold the proverbial candle to Mr. Holcroft when it comes to valve gear design.

In due course, Mr. Holcroft had drawn out a suitable arrangement and explained all about it. He did the trick by using two overlapping combinations of levers. Each combination is actuated by *both* the outside valve-spindles, and the levers are very ingeniously superimposed, so that whilst they are all in the same plane, each set can operate quite independently of the other, without any chance of fouling. The accompanying illustrations show the complete assembly, also the two separate sections (Fig. 7-18) so that the action can easily be followed.

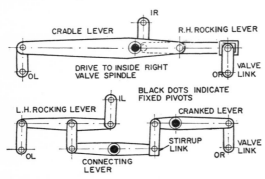

Fig. 7-18
The gear dissected.

How the Gear Works

As the cranks are set at 135 deg. instead of the 120 deg. of a three-cylinder engine, the centres and lengths of the levers are a little different. If you take a look at that half of the gear which drives the inside right valve, you will recognize immediately the long lever that corresponds to the long Gresley "two-to-one" lever on the three-cylinder engine, also, the short floating lever coupled to the end of it corresponding to the floating equal-armed lever on the Gresley gear. This one however isn't equal. Please note, I refer to the "Gresley" gear in a descriptive or distinguishing sense only. As a matter of fact, Mr. Holcroft anticipated Sir Nigel, and was the pioneer "conjugationalist". Now take a look at the second half. Here we have practically the same arrangement, but with the action reversed, the whole lot being "turned over", in a manner of speaking. It would be mechanically impossible to use the same arrangement of long and short levers, and reverse the action by changing the fixed and moving pivots, as the levers would naturally foul, so Mr. Holcroft got over the trouble by an ingenious bit of "wangling", and killed all the birds with one shot.

The long "Gresley" lever is all-present-and-correct-sergeant, but transferred to the right and rather shrunk in size, although the proportions are O.K., and the floating lever is conspicuous by its presence on the other side, being practically the same size as its fellow-conspirator or opposite member; but the two levers, instead of being directly connected, are coupled by a third lever with equal arms, mounted on a fixed pivot to the rear of the main assembly. That leaves a gap on the horizontal line of the fixed and floating levers, which very nicely accommodates the fulcrum of the big lever. The combined movements of the outside valve-spindles on the outer ends of the levers produce corresponding movements of the inside ends which are coupled to the inside valve-spindles; and these movements are absolutely uncanny to watch. It looks as if the blessed gear itself had brains of its own, and *knew* just how and when to waggle the inside spindles back and forth. Though Mr. Holcroft explained the working of the gear to me, and I made it, yet I was fascinated beyond all measure when I got it erected and tried it on the air pump. The biggest shock I got was after I set the valves of the outside cylinders to my pet timing. I took off the cover of the inside steam-chest, took one look inside, and very nearly fainted. *The valves were already set—* the gear had done it!

How the Gear was Made

The whole of the levers were cut from steel strip of requisite width and thickness, and the pins and pivots, which were a fixture, were made a press fit, so that the gear, when assembled complete, had a very clean appearance, and was entirely innocent of brazing marks, or excessively-rounded corners due to cleaning off burnt borax. The long cradle lever was made in two pieces, each $\frac{3}{8}$ in. wide and $\frac{3}{32}$ in. thick, drilled and filed to shape whilst clamped together. The distance-piece was turned from an odd scrap of $\frac{3}{8}$ in. round steel. It was shouldered each end to fit $\frac{1}{4}$ in. holes drilled in the levers, the holes being very slightly countersunk. The piece was then pressed in, temporary pins being placed in the end pinholes to keep the levers in line; the projecting edges of the distance-piece were hammered into the countersinks and filed off flush, and the whole job polished on the linisher. The fulcrum-pins, which have a collar at the side next the lever only, were turned from $\frac{1}{4}$ in. silver-steel and pressed home under the ram of the bush and mandrel press.

The right and left-hand rocking levers, both of which float, were filed up from $\frac{1}{8}$ in. by $\frac{5}{16}$ in. strip, as they are single levers. The left-hand one has three plain pinholes in it, but the outer end of the right-hand one has a rectangular end with a slot in it, in which works a small bronze die-block. This is necessary because the lever works on a floating fulcrum-pin; and the end carrying the die-block works on the pin attached to the cranked lever which works on a fixed fulcrum on the engine frame, so that the ends of the two levers describe arcs of different radii. The difference is very slight, but without the die-block we should stand a chance of what "Bert Smiff" would call "bustin' up the 'ole blinkin' works".

The two cranked levers were cut from $\frac{3}{8}$ in. by $\frac{3}{32}$ in. strip, and as the offset is the same as the thickness, the levers were simply placed between the vice-jaws with a piece of the same strip ahead of and behind the bend, and one good wrench at the vice screw-handle did the needful. The pins were turned from silver-steel rod and pressed into countersunk holes, riveted over slightly on the opposite side, and filed flush.

The connecting lever has two long bosses on it, so a spot of "brazing" was called for here. Holes were drilled at the correct centres in a piece of $\frac{1}{8}$ in. by $\frac{3}{4}$ in. strip, the two bushes turned up, and pressed in. A tiny fillet of Sifbronze flux mixed to a paste with water was laid around each; then a touch with the oxy-acetylene blowpipe, using 75-litre tip, and a small bead of white Sifbronze was applied, and flashed into a fillet clean around each bush. The lever was then filed to shape and polished, and the joints are practically invisible. The lever looks as though it had been milled out of the solid.

The stirrup-link was made from a piece of $\frac{1}{16}$ in. by $\frac{1}{4}$ in. steel strip very carefully bent to shape, and drilled after bending, extra care being taken with the marking-out. There are four pairs of small connecting links needed for coupling up the gear to the valve-spindles, and these were filed up from $\frac{1}{4}$ in. by $\frac{1}{16}$ in. strip, whilst the four little crossheads were made from $\frac{1}{4}$ in. square rod. All the straight pins are $\frac{1}{8}$ in. silver-steel; those in the valve-gear are press fits in the levers in which they are a fixture, and work in reamed holes in the levers in which they move. The pins in the valve crossheads are made from the same material, but are shouldered at each end and furnished with nuts and washers. All the parts are shown separately in Fig. 7-19.

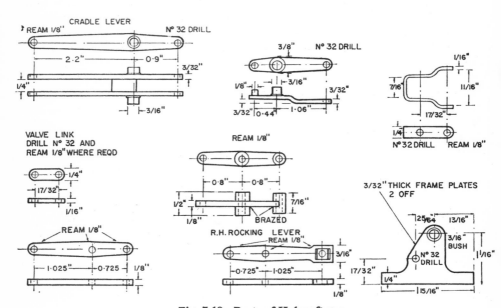

Fig. 7-19 Parts of Holcroft gear.

How the Gear is Erected

Two frame plates were cut out of $\frac{3}{32}$ in. steel sheet, to fit between the engine frames, and these were fixed at a distance of $\frac{1}{2}$ in. apart by a piece of $\frac{1}{2}$ in. brass rod, to which the frames were bolted by 6 BA bolts made from silver-steel of that thickness, screwed and nutted at each end. Each frame plate has a projecting tongue which is drilled and bushed to carry the pivots of the cradle lever. The pivot bush of the connecting-link works on a plain pin made a press fit in the frame plates. The whole issue is located at a point level with the front end of the outside cylinders, and is kept in position by two roundhead screws put through clearing holes in the main frames at each side, into tapped holes in the brass rod. The fixed pivots of the cranked levers are carried by two small steel brackets milled from $\frac{3}{8}$ in. square steel, and screwed to the right-hand main frame of the engine. The complete valve-gear assembly, frame and all, can be completely removed by disconnecting the small links from the valve crossheads, and taking out six screws. On a full-sized engine, the whole set could be changed by a fitter and mate with a hand crane, in a single night, so that no engine fitted with a Holcroft gear need ever be laid up for repairs to it.

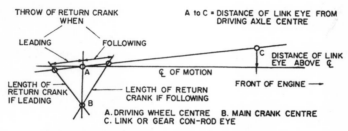

Fig. 7-20   Diagram of return crank settings.

Fitting Up Return or Eccentric Cranks

One essential point on any valve-gear using a return crank to operate it is that the said crank *must be an absolute fixture on the crankpin;* and the latter, ditto in the wheel boss, or else the timing stands a very good chance of being thrown out. Fig. 7-20 is a diagram showing how to find the length of return cranks. The crankpin should be pressed into the wheel boss and have a little key in it at the back of the wheel; in the smaller sizes a piece of steel wire will do, fitted in the usual manner by drilling a hole half in boss and half in pin (that is, on the joint line) and driving in the wire key. There are three good ways of fitting the return crank to the pin. The simplest is to have the pin parallel throughout, and the boss of the return crank drilled a drive fit to go on the pin. When the crank is set right, a pin is driven through both boss and crankpin (*A* in Fig. 7-21), which prevents it turning or coming off. Method No. 2, shown at *B*, is similar to big practice and was used on *Fayette*. The end of the crankpin is shouldered down, and the return crank

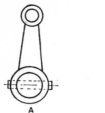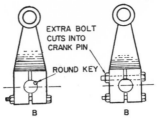

Fig. 7-21   Return cranks.

boss, after being bored a drive fit on the reduced diameter, is split down with a saw and fitted with a bolt. This method makes for ease of setting, as the bolt can be tightened sufficiently to make the crank "stay put" while adjustments are being checked off, and it can be easily shifted to correct. When all O.K., a little screwed key is put between boss and pin in the usual manner, or, alternatively, a second bolt can be put right through the boss, the hole being drilled so that it just catches the crank pin and cuts a groove in it. The third method, shown at C, is to bore out the boss to suit a shouldered crank pin as before; but the split section does not extend to the edge of the boss. It can be cut with a metal fret-saw, starting in the hole; but care must be taken to saw straight. After setting, it may be either keyed or have another bolt put in to make sure it does not turn. Either type may be used with a crankpin having a squared end, in which case no key is required.

CHAPTER VIII

Miscellaneous Details

ON THE FULL-SIZE L.N.E.R. Gresley "Pacifics", the driver's reversing gear consists of a vertical screw, operated by a handle like a tender brake handle, located close to the backhead. The nut is connected to the horizontal reach rod by a link and a bell crank. Whilst this is O.K. in full size, on a little engine it is about the worst possible position, having to be operated by a driver riding behind the tender, instead of on the footplate. It is, therefore, a good plan to substitute an ordinary horizontal wheel and screw reverser, and here are the details of one especially arranged for this particular type of engine. The complete arrangement is shown in Fig. 8-1.

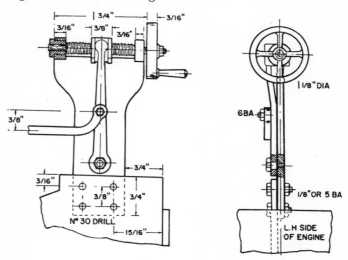

Fig. 8-1
Wheel and screw
reverser.

Stand and Bearings

The stand may either be a casting with the bearings cast on, or it may be built up. If a casting is used, clean up with a file, and centre-pop the two bearings. Put a $\frac{1}{8}$ in. drill through both, and see that it lines up with the top edge of the stand, both vertically and horizontally. If it doesn't, correct with a rat-tail file, and try with a little larger drill. When O.K., open out one bearing to $\frac{3}{16}$ in., and the other to $\frac{9}{32}$ in., tapping this $\frac{5}{16}$ in. by 40. If the stand is to be built up, cut out a piece of $\frac{1}{8}$ in. bright steel plate to the given

119

dimensions. Turn up the two bearings from a bit of $\frac{7}{16}$ in. bronze or gunmetal rod and mill, plane or file a groove in each, so that they will fit tightly at each end of the top edge of the stand; then silver-solder them in position. Turn up a little nipple from a bit of $\frac{3}{8}$ in. hexagaon bronze or gunmetal rod, drilling it $\frac{5}{32}$ in., and screwing the outside $\frac{5}{16}$ in. by 40. At 1 in. from the bottom, on the centre-line, drill a No. 40 hole and tap it either $\frac{1}{8}$ in. or 5 BA for the fulcrum pin.

Screw and Nut

The reversing screws on most full-sized engines are left-handed; that is, you turn the wheel clockwise to put her in forward gear, just as you turn the handle of your lathe cross-slide clockwise to advance the tool into cut. Therefore, if you have a $\frac{1}{4}$ in. Whitworth tap and die with left-hand threads, you may as well use them for the screw and nut; but if not, use the ordinary right-hand tap and die. Chuck a bit of $\frac{1}{4}$ in. round mild-steel in the three-jaw, and turn down $\frac{1}{4}$ in. of it to a nice running fit; without shake, in the screwed nipple and of the front bearing; use the nipple itself for a gauge. Now pull the steel out of the chuck, exposing about $1\frac{1}{2}$ in. of it beyond the shoulder of the little journal just turned, and carefully screw it $\frac{1}{4}$ in. Whitworth left-hand if possible, with the die in tailstock holder. Use plenty of cutting oil, and work the mandrel back and forth by pulling the lathe belt by hand. A good clean thread is essential. Pull the steel out a bit more, and part off $2\frac{3}{16}$ in. from the extreme end. Reverse in chuck; you can hold by the threads, if the chuck is not tightened excessively, to machine the other end. Turn down $\frac{9}{16}$ in. length to $\frac{3}{16}$ in. diameter, a proper running fit in the back

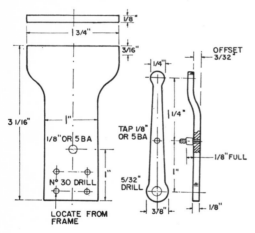

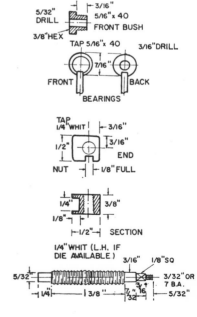

Fig. 8-2
(above) Reverser stand and lever.
(right) Bearings, screw and nut.

bearing; then turn down $\frac{5}{32}$ in. of the end to $\frac{3}{32}$ in. diameter, and screw it 7 BA. Set the screw back in the chuck until $\frac{3}{16}$ in. of the plain part behind the small thread projects from the chuck jaws; file that bit $\frac{1}{8}$ in. square, using one of the chuck jaws as guide. The length of the screwed part should be $1\frac{3}{8}$ in., and should fit nicely between the bearings on the stand.

To make the nut, chuck a bit of $\frac{1}{2}$ in. square bronze or gunmetal rod in the four-jaw (doesn't matter about it being exactly true) face the end, and part off a $\frac{3}{8}$ in. length. On one end of this, make a centre-pop $\frac{3}{16}$ in. from two adjacent sides (see Fig. 8-2), then rechuck with this mark running truly. Centre, drill $\frac{3}{16}$ in. or No. 12, and tap to suit the screw. At the bottom, plane, mill or file a groove a shade over $\frac{1}{8}$ in. wide, just enough to let the nut slide along the top of the stand. In the side opposite to the tapped hole, form a groove $\frac{1}{4}$ in. wide and $\frac{1}{8}$ in. deep; this could be done by end-milling, or by a cutter on an arbor between centres, holding the nut in a machine-vice on the saddle. Failing any other means, a file will make a good job of it if properly handled—in more senses than one!

To assemble, put the nut in the middle of the stand; if the plain bearing is to your right, the recess in the side of the nut should face you. Put the screw through the tapped bearing, squared end first; screw it through the nut, push the end through the plain bearing, and screw in the nipple. When the nipple is right home, the screw should turn freely, without any end-play, moving the nut easily up and down the stand. File a shade off the screwed end of the nipple if the screw is stiff between bearings.

The wheel may be a casting or it may be cut from a $\frac{3}{16}$ in. slice of $1\frac{1}{4}$ in. diameter rod. Dural makes nice wheels. The spokes on one I made were formed by drilling four $\frac{7}{32}$ in. holes and opening them out triangular shape with an "Abrafile", leaving four spokes which were rounded off with a strip of Aloxite cloth, the result being neat and pleasing. A $\frac{1}{16}$ in. hole was drilled in the rim for the handle, which was turned from a bit of $\frac{1}{8}$ in. nickel-silver rod, with a pip on the end a tight drive fit for the $\frac{1}{16}$ in. hole. The wheel was chucked in the three-jaw, centred, and drilled $\frac{1}{8}$ in., the hole was squared by driving a punch through it. The punch is simply a 2 in. length of $\frac{1}{8}$ in. square silver-steel, squared off truly at one end, hardened, and tempered to dark yellow. The other end is bevelled off, so that it doesn't become burred with hammer blows, and can be driven clean through the hole in the wheel boss. I have a small round block of cast-iron with holes of various sizes in it; wheels are laid on this for punching, over a hole of appropriate size to suit wheel boss and punch. The finished wheel is pushed on to the squared end of the reversing screw, and secured with an ordinary commercial nut.

Lever and Reach Rod

The lever is milled or filed up from a piece of $\frac{3}{8}$ in. by $\frac{1}{8}$ in. mild steel about $2\frac{5}{8}$ in. long, to the shape and dimensions shown (Fig. 8-2). The upper end should be a nice fit in the groove in the nut, and is offset $\frac{3}{32}$ in. The lower end is drilled $\frac{5}{32}$ in. for the fulcrum pin. At 1 in. from this hole, drill another

No. 40 and tap it $\frac{1}{8}$ in. or 5 BA, for the reach-rod pin. To make this, chuck a piece of $\frac{1}{8}$ in. silver-steel in three-jaw, and put $\frac{1}{8}$ in. of thread on the end to match the tapped hole in the lever. Part off about $\frac{3}{8}$ in. from the end, reverse in chuck, and turn down $\frac{1}{8}$ in. of the other end to $\frac{7}{64}$ in. full diameter, screwing it 6 BA. Screw this tightly into the hole in the lever, and file off flush at the back. There should be just enough plain part projecting to allow a 6 BA nut to screw tight up to the shoulder without gripping the boss of the reach-rod. For the fulcrum pin, chuck a bit of $\frac{5}{16}$ in. hexagon steel rod in the three-jaw, and turn down a full $\frac{1}{4}$ in. to an exact running fit in the hole in the bottom of the lever; then further reduce $\frac{1}{8}$ in. length to $\frac{1}{8}$ in. diameter and screw $\frac{1}{8}$ in. or 5 BA to match the tapped hole in the stand. Part off to leave a head about $\frac{1}{8}$ in. thick; reverse in chuck, and chamfer the corners. When the fulcrum pin is right home, it should hold the lever close to the stand, but not interfere with its back and forth movement, so the plain part wants to be exactly $\frac{1}{8}$ in long. My way of doing this is not to measure it, but slip a $\frac{1}{8}$ in. washer over the plain part, and then, when turning the end for the screw, run the knife tool right up to the washer, and follow with the die. The plain part will then be exactly the correct length. To assemble, simply put the offset head in the groove in the nut, and screw the fulcrum pin home. When the hand-wheel is rotated, the lever should move back and forth easily, yet keeping in close contact with the stand. Don't forget a spot of oil!

Erection is simple. Drill four No. 30 holes in the left-hand side of the trailing cradle, as indicated in the illustration; then place the stand in position $\frac{3}{4}$ in. from the back (it will just touch the rear angles of a built-up cradle) and $\frac{3}{4}$ in. below the top. Hold in position temporarily with a toolmaker's clamp, run the No. 30 drill through the stand, using the holes in the cradle plates as guides, and put in $\frac{1}{8}$ in. or 5 BA bolts, as shown in the end view of the complete assembly (Fig. 8-1).

To save milling a long length of steel rod, the reach-rod can be made from a piece of $\frac{1}{8}$ in. by $\frac{3}{16}$ in. rectangular steel, with a small block of $\frac{1}{4}$ in. by $\frac{5}{16}$ in. rod brazed on at one end and machined to form the fork or clevis, and a boss at the other for attaching to the lever. The boss is merely a $\frac{1}{8}$ in. slice of steel, parted off a piece of $\frac{5}{16}$ in. round rod held in the three-jaw; the hole is reamed $\frac{1}{8}$ in.

To get the correct length of rod, take your measurement from the actual job. Put the reverser in mid-position, that is with the nut in the middle of the screw, and the lever vertical. Set the valve gear in mid-position also, with the die-blocks exactly in the centres of the links. Then measure the distance from the centre of the hole in the reverse arm on the weighshaft, to the centre of the pin in the lever on the reversing gear; this will give the exact dimension required. For connecting the fork to the reverse-arm on the weighshaft, use a bolt made from $\frac{1}{8}$ in. silver-steel, turned down to $\frac{3}{32}$ in. at each end and furnished with small nuts, same as the top of combination lever and other parts of the gear; the boss end is merely slipped over the pin in the lever, and secured with an ordinary commercial nut. When the reversing wheel is

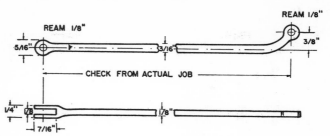

Fig. 8-3
Reversing rod or
reach rod.

operated, the valve gears should respond, working evenly, smoothly, and in unison; there should be no tight places anywhere, and reversing should be equally easy in any position of the cranks.

Centre-Pivoted Reverser

It sometimes happens that a reverse shaft and arms have to be fixed up in such a manner that if the reverse lever is directly connected to the arm on the shaft, the engine goes in the opposite direction to the inclination of the lever. In full size, in days gone by, this state of affairs was responsible for several bad smashes; on a dark night, or in fog, a driver used to an engine which "went the same way as the lever", as he would say, might temporarily forget that he was driving one of the "back-to-front" type, and not notice that he had started backwards until the train collided with the one following. It is more easily done than a layman would ever imagine! To obviate this, the lever of a reversing gear of the kind just described, should be pivoted in the middle, as shown in Fig. 8-4, which gives all the necessary details; this particular one is especially suited for the "Petrolea" class 2-4-0 type on the old Great Eastern Railway.

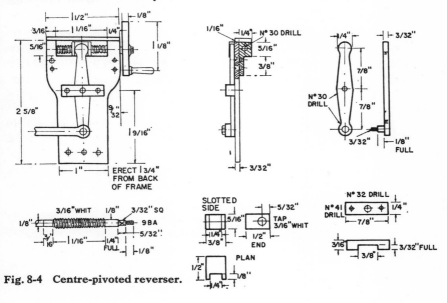

Fig. 8-4   Centre-pivoted reverser.

Fig. 8-5
Reverse rod for wide
firebox engine.

On some engines with wide fireboxes, the firebox comes out almost to the edge of the running-board, preventing the use of the ordinary type of reach rod or reversing rod. This can be overcome by using a rod set over as shown in Fig. 8-5, which is self-explanatory.

Simple Disc Regulator

This can be fitted to any domeless boiler, and for the water-tube type especially, it is miles in front of the wretched leaky-sticking plug cock. The stops are self-contained in the valve, which allows a plain and neat gland without any external stops or pins on the backhead. Any type of driver's handle can be fitted as desired. Just one more little advantage which will appeal to many who are familiar with the "superheated sneezing blower" usually fitted to water-tube boilers. With this arrangement and the special fountain, *all* the steam used for blower, whistle, etc., has to come through the numerous tiny holes in the regulator collecting pipe; so that, despite the almost unavoidable surging of the water as the engine starts, stops, or varies in speed, the blower does not "sneeze" nor the whistle "bobble". To make the regulator, kick off with the collecting pipe (Fig. 8-6). This will be a 3 in. length of $\frac{7}{16}$ in. treblet tube; but if anyone is not certain about being able to drill little holes in exact positions on a $\frac{7}{16}$ in. diameter valve face, the tube can be made $\frac{1}{2}$ in. or even $\frac{9}{16}$ in. in diameter. The latter size is correct for a $2\frac{1}{2}$ in. gauge engine. Chuck the tube lightly and face off both ends; then drill a couple of dozen $\frac{1}{32}$ in. holes in it in three rows $\frac{1}{8}$ in. apart and spacing each hole just under $\frac{1}{4}$ in. apart from its next-door neighbour in the same row. Stagger the holes with those of the next row. Do not forget to file the burrs off inside the pipe.

Port Face and Valve

Chuck a length of $\frac{1}{8}$ in. gunmetal rod, face up the end and turn down to about $\frac{5}{16}$ in. diameter for $\frac{1}{4}$ in. length. Centre, drill down No. 21 for $\frac{5}{16}$ in. depth, and tap $\frac{3}{16}$ in. by 40 for the steam pipe. Part off at $\frac{9}{16}$ in. from the end. Reverse and chuck the piece by the little boss; turn down $\frac{3}{16}$ in. of the large diameter to fit the collecting pipe tightly. Carefully face off, centre, and

Fig. 8-6
Simple disc
regulator for
Guage "1"
engine.

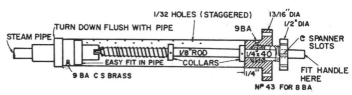

drill and tap a hole 7 BA by $\frac{1}{8}$ in. deep for the pivot or valve pin. Countersink this hole just a shade. Now drill the steam ports; it seems a ticklish job, but only requires care and patience, and feed very lightly as the drill breaks through into the tapped hole. The position and sizes of holes are given on the sketch (Fig. 8-7).

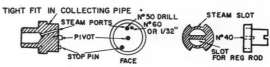

Fig. 8-7
Details of regulator valve.

To make the valve, chuck the piece of $\frac{1}{2}$ in. rod again and turn down a piece $\frac{1}{4}$ in. diameter and $\frac{1}{4}$ in. long; then slightly reduce another $\frac{3}{16}$ in. or so of the rod till it will slip easily into the tube. Part off at $\frac{3}{8}$ in. from the end of the boss; reverse, face up the disc, and put a No. 40 hole in the centre $\frac{3}{16}$ in. deep. Countersink slightly. File the steam and stop-pin slots as shown; put a hacksaw cut across the boss to take the flattened end of the regulator-rod, which actuates the valve, and finally true the working face on a bit of plate glass or other flat surface, using pumice powder and water as a grinding medium. Now fit a $\frac{3}{32}$ in. brass pin screwed 7 BA to the centre hole of the port face, and leave about $\frac{1}{8}$ in. of plain rod standing out. Slip the valve over with the steam slot exposing the ports fully; then at the left-hand side of the lower slot make a mark. Remove valve and fit a $\frac{1}{16}$ in. brass pin at this spot. Now if the valve be replaced again it will be seen that the ends of the slot coming into contact with this pin determine the "full on" and "shut off" points, and the slot should be carefully filed until at one end of the travel the ports are entirely covered, and the other end fully exposed. Remove pins, true up the port face same as you did the valve, and carefully replace the pins.

Gland and Rod

The gland is plainly shown in Fig. 8-6, and I need not go into full details of it. The only point is that the spigot should be a tight fit in the regulator collecting pipe. The flange can be altered to suit any builder's individual wishes and can be oval in shape if desired; for a small-boilered locomotive it may be circular, $\frac{13}{16}$ in. diameter, and attached to the backhead by four 8 BA screws. The regulator spindle is of German silver rod $\frac{1}{8}$ in. diameter; one end is flattened to engage with the valve slot, a light coiled spring of 22 gauge brass wire and 1 in. long is slipped over the flattened end and prevented slipping too far back by a little collar pinned to the rod. Another collar at the gland end stops the rod from slipping back out of the valve slot.

Assembling and Fitting Up

Carefully drive the port block into the collecting pipe, taking care that the ports come at the top where the small holes are drilled in the pipe; secure it with a 8 BA countersunk brass screw. Insert the valve in its correct position; this is quite easily done by aid of a screwdriver, and see that it works freely.

Put the spring on the regulator-rod against the pinned collar; do not pin the other collar at first, but make it a fairly tight fit and leave it in its approximate position. Now assemble the gland and push it into place, meanwhile holding the regulator-rod in position against the valve. The gland will drive the collar before it and leave it on the rod in correct position. Remove the gland again, take the rod out, pin the collar where you find it, file $\frac{1}{32}$ in. off the flattened end to allow for expansion, replace, and refit the gland-piece, fixing same with a 8 BA countersunk brass screw. File a little off both screwheads if they project too much above the surface of the collecting pipe. Cut a $\frac{7}{16}$ in. hole in the backhead, insert regulator and mark off position of screws through the holes in the flange; drill and tap 8 BA. Screw a length of $\frac{3}{16}$ in. seamless copper tube (20 gauge) into the steam outlet of the regulator; insert into the big hole in the boiler, letting it pass through the hole in front end until the regulator gland flange is hard up against the backhead. Don't forget a jointing washer, and finally secure by brass screws through the flange. Pack the gland at the footplate end; cut off the rod about $\frac{3}{16}$ in. from the gland, and fit any type of handle you fancy. The pipe may pass through an asbestos-packed gland at the front end, or have a flange fixing.

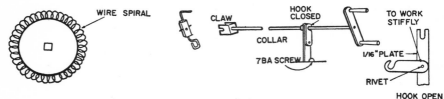

Fig. 8-8   Cool valve wheel.   Regulator extension handle.

Cool Handles

The late Mr. H. G. Conybeare devised a little fitting which he called a "cool handle" (Fig. 8-8), and I hasten to pass it on for the benefit of anyone whose fingers are not fireproof enough to operate little wheel valves of the usual type without discomfort. The device is a miniature reproduction of the wire-rimmed hand-wheels sometimes found on American and Continental engines, and largely used in stationary work.

They are quite easy to make. Chuck a length of $\frac{1}{4}$ in. diameter brass or "screw" rod, centre and drill up according to size of valve needle spindles; $\frac{3}{32}$ in. is the best size for $\frac{5}{32}$ in. spindle, this allowing the wheel to be fitted either to a turned spigot or on a square. With a round-nose tool about $\frac{3}{32}$ in. wide make a shallow groove at the end of the rod and part off; this produces a sort of grooved pulley wheel $\frac{1}{8}$ in. thick. Repeat for as many wheels as required. Now chuck a piece of $\frac{1}{16}$ in. stiff wire and wind on it a length of 24-gauge tinned music wire to form a fairly closely-coiled spring; don't make the coils *too* close, however, or the spiral will not keep cool. Cut off a sufficient length to go round the groove in the wheel, and join the ends. Tin the groove; apply a drop of soldering fluid to the inside of the spiral ring, spring it over the wheel and heat the whole lot carefully till the solder melts and secures the spiral in place. Clean off the superfluous solder, square the hole if required, and fit to spindle. Holes may be drilled in the wheel between centre and rim. Fig. 8-8 gives an idea of the finished wheel. Note—Don't use German silver wire for the spiral or you will be as badly off as you were before. The tinned steel wire is the most satisfactory non-conductor of heat.

A Regulator Extension Handle

The following small contrivance was designed by a girl of eight who objected to a hot regulator handle. Apart from its primary object, it saves leaning forward over the tender, which is a great consideration with a short but heavy driver not being used to sitting on a $2\frac{1}{2}$ in. gauge flat car. Fig. 8-8 shows the arrangement, which is simply a $\frac{1}{8}$ in. steel rod sufficiently long to extend from the regulator handle in the cab to a bracket just in front of the filling hole on the tender. The regulator end is provided with a claw, which slips over the centre portion of the regulator handle. The claw is not fixed to the regulator handle in any way; it simply has a slot to clear the end of the taper pin and this prevents it falling down. The other end is provided with a double handle an inch long. The rod rests in a slotted bracket secured to the tender top by a single 7 BA screw, and the top of the slot has a swing hook to prevent the rod being accidentally jerked out. In front of the bracket a little collar is pinned on to the rod, and this prevents the claw slipping backwards off the regulator handle.

The device is certainly much better than a big unsightly handle sticking through the roof of the cab. It is not in the way when firing up, as it can be taken off and re-attached in a couple of seconds or so. It normally lies on top of the tender along with the fire irons, ready for instant use if anybody wants it. A somewhat similar device could be used for operating the ordinary type of disc wheel valve, which has four holes in the web. A short rod of any convenient length, having a forked end made to fit two of the holes, would be very handy for intermittent use, such as on the injector steam valve; no outer support would be required, the end being simply bent over to form a handle, or else fitted with a wheel.

Brakes for $2\frac{1}{2}$ in. Gauge Engines

On a locomotive built for heavy passenger hauling on a small gauge, brake gear on the engine itself is not of much use, and may even spoil the whole outfit, because the wheels would lock and slide even on sanded rails, resulting in flats on the tyres and other troubles. As the weight of a little engine is so much out of proportion to the load it can shift, it is far more effective to brake wagons and utilise the dead load for retardation, same as in full-size practice, on passenger trains and "fitted" goods trains used for fast perishable traffic. However, the brake gear on many engines is a conspicuous feature. The hangers for $2\frac{1}{2}$ in. gauge locomotives can be filed up from 16 gauge steel and slung from the main frames by shouldered bolts. The bottoms of each

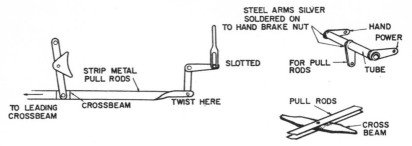

Fig. 8-9   Brake gear for smaller engines and simple brake rigging.

pair of hangers are connected by a fish-bellied cross beam (see Fig. 8-9), filed up from flat steel and turned down at the ends to work in holes drilled at the bottom of the hangers. A washer and tiny pin through each will stop them coming adrift, or they may be nutted. The brake blocks may be chopped out of the solid or may be cast. I am rather in favour of fibre blocks; they grip like Old Nick without damaging the tread of the wheel and need no great pressure. I always use them on flat cars. Anyway, they are of the well-known "flat-triangular" shape and slotted at the back for the hanger, to which they are secured by a $\frac{3}{32}$ in. bolt or pin through each. The cross-beams are connected by two strips of $\frac{3}{16}$ in. by $\frac{1}{16}$ in. bright steel, above and below, to save the fag of making a brake-rod with four slots in it. Compensating gear may be omitted "for the sake of simplicity"—with apologies to a famous catalogue. One of the strips is drilled with four holes, approximately coinciding with the centres of the cross-beams with brakes in "on" position. The blocks are then temporarily jammed "on", the strip laid on the cross-beams in position, and holes drilled in the latter to correspond with those in the strip, which is then used as a jig to drill the other strip. The whole is assembled with small bolts or pins.

Combined hand and Power Operation

For a $2\frac{1}{2}$ in. gauge engine, fix a $\frac{3}{16}$ in. round steel bar across the frames just behind the firebox, and on it mount a piece of tube or long bush carrying three arms, the middle one hanging vertically and the others pointing to the rear (Fig. 8-9). The vertical one is connected to the strips operating the cross-beams; each strip has a half turn twist in it and the arm is located between the ends, a pin or bolt passing through the lot. The left-hand horizontal arm is connected to a steam or vacuum cylinder under the footplate; if steam, the pressure must be applied *underneath* the piston, and the rod must pass through a stuffing box and gland. The other arm is connected to a hand-brake column, of the well-known type, having a vertical screw carried in brackets and surmounted by a cross handle. The screw carries a long nut, from which two connecting links extend down to the brake-actuating arm. The ends of these links are slotted, and the pin in the arm passes through the slots. When the brake handle is turned to the right, the nut rises, pulls up the links and arm and applies the brakes. When the power cylinder is operated and pulls up the other arm, the pin in the end of the hand-brake arm simply travels up the slots without affecting the hand-brake screw at all. It does not matter about making a slotted connection on the power side, as applying the hand brake merely moves the piston in the power cylinder and the required extra effort is practically nil.

Tender Brake for 5 in. Gauge

On the usual type of outside-framed tender, the whole of the brake gear is fitted between the frames, the hanger pins being put through from the inside, and nutted on the outside. There is no need to go into details of the hangers, pins, and brake blocks, as these are all shown in Fig. 8-10. Some of the suppliers of castings and parts for my engines stock cast-iron brake blocks, and these should be used for best results.

The brake column may be turned from a piece of $\frac{5}{8}$ in. round brass rod a shade over finished length, $4\frac{3}{8}$ in. Chuck in three-jaw, face the end, turn

Fig, 8-10   Tender brake for 5-in. gauge engine.

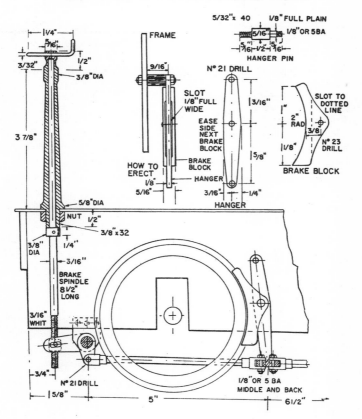

down $\frac{1}{2}$ in. length to $\frac{3}{8}$ in. diameter, and screw $\frac{3}{8}$ in. by 32. Then centre the end, and drill a $\frac{3}{16}$ in. hole clean through it. Placing my $\frac{3}{16}$ in. drill in the tailstock chuck, I find that there is $2\frac{3}{4}$ in. of it projecting; the clearing drill, No. 11, projects still more. Therefore, either of these drills will do the needful if put in from one end as far as they will go; the piece of rod is then reversed in the chuck, the other end faced and centred, and the drill put in from that end until the bores meet in the middle. Tip for beginners: keep withdrawing the drill every $\frac{1}{16}$ in. or so, and clear the chips out of the flutes, especially when they are in the hole to full depth. If anybody wants to make certain of a good bore and absolute accuracy, it would be policy to make a long $\frac{3}{16}$ in. D-bit, which is only a few minutes' work. The hole can then be started by the drill and finished with the D-bit, without reversing the piece of metal, if you so desire; but keep on withdrawing, and clearing chippings, or else the whole will seize up.

Now chuck a short bit of rod, any size above $\frac{1}{2}$ in. diameter, and about $\frac{1}{2}$ in. long, in the three-jaw. Face, centre, drill through with letter "R" or $\frac{11}{32}$ in. drill, tap $\frac{3}{8}$ in. by 32, countersink slightly, and skim off any burrs. Screw the end of the embryo brake column into this, support the other end by bringing up the tailstock centre and letting the point enter the hole in the end, and turn the outside to the outline shown. Just slew your top slide around a little, and use a round-nose tool. Finally, make a $\frac{3}{8}$ in. by 32 nut from a bit of $\frac{1}{2}$ in. hexagon brass rod.

The spindle is an $8\frac{1}{2}$ in. length of $\frac{3}{16}$ in. round steel rod; either silver-steel or ground rustless will do. Screw one end $\frac{3}{16}$ in. Whitworth, for a length of about $1\frac{1}{4}$ in. The upper end is furnished with a fancy boss, to carry the cross handle. Chuck a bit of $\frac{3}{8}$ in. round steel, face the end, centre, and drill down about $\frac{5}{16}$ in. with No. 14 drill. Turn to shape shown, and part off at $\frac{1}{2}$ in. from the end. Squeeze this on to the plain end of the brake spindle. A No. 48 cross-hole can be drilled in the neck, and a bit of 15-gauge spoke wire pressed in for a pin; file flush both sides. If you like, you could leave the turning to shape until after the boss was pressed on and pinned; chuck the spindle with the boss close to the jaws, turn the outline, face the end, and the pin will be invisible. Drill a No. 43 hole across the upper part, squeeze in a $1\frac{5}{8}$ in. length of $\frac{3}{32}$ in. round or rustless silver-steel, rounded off a little at both ends. Bend up $\frac{3}{8}$ in. of the cross wire at one end, and you have a dinky handle.

Chuck the $\frac{3}{8}$ in. rod again, centre, and drill No. 13 for about $\frac{3}{8}$ in. depth; part off a $\frac{1}{4}$ in. slice to form the collar. Put the spindle down the column, push the collar over the screw, and slide it along until it touched the bottom of the column, and pin it, same as the handle boss. The spindle should be free to turn, without any up-and-down play. The collar should be just small enough to pass through the nut.

Now watch your step. At $3\frac{9}{16}$ in. from the tender centre-line, to your left, as you look at the front of the tender, and 1 in. from the front edge of the soleplate (that is, $\frac{3}{4}$ in. from front edge of frame plates) drill a $\frac{3}{8}$ in. clearing hole clean through soleplate and top of drag beam. Clean off any burr, then

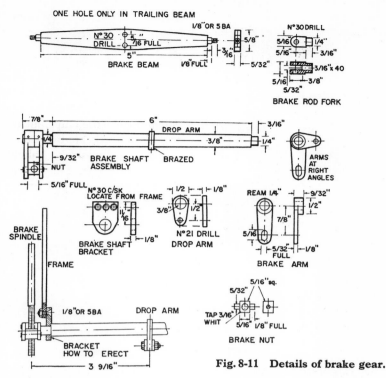

Fig. 8-11   Details of brake gear.

put the screwed part of the brake column through it, and fix with the nut (Fig. 8-10). If you have made a right-hand-drive engine, the column will be fitted in a corresponding position on the other side of the tender.

Brake Shaft

The brake shaft is made from a piece of $\frac{3}{8}$ in. round mild-steel rod, $\frac{7}{8}$ in. long. Chuck in three-jaw, face the end, and turn $\frac{7}{8}$ in. length to $\frac{1}{4}$ in. diameter. Reverse in chuck, face, and turn $\frac{1}{4}$ in. spigot $\frac{3}{16}$ in. long. The distance between shoulders should be 6 in.

The drop-arm is an easy job, filed up from a bit of $\frac{1}{8}$ in. steel plate (odd scrap of frame steel does fine) and drilled and reamed as shown. It should be a tight fit on the shaft. The brake arms are just as easy. File or mill them from $\frac{1}{8}$ in. steel plate. The slot is formed by drilling two No. 21 holes close together, and joining them by judicious application of a rat-tail file. Drill a $\frac{1}{8}$ in. hole in the other end; then chuck a bit of $\frac{1}{2}$ in. round mild-steel in the three-jaw, and turn a $\frac{1}{8}$ in. pip on the end, to a tight fit in the hole. Part off at $\frac{5}{32}$ in. from the shoulder. Ditto repeato, then squeeze the pips into the holes in the arms, and braze them; just apply a little wet flux, heat to bright red, and touch with a bit of soft brass wire, or Sifbronze rod, which will melt and form a fillet. Quench in water, wash off, and clean up; then chuck the bosses in the three-jaw, making sure the arm of each runs truly. Face off

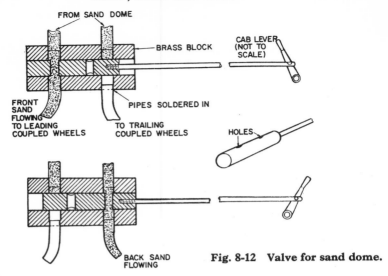

Fig. 8-12   Valve for sand dome.

any of the pip which protrudes beyond the arm; centre, drill letter "C" or $\frac{15}{64}$ in., and ream $\frac{1}{4}$ in. Put the drop-arm right in the middle of the shaft, and braze that too, in similar fashion. You can use silver-solder if you like for both jobs, but brazing is best (Fig. 8-11).

Brake Nut and Brackets

For the brake nut, chuck a piece of $\frac{5}{16}$ in. square steel, or hard bronze, in four-jaw, and set to run truly; face the end, and turn down a full $\frac{1}{8}$ in. length to $\frac{5}{32}$ in. diameter. Part off at a full $\frac{7}{16}$ in. from the shoulder; reverse in chuck, and repeat operation. Drill a No. 21 hole through the cube and tap $\frac{3}{16}$ in. Whitworth. The coarse thread makes for quick action, and there is no chance of stripping.

The brackets are milled or filed up from $\frac{1}{8}$ in. steel plate. Drill and ream the $\frac{1}{4}$ in. hole, then locate and drill the screwholes from the tender frame. To drill these, mark off a point $1\frac{5}{8}$ in. from front edge of frame, and $\frac{1}{8}$ in. from the bottom edge; drill a No. 30 hole there, and another one each side of it, on the same level, and $\frac{1}{4}$ in. away. File off any burr, then put a bracket in the position shown (Fig. 8-10), hold it with a toolmaker's clamp, and drill it, using the holes in frame to guide the drill. Ditto repeato on the other side of frame; but before drilling the screw holes in the second bracket, poke a piece of $\frac{1}{4}$ in. steel through both the bigger holes, and see that it lies fair and square across the frames, and is quite level. Adjust bracket if necessary, then tighten clamp, and go ahead with the drilling. Countersink both brackets on the inside, and mark which is which.

How to Erect Brake Shaft

Put the correct bracket on the longer end of the brake shaft, countersinks on the inside, then put on a brake-arm, boss outwards; place nut in position, and put on the other arm, as shown in the assembly Fig. 8-11. The centre of nut must be $3\frac{9}{16}$ in. from the centre of drop-arm, and the arms at right-angles to it. The nut must be free to move the full extent of the slots. The bosses of the brake-arms can be pinned to the shaft by bits of 15-gauge spoke wire.

Put the other bracket on the other end of shaft, hold it in position with the nut under the screw on the spindle; turn the handle, and the screw will pull up the nut, so that the brake shaft comes into position. All you then have to do, is to line up the holes in the brackets with those in the frame, and put three $\frac{1}{8}$ in. or 5 BA countersunk-head screws through the holes, with nuts outside the frame. Where there is a lot of vibration, as in the present position, I recommend the use of weeny spring washers under the nuts. The brake shaft should now operate easily by turning the handle. If the spindle is oiled before inserting in the column, it will not need any more for a very long period; but a hole can be drilled in the column near the top, through which a spot of oil may occasionally be introduced via the driver's bosom companion.

Pull-Rods

All we now need, are six forks and three pieces of $\frac{3}{16}$ in. steel rod, to connect up. A drawing of the forks is given in Fig. 8-11. The exact lengths of the pieces of rod are easily obtained by measuring on the actual tender; screw them about $\frac{1}{4}$ in. each end. Note that the front fork is drilled No. 21, and attached to the drop-arm by a bolt made from a piece of $\frac{5}{32}$ in. round silver-steel, shouldered down to $\frac{1}{8}$ in. at both ends, screwed $\frac{1}{8}$ in. or 5 BA, and furnished with commercial nuts. When these are right home, the pin should be free to turn with your fingers. The other forks can be attached to the beams, by $\frac{1}{8}$ in. or 5 BA bolts and nuts, as shown; or if you prefer, $\frac{1}{8}$ in. by $\frac{1}{2}$ in. ordinary commercial split-pins can be used. Just poke through from the top, and spread the points just enough to prevent them coming out. If the blocks do not all touch the wheels at the same time when the handle is turned, merely adjust the forks on the rods until they do.

Sand Valves

Sand valves on American and some Continental engines are usually located at the base of the sand dome. In the case of only one dome serving both leading and trailing sand pipes, a single valve, as shown in Fig. 8-12, serves to feed either pipe, according to whether the lever in the cab is pushed forward or pulled back. In mid-position both sands are shut off. The body of the valve is filed up from a scrap of brass and may be either soldered direct to the sandbox or screwed by a lug each end to the boiler barrel and connected to the sandbox by a couple of short lengths of pipe. The hole for the circular sliding valve is drilled either $\frac{1}{8}$ in. or $\frac{5}{32}$ in., according to the size of engine, and the holes for the sand pipes (10 or 11-gauge treblet tube) are put in next. Fit the valve and set it in "front sanding" position, put a drill in the sand-pipe hole and make a mark on the valve with the point; then remove valve

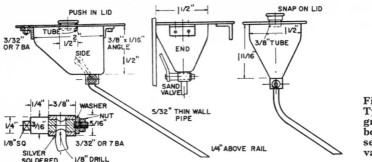

Fig. 8-13
Types of
gravity sand-
boxes and
sections of
valve.

and drill through with a drill a little smaller. If the holes in the valve are drilled the full bore of the sand-pipe holes, the valve has a tendency to jam. Repeat the process for the back sanding position. Run a $\frac{1}{16}$ in. rod from each sand valve to the cab—two or three small handrail pillars will make admirable guides—and fit a couple of little levers which should be connected by a transverse rod so that the sands can be operated from either side of the engine, a great convenience in "real life", when on heavy shunting.

Where separate sand domes are employed, one for front and one for back sand, as on ten or twelve-coupled locomotives, and articulated engines of the "Mallet" type, the sand valves can be made in the same way; but of course, there will be only one pipe to each, and only one hole in the valve. Both valves on the same side should, however, be coupled together by a $\frac{1}{16}$ in. rod and arranged for "forward sand, back sand, or off", in the same way as the single two-way valve. Maybe a good many folk will be wondering why sanding gear is used, and is sand of any value on small locomotives at all? If they did much driving, they would soon realise what a difference a pinch of sand can make to the tractive effort at the drawbar. The sliding valve can also be used with ordinary British sandboxes either forming part of the splasher, or separate hoppers below the running-board. Simply use half the valve shown. A plug-cock sand valve may also be used with these sand boxes, as shown in Fig. 8-13, which explains itself. It is operated by a lever in the cab, shown in Fig. 8-14.

A Working Steam Sander

I believe the sanding gear fitted to my original $2\frac{1}{2}$ in. gauge G.W.R. 4-2-2 is one of the smallest ever made for work as well as ornament; and as the arrangement is practically the same for the usual sizes of small engines, anyone who wishes to use same for other sizes than $2\frac{1}{2}$ in. gauge can do so by simply altering the dimensions. The boxes are of the usual hopper pattern, 1 in. long at the top, 1 in. deep at the longest side, and $\frac{3}{8}$ in. wide. Each is made from two pieces of thin sheet brass, as shown in Fig. 8-14. Cut out the piece forming one end and both sides of the box, bend at the dotted lines and solder in a $\frac{3}{8}$ in. wide strip to complete. A piece of $\frac{5}{16}$ in. thin tube forms the filling orifice, and a flanged push-in cap is turned from a scrap of brass rod.

Make it a good fit and leave the top fairly large to keep water out; no airhole is needed. Solder a couple of little angle-brackets back and front, or each end to enable the box to be attached to the underside of the running plate, or the side frames, as may be most convenient.

The Sand Trap

There is no sand valve in a steam or air sander; the action is similar to a vacuum brake ejector. The sand runs from the box into a trap, where it remains until brought down by a rush of air induced by the steam jet at the bottom of the pipe; the steam jet gives it the final "kick" on its way to the point of contact between wheel and rail. The trap is made from a piece of $\frac{3}{16}$ in. square brass rod, and is drilled as shown in Fig. 8-14. Drill the long hole right through with a No. 40 or $\frac{7}{64}$ in. drill, and tap both ends either $\frac{1}{8}$ in. or 5 BA, closing each with a short screw. This will allow for the easy removal of any damp sand that may tend to choke the trap up. The sand pipes are pieces of $\frac{1}{8}$ in. treblet tube; this has very thin walls and is best silver-soldered into the sand trap.

The Steam Jets

There are alternative methods of making these. In $2\frac{1}{2}$ in. gauge, use $\frac{3}{32}$ in. copper tube; larger sizes in proportion. When softened, it can be bent into practically any shape without kinking by means of fingers alone. Take a short length and soften it in the usual manner by making red-hot and plunging into water; then close up one end carefully until the point of a pin can just be inserted. Bend the sand pipe as shown in the top section (a) of Fig. 8-14,

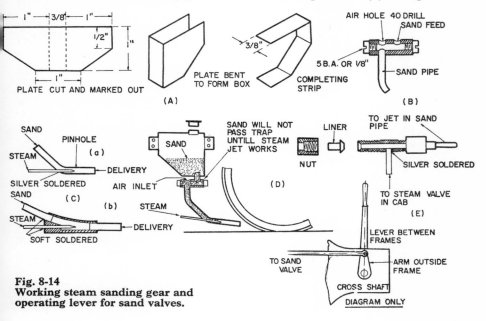

Fig. 8-14
Working steam sanding gear and operating lever for sand valves.

drill a hole a tight fit for the steam pipe and silver-solder in, with great care. The lower section (*b*) in Fig. 8-14 shows a fitting somewhat similar to those used on a big engine. It can be filed up from a piece of $\frac{3}{8}$ in. by $\frac{3}{16}$ in. brass rod. The action is the same, so detailed description is unnecessary.

Assembly

Drill a hole in the bottom of the sandbox hopper a driving fit for the size tube used for sand pipes, and insert the tube about $\frac{1}{8}$ in. This is a "safety first" precaution in case you are heavy-handed with the soldering-bit and extra liberal with the solder when attaching the traps to the hoppers, which operation can then be performed. Now give the complete sandboxes a good wash out in running water and leave them in front of the fire for half an hour or so to dry thoroughly before erecting on the engine. (If you happen to be a full size driver or fireman, you won't need to read *that* twice!) The erection calls for no special instructions; just drill the holes in the running plate for the fillers to project through, and bolt the boxes on by means of the brackets already fixed, taking care to bend the lower ends of the sandpipe in such a manner that they "fire" straight at the wheel and rail contact (Fig. 8-14).

Steam Connections

The piping up will, of course, vary according to the type of engine. Small passenger tender engines usually work chimney first, so a pair of boxes in front of the leading coupled wheels are usually sufficient. A tank, or goods engine, is usually provided with boxes for either direction. Anyhow, each pair of boxes can have their steam pipes connected by a little union fitting made as follows: Cut off a piece of $\frac{7}{32}$ in. round brass rod $\frac{5}{8}$ in. long; drill through No. 50, after making a deep centre in each end; screw each end $\frac{7}{32}$ in. by 40 threads for $\frac{1}{4}$ in. down, and drill a $\frac{3}{32}$ in. hole in the middle (Fig. 8-14). Make two union nuts from $\frac{5}{16}$ in. hexagon rod; cut off two pieces $\frac{1}{4}$ in. long, centre and drill through $\frac{1}{8}$ in. or No. 30, open out with No. 12 drill or $\frac{3}{16}$ in., tap $\frac{7}{32}$ in. by 40, and chamfer the ends. Make two little liners as shown from $\frac{3}{16}$ in. round rod; drill through a tight fit for the steam pipes, which are soft-soldered in. Silver-solder a length of $\frac{3}{32}$ in. pipe into the $\frac{3}{32}$ in. hole in the centre; this pipe is led away to the cab and attached to a wheel valve. In the case of a front and back sanding gear, the pipes from the respective pairs of boxes can be led to either side of a two-way valve, or else two separate wheel valves can be used. Needless to say, very finely sifted sand must be used with this device. It requires careful "wangling" to work such a tiny steam sander properly—if you give her too much steam you sand the motion, driver and passengers as well! Still, the gadget well repays the work of fitting, and is one more link between the "engine" and the "enginette".

Boiler Lagging on Small Engines

The easiest way to lag a boiler is to do the job before erecting it on the frames. If asbestos is used, simply cover the barrel with a layer of asbestos string wound on to the correct thickness; and a bit of asbestos millboard, wetted and moulded to the correct shape, will do for the firebox wrapper. Felt or fabric lagging can be wound on the barrel in strips, and secured by a coil or two of fine iron binding wire. The outside covering or cleading plates should be of hard-rolled sheet brass. This does not rust, will stand fairly rough usage without denting, and takes paint beautifully. Very thin sheet, say, about 30 gauge, will be found quite satisfactory for $2\frac{1}{2}$ in. gauge engines. Before cutting to size, make paper patterns showing exact size of sheets and location of all holes. Remove clack boxes, dome cover and any other excrescences; cut strips of paper to the desired width of lagging plates and lay round boiler. Rub your finger over the places where the clack-box bushes, etc. are and then remove the paper template and cut out around the markings.

When the paper "lagging" fits snugly and all holes are in the right place, cut your brass to exactly the same dimensions, with the certain knowledge that all will be O.K. and no metal will be wasted. Lap the brass sheets around the boiler and temporarily tie with binding wire or string; then secure the edges with a few touches of solder (Fig. 8-15) at points which will not show on the finished engine. Finally, fit bands of spring steel, or hard-rolled thin brass strip, over the circumferential joints, securing these by 10 BA bolts and nuts under the barrel. The bands over the firebox may either be fixed by a screw tapped into the wrapper plate itself, or little bolts through the running board as close to the boiler as possible. The latter, of course, must be done after erecting boiler and before fitting tanks. To get the sharp angle bends on the spring steel bands, heat the ends in a gas or spirit flame till bright red, and sharply bend with pliers. The bolt holes should be punched on a block of lead, with a punch shaped as sketch (Fig. 8-15), before the ends are bent. Hold the punch vertical and hit sharply.

A Two-Element Superheater

This particular superheater was designed for a $2\frac{1}{2}$ in. gauge "Austerity" type 2-8-0 goods engine, but is suitable for practically any type in that gauge. The steam flange is the same as used for single elements; the latter have

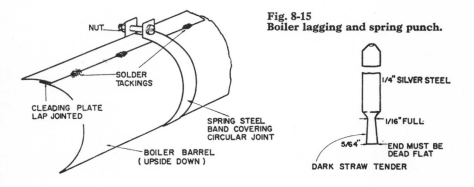

Fig. 8-15
Boiler lagging and spring punch.

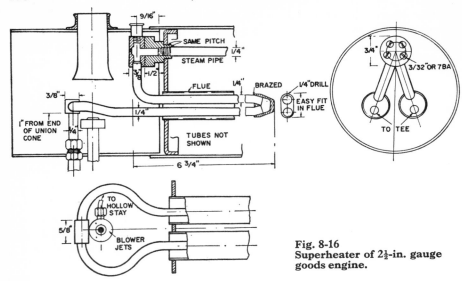

Fig. 8-16
Superheater of 2½-in. gauge
goods engine.

block return bends, which are not so liable to become choked solid with
brazing metal when assembling, as is the spearhead pattern—a welcome
advantage for beginners! The lower ends of the elements encircle the blastpipe, and are attached to a vertical pipe which goes straight down to the cross-
pipe between outside cylinders, or is screwed into the top of the steam chest
on an inside cylinder engine.

The steam flange is made from a piece of $\frac{3}{4}$ in. round or hexagon brass
$\frac{11}{16}$ in. long. Chuck in three-jaw, face, centre, and drill through with $\frac{7}{32}$ in.
drill, tapping $\frac{1}{4}$ in. by 40. Turn down $\frac{3}{8}$ in. length fo $\frac{9}{16}$ in. diameter, and
further reduce $\frac{3}{16}$ in. length to $\frac{3}{8}$ in. diameter, screwing $\frac{3}{8}$ in. by 40. Inner
and outer threads *must* be same pitch; beginners please note! Reverse in
chuck, and face the other side truly. Put a smear of plumbers' jointing on the
threads, start the inner thread on the projecting bit of steam pipe, and screw
right home. The outer threads engage in the hole in the tubeplate, and the
lot is locked up solid (Fig. 8-16).

How to make up the Elements

Four pieces of $\frac{1}{4}$ in. copper tube are needed, 20 or 22-gauge; two 7 in.
long, and two 9 in. long. Square off the ends, and brighten up one end of
each with a file or rough emery cloth. For the return bends, you need two
pieces of copper, each $\frac{5}{8}$ in. square, and $\frac{5}{16}$ in. in thickness; brass *could* be
used at a pinch, but it would need extra care in brazing, silver-solder not
being permissible on superheater element joints near the firebox. On one
narrow side of each, $\frac{5}{16}$ in. apart, make two centrepops, and then drill two
$\frac{1}{4}$ in. holes at such an angle that they break into each other about $\frac{3}{16}$ in.
below the surface of the metal; you will have to drill about $\frac{7}{16}$ in. deep to
get a clear passage for the steam, see Fig. 8-16. Now insert one long tube

and one short tube into each, for a bare $\frac{3}{16}$ in. Put a little flux, such as wet Boron compo, or borax-and-water paste, around each tube; blow up to bright red, and touch with a piece of thin soft brass wire. Sifbronze can be used with advantage; a job like this doesn't need the oxy-acetylene flame, as a blowlamp or air-gas blowpipe will make such a small piece hot enough to run Sifbronze. When the jointing material has made a small fillet around each pipe, let cool to black, dip in acid pickle and wash off. Note—if the pipes are hard, heat them to redness full length before quenching out.

Bend the pipes parallel for a distance of approximately 6 in. from the return bend blocks, then carefully set the ends to the curves shown in the plan and elevation illustrations. If the pipes go hard whilst being bent, soften them again by reheating and quenching. If you poke a piece of steel rod about 6 in. long, into the end of each pipe, you can form the curves around your finger and thumb quite easily, eliminating all risk of kinking. Don't forget that whilst both the short ends are bent upwards to meet the wet header, the longer ends are bent to right and left, the shape being like the "pairs of pliers" carried by the trailing end of the common or garden earwig. Now carefully file away the surplus metal around the return bends, rounding off the top and bottom so that they fit the flues loosely, and tapering off the blind ends to the shape shown in Fig. 8-16.

Wet Header

Chuck a piece of $\frac{3}{4}$ in. round or hexagon brass in the three-jaw; face the end, centre, drill a bare $\frac{5}{16}$ in. depth with No. 2 or $\frac{7}{32}$ in. drill, and part off at $\frac{3}{8}$ in. from the end. Make two centrepops in the edge, at a shade over $\frac{1}{4}$ in. centres, and drill them out $\frac{3}{16}$ in., aiming the drill so that it breaks into the blind hole in the middle. Counterbore these holes with $\frac{1}{4}$ in. drill for about $\frac{1}{8}$ in. depth. The four screwholes are drilled No. 40; their exact position does not matter, so long as they clear the holes mentioned above, and will not cross the tapped hole for the snifting valve. This hole must be left for the time being, as it cannot be located correctly until the superheater is temporarily erected, and the smokebox put on. Clean the ends of the upturned pipes, fit them to the holes in the edge of the wet header (see illustrations) and silver-solder them in.

Hot Header or Tee Fitting

This is very simple, being merely a piece of $\frac{3}{8}$ in. square brass rod $\frac{5}{8}$ in. long. Chuck it truly in the four-jaw, centre, and drill a $\frac{1}{4}$ in. hole clean through; then, in the middle of one of the sides, drill another $\frac{1}{4}$ in. hole to meet it. The two ends of the "earwig's tail" are fitted to the ends, as shown in the plan. A piece of copper tube about 1 in. long, is fitted to the hole in the side Make a nut to fit the top of the steam connection to the cross pipe, and put it on the tube; also fit a union cone to the bottom, the distance between the end of the union cone and the bottom of the tee fitting being approximately 1 in. The three pipe joints and the union cone can then be silver-soldered at one heat.

After pickling and cleaning up, put the complete superheater assembly in place as shown in the illustration, the wet header butting up against the flange on the end of the steam pipe; fix it temporarily with a toolmaker's clamp. Run the 40 drill through the screwholes in the header, and make counter-sinks on the flange; remove superheater, drill the countersinks No. 48 and tap 7 BA, and replace superheater with a $\frac{1}{64}$ in. jointing washer or gasket between the faces, securing with four screws. Now put the smokebox tem-porarily in place; and see it *is* in place, at that, with the chimney vertical, and not lopping over to one side, a condition of things I have seen on both commercially and professionally-made locomotives costing big money. It should enter the boiler shell to $\frac{1}{4}$ in. depth. Next, at $\frac{9}{16}$ in. from the end of the smokebox (that is, $\frac{5}{16}$ in. from the end of the boiler) and dead in line with the chimney, drill a $\frac{5}{16}$ in. clearing hole, and let the drill penetrate far enough to make a countersink on the top of the wet header. Don't take anything apart, but drill a $\frac{5}{32}$ in. hole in the wet header right down to the steam way in the middle, and tap it $\frac{3}{16}$ in. by 40, taking care to keep both drill and tap exactly vertical in the middle of the $\frac{5}{16}$ in. hole; then you'll be certain that the snifting valve will screw in straight. Now remove the whole bag of tricks, and carefully blow out any chippings that might possibly have got down into the ends of the superheater elements, after which the super-heater and smokebox can be replaced.

Note—The measurements for locating the hole for snifting valve, are suited to the "Austerity" engine mentioned at the beginning. For any other type of engine, it is only necessary to drill the $\frac{5}{16}$ in. hole exactly above the wet header.

Snifting Valve

The snifting valve is slightly different in construction, to that already shown in Fig. 6-9, but its function and action is exactly the same. To make it, chuck a bit of $\frac{3}{8}$ in. round brass rod in the three-jaw, face the end, centre, drill down about $\frac{1}{2}$ in. with No. 43 drill, open out to $\frac{1}{4}$ in. depth with $\frac{5}{32}$ in. drill, and bottom the hole with a $\frac{5}{32}$ in. D-bit, making the total depth about $\frac{9}{32}$ in. full. Tape the hole about halfway down, with $\frac{3}{16}$ in. by 40 tap. Turn down the outside to $\frac{5}{16}$ in. diameter for a bare $\frac{5}{16}$ in. length, part off $\frac{3}{8}$ in. from the end, reverse, and round off the bead. Put a $\frac{3}{32}$ in. reamer through the remains of the 43 hole; or if you haven't a reamer, broach it very slightly

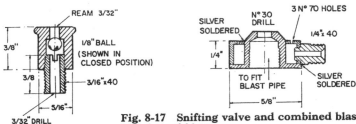

Fig. 8-17 Snifting valve and combined blast nozzle and blower.

to form a true seating for the $\frac{1}{8}$ in. ball. This can be rustless steel or bronze; if the latter, use a steel cycle ball to take the "biff" which forms the seating on the edge of the hole.

For the nipple, chuck a piece of $\frac{3}{16}$ in. rod, centre, drill down about $\frac{1}{2}$ in. with $\frac{3}{32}$ in. drill, screw the outside a full $\frac{3}{8}$ in. long with a $\frac{3}{16}$ in. by 40 die in the tailstock holder, part off $\frac{3}{8}$ in. from the end, and crossnick one end with a saw or a watchmaker's flat file. Put the ball in the cap, and screw in the nipple, nicked end first, with a smear of plumbers' jointing on the threads (Fig. 8-17). If you haven't any, red lead mixed to a paste with gold size or boiled oil will do as a substitute. Don't screw the snifter permanently into the header yet; leave it until the boiler is properly erected on the chassis "for keeps".

Combined Blastpipe and Blower Nozzle

The only other ornament required in the smokebox will be the fitting combining blastpipe nozzle and blower ring. Chuck a piece of $\frac{5}{8}$ in. round brass in the three-jaw; turn down $\frac{5}{16}$ in. full to $\frac{13}{32}$ in. diameter, face the end and chamfer it, and part off $\frac{3}{8}$ in. from the end, so as to leave a flange $\frac{5}{8}$ in. diameter and a bare $\frac{1}{16}$ in. in thickness. Reverse in chuck, centre, drill right through with No. 30 drill, open out to $\frac{1}{4}$ in. depth with $\frac{9}{32}$ in. drill, and tap 32 or 40 to fit top of blastpipe. Chuck the $\frac{5}{8}$ in. rod again, centre, and drill a $\frac{13}{32}$ in. hole a full $\frac{1}{4}$ in. deep; then open out to $\frac{3}{16}$ in. depth with a $\frac{17}{32}$ in. drill. If you have a D-bit that size, it would be an advantage to bottom the hole, as shown in Fig. 8-17, but this is not absolutely essential. Part off at $\frac{1}{4}$ in. from the end; the bit that comes off will be an angle ring, which is placed over the other part of the nozzle, leaving an annular space between the two parts, as shown in the section. Drill a $\frac{5}{32}$ in. hole in the side of the ring, and fit a $\frac{1}{4}$ in. by 40 countersunk union screw into it, as shown in Fig. 8-17; the whole lot can then be silver-soldered at one heat. For the blower jets, drill three No. 70 holes in the top of the angle ring, penetrating the annular space, as shown in the plan sketch.

The blower pipe connection is merely a piece of $\frac{1}{8}$ in. tube, long enough to reach from the end of the hollow stay to the blastpipe cap, and having a union nut and coned nipple at each end.

Superheater for Three-Cylinder Engine

This superheater, which is of the multiple-element firetube type, is a simplified edition of that used on full-sized locomotives. There are three distinct sections in this superheater assembly, viz., the wet header, which carries the vacuum relief or snifting valve, and which is attached to the flange of the main steam pipe; the four elements, which reach to the combustion chamber; and the hot header, from which diverge the pipes conveying the hotted-up steam to the cylinders. Dimensions are for a $3\frac{1}{2}$ in. gauge engine.

For the elements, four pieces of $\frac{1}{4}$ in. by 20 or 22-gauge copper tube approximately 13 in. long, are needed for the upper members, and four ditto

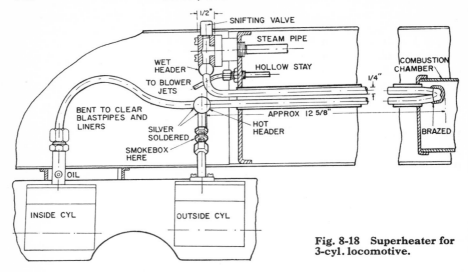

Fig. 8-18 Superheater for 3-cyl. locomotive.

$12\frac{1}{4}$ in. long for the lower. One end of each longer piece is bent to a right-angle, as shown. The leading ends of the shorter tubes are left straight. The rear ends may also be left straight until the block return bends are brazed on; these are made and fitted exactly as shown previously, in Fig. 8-16.

Steam Flange and Wet Header

A casting may be provided for the flange, in which case it will need only facing and drilling. If not, chuck a piece of 1-in. round brass rod in the three-jaw; face the end, centre, and drill down $\frac{3}{8}$ in. depth with $\frac{9}{32}$ in. drill. Part off at $\frac{1}{2}$ in. from the end; if a casting is used, reverse in chuck and face the other side, to give the screws a smooth bed for their heads. File a half-round groove a full $\frac{1}{8}$ in. deep in the edge, with a $\frac{1}{2}$ in. round file; or put the header flange under the slide-rest tool-holder and run it up to the side of a $\frac{1}{2}$ in. end-mill in the three-jaw. At the bottom of the semi-circular groove, drill a $\frac{9}{32}$ in. hole, breaking into the blind centre hole. Never mind about the snifting-valve hole for the time being.

The next requirement is a piece of $\frac{1}{2}$ in. by 20-gauge copper tube, $3\frac{1}{4}$ in. long; in the middle of this, drill a $\frac{9}{32}$ in. hole, and then, diametrically opposite, drill four holes at $\frac{7}{8}$ in. centres, as indicated in the end view, Fig. 8-19, so that they come opposite the flues. Use letter "D" or $\frac{1}{4}$ in. drill, same as for block bends. Plug each end of the tube either with discs of $\frac{3}{32}$ in. sheet copper, or a couple of slices parted off a piece of brass rod turned to a tight fit in the tube. Fit the four bent-up ends of the elements into the four holes; tie the flange to the top of the header tube with some thin iron binding-wire, or hold it in place with a brazing clamp, and silver-solder the whole issue—flange, tubes, and ends of header tube—at one fell swoop. Silver-soldering is quite O.K. for the joints in the superheater at the smokebox end, as it is well away from the fire; and the joints will be of ample strength.

Hot Header and Distribution Pipes

The hot header is an exactly similar piece of $\frac{1}{2}$ in. tube to that used for the wet header, with four holes for $\frac{1}{4}$ in. tubes at $\frac{7}{8}$ in. centres, and plugged ends. Now diametrically opposite and right in the centre, drill another hole for $\frac{1}{4}$ in. tube; the pipe feeding the middle cylinder goes in that one. The two pipes for feeding the outside cylinders are attached at the bottoms and note carefully—the composite illustration shows the rig-up for both piston-valve cylinders and slide-valves. That on the left is for piston-valves, and that on the right is for slides. The steam-pipe hole for the former is drilled approximately $\frac{7}{8}$ in. from the end, and for the latter $\frac{1}{2}$ in.

Two brass fittings are needed, to poke through the sides of the smoke-box. To make these, chuck a bit of $\frac{1}{2}$ in. hexagon—or round will do at a pinch—brass rod in three-jaw; face the end and centre deeply; drill down about $\frac{3}{4}$ in. depth with $\frac{13}{64}$ in. drill. Turn down $\frac{1}{2}$ in. of the outside to $\frac{3}{8}$ in. diameter, and screw $\frac{3}{8}$ in. by 32; part-off $\frac{5}{8}$ in. from the end. Reverse in chuck, and open out the hole for about $\frac{3}{32}$ in. depth with letter "D" or $\frac{1}{4}$ in. drill. Fit a short piece of $\frac{1}{4}$ in. tube in each, as shown in the illustration, 1 in. for slide-valve cylinders, and $1\frac{1}{4}$ in. for piston-valve cylinders. Silver-solder the tubes to the fittings, bend slightly as shown, and insert in bottom holes in the hot header. The pipe for feeding the inside cylinder is approximately $6\frac{1}{2}$ in. long, $\frac{1}{4}$ in. diameter, and carries a $\frac{3}{8}$ in. by 32 union nut and cone on

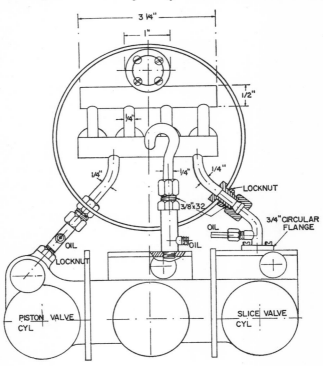

Fig. 8-19 Pipe arrangement.

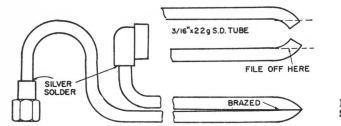

Fig. 8-20
Simple superheater.

its outer end. The inner end is fitted into the middle hole in the hot header; the four straight members of the elements are also fitted into the four holes in the back of the header, and the whole of the joints silver-soldered at one heating as before. Figs 8-18 and 8-19 show how the complete superheater is erected.

Simple Superheater and Blower Ring

A simple single-element superheater for engines of $2\frac{1}{2}$ in. gauge and below is shown in Fig. 8-20. The element is made from $\frac{3}{16}$ in. by 22-gauge copper tube, the ends being slightly bent over, filed off straight, put together in the form of a spearhead, and the joint brazed. The front end is bent up, and silver-soldered to an oval flange, which may be fixed to the smoke-box tubeplate by two screws; or else to a round flange, attached by three screws to a flange fitting on the end of the main steam pipe, as shown in the superheaters previously described. The lower half of the element is bent into a swan-neck, as shown, and attached to the steam pipe leading to the cylinders, by an ordinary union. This superheater needs a flue not less than $\frac{1}{2}$ in. diameter.

Fig. 8-21 shows the simplest form of ring blower, viz., a ring of $\frac{1}{8}$ in. copper tube with two or three No. 70 holes in it, and a short pipe terminating in a union nut and cone, for attaching to the union at the smokebox end of the hollow stay. The ring rests on top of the blastpipe nozzle when erected.

Blower Valves

In Fig. 8-21 is shown a section of a wheel valve arranged for fitting to the hollow stay carrying steam for the blower. It is made from $\frac{5}{16}$ in. hexagon rod, and has a hole drilled and tapped to suit the stay as shown; it may also be used on a water-tube boiler. Where this is done, the hole should be $\frac{1}{8}$ in. and the fitting screwed to the end of a length of pipe passing through the inner barrel itself, emerging at the farther end and terminating in a $\frac{1}{32}$ in. nipple or a ring. Do not pass the pipe through the space between the inner

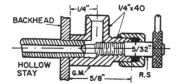

Fig. 8-21 Blower valve.

barrel and outer shell, or the engine will keep "sneezing" all the time the blower is in operation. Fig. 8-22 shows a valve adapted to screw anywhere on the backhead. It has a "blind" end terminating in a $\frac{5}{32}$ in. spigot. Ascertain the most handy place for the valve, or one where its appearance is symmetrical with the other fittings on the backhead; drill and tap a $\frac{5}{32}$ in. by 40 thread hole and screw the fitting in, connecting up as shown. Another satisfactory arrangement, is to silver-solder the hollow stay into the end of the blower valve, the boss of which is made large enough for the purpose, and screwed externally to fit a tapped hole in the backhead (Fig. 8-22).

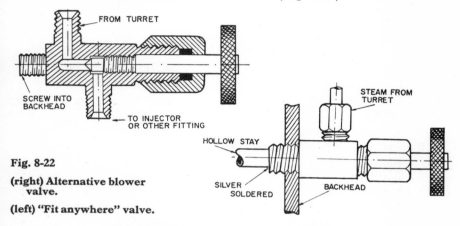

Fig. 8-22

(right) Alternative blower valve.

(left) "Fit anywhere" valve.

Oval Buffers for 2½ in. Gauge Engines

Oval buffers, besides being "fashionable", are very desirable fitments on small engines and rolling stock, as they minimise the buffer-locking trouble when shunting. They need, however, to be fitted up so that the heads do not go round, or else they look ridiculous. As I have seen several small engines with crude or clumsy non-turning arrangements, the following notes and sketches (Fig. 8-23) on the construction of a set of neat and easily-made oval buffers will be useful. Cut off four pieces of $\frac{1}{2}$ in. round brass or screw rod, each $\frac{7}{8}$ in. long. Turn down $\frac{1}{4}$ in. of one end to $\frac{1}{4}$ in. diameter, and screw $\frac{1}{4}$ in. by 26 or 40. Chuck a short bit of $\frac{1}{2}$ in. rod; centre, drill and tap to match; screw the embryo buffer sockets in it and turn the outsides either taper or parallel with lip or bead, as the case may be. Then centre and drill right through with $\frac{3}{32}$ in. or No. 43 drill, open out to $\frac{3}{4}$ in. depth with No. 30 drill and again to $\frac{9}{16}$ in. with No. 12 drill. Turn the heads from $\frac{7}{8}$ in. round mild-steel rod, as per sketch; drill and tap the shanks 7 BA and file the heads oval. Get a length of $\frac{3}{32}$ in. square silver-steel; cut four pieces each 1 in. long, turn the corners off one end of each to $\frac{3}{32}$ in. diameter for $\frac{1}{8}$ in. long and the other ends to $\frac{3}{16}$ in. long. Thread all the turned ends 7 BA, screw the $\frac{1}{8}$ in. ends into the buffer shanks and secure with a touch of solder if the threads do not fit tightly. File the remaining piece of $\frac{3}{32}$ in. square silver-steel down to a sufficient taper to easily enter the small hole in the buffer socket.

Fig. 8-23 Oval buffers.

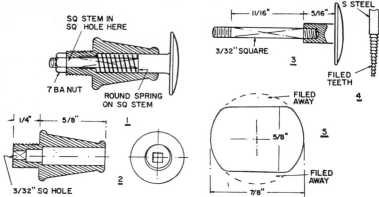

Then cut a few teeth on all four sides (Fig. 8-23), harden and temper to dark straw, and carefully drive it through the socket hole, which it will leave nice and square. These square holes may need easing out a shade with a watch-maker's file to allow the square buffer stems to slide easily. Wind a length of 24-gauge music wire round a piece of $\frac{1}{8}$ in. rod, cut off four $\frac{5}{8}$ in. lengths and slip one into each buffer casing. Put the buffer shanks in place with the square stems protruding through the square holes, secure with a 7 BA nut on the screwed extremities, and the job will be finished. The heads won't turn!

Screw Couplings for $3\frac{1}{2}$ in. Gauge

These are easy enough to make, and give a finish to the front of the engine. The shackles are bent up from $\frac{3}{32}$ in. steel wire; just the ordinary mild-steel will do. To make the eyes, file away half the diameter of the wire for about $\frac{3}{8}$ in. at each end; bend the resulting half-round section into a loop with a pair of round-nose pliers, and braze or silver-solder the joint. Don't worry if you stop up the eye; just poke a No. 40 drill through it. Before bending the eyes on the shorter shackle, poke it through the hole in the hook, otherwise you won't get it in. Lengths and width of shackles are given on the drawing; I got the right sizes from a working drawing of the full-sized engine, so they should "look right"! (Fig. 8-24).

The four swivels are turned up from $\frac{1}{4}$ in. round rod. Chuck in three-jaw, face the end, and turn down a full $\frac{1}{8}$ in. length to an easy fit in the hole in the shackle, and part off $\frac{1}{2}$ in. from the end. Reverse in chuck, and turn down a full $\frac{1}{8}$ in. of the other end to fit the shackle; then file a small flat on opposite sides of the full-sized centre portion. Centre-pop one side of each, and drill all four No. 40; tap two of them $\frac{1}{8}$ in. or 5 BA. The tapped ones go between the ends of the longer shackles. The latter can easily be sprung over the ends of the swivels, by a little judicious wangling, and the joints should be quite free.

The screw is also turned from $\frac{1}{4}$ in. rod. Chuck in three-jaw, and turn down $\frac{1}{2}$ in. length to $\frac{1}{8}$ in. diameter; screw $\frac{1}{8}$ in. or 5 BA. Part off about $\frac{3}{8}$ in. from the shoulder, reverse in chuck, and turn down $\frac{1}{4}$ in. of the other end to an easy fit in the drilled swivel. Put it through, and slightly rivet over the end to prevent it coming out, but leave it free to turn. Drill a No. 48 hole in the part between screw and shackle; tap it 7 BA and screw in an inch of $\frac{3}{32}$ in. steel wire, threaded both ends. On the outer end, fit a ball about $\frac{7}{32}$ in. diameter, turned up from $\frac{1}{4}$ in. rod, and drilled and tapped to suit. Screw on the shackle with the tapped swivel in it, and the coupling is complete. Always hang the loose shackle over the drawhook when the engine is not coupled to a car. Warning—don't use these little couplings for hauling a load of heavy cars full of passengers, as they aren't strong enough for hard work, being of "scale" size and more for ornament than use, as in the case of the working brakes. For passenger-hauling, fit an ordinary three-link coupling to the passenger car, and throw the little shackle off the drawhook before coupling the car to the engine.

Brake Pipes

I have seen many small locomotives fitted with imitation brake pipes, but none of them seem to have the correct appearance of their big sisters' accessories—the hose clips are usually missed out, for one thing. A realistic hose coupling for $2\frac{1}{2}$ in. gauge locomotive can be made from a piece of $\frac{3}{32}$ in. copper wire or tube, with a short length of ordinary cycle valve tubing slipped over it to represent the hose itself. The wire or tube should be bent to the shape shown; most of the miniature dummy hoses hang straight down, and this is not always correct. The brake fitters do not trouble to put the "dollies" on so exactly! A little copper clip can be made and soldered to the vertical part of the pipe; this allows it to be fixed to the buffer beam by a couple of 10 BA screws, hexagon-headed for preference. Two clips of soft sheet brass or German-silver about 30 gauge and $\frac{1}{16}$ in. wide are slipped over the ends of the hose and gently squeezed up with a small pair of pliers. They will "stay put" and give the finishing touch to a prominent though small fitting. Don't forget Westinghouse pipes are smaller and shorter than those used for the vacuum brake.

Lamps for $2\frac{1}{2}$ in. Gauge Engines

Another eyesore to all real enginemen is a tiny locomotive fitted with lamps having *painted* bullseyes. There isn't the slightest need for this; most drapers and fancy shops sell pins having glass heads about $\frac{3}{16}$ in. diameter, either green, red or colourless. These make excellent lamp bulls.

For a set of square Great Western lamps (Fig. 8-24), part off three pieces of $\frac{5}{16}$ in. square brass rod, each $\frac{1}{2}$ in. long. Turn $\frac{1}{8}$ in. of each down to $\frac{7}{32}$ in. diameter, and drill a No. 57 hole through the turned part to take the wire handles made from a hairpin. In each of the lamp bodies drill a $\frac{1}{4}$ in. hole half way through, completing right through with a No. 60 drill. Into the $\frac{1}{4}$ in. holes force short lengths of $\frac{1}{4}$ in. brass tube and file off so that $\frac{1}{16}$ in. stands out from the lamp body to form the bezel flange. Insert the stems of

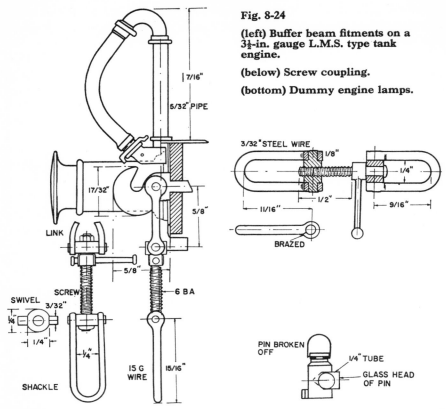

Fig. 8-24

(left) Buffer beam fitments on a 3½-in. gauge L.M.S. type tank engine.

(below) Screw coupling.

(bottom) Dummy engine lamps.

the pins into the No. 60 drill holes, and force through until the glass heads (one of each colour) are sunk just inside the pieces of tube; break off the pins flush with the back of the lamp; file off any burr, and solder little sheet-metal clips on the back to suit the lamp irons fitted to the engine (Fig. 8-24). The bright countersink left by the ¼ in. drill reflects light through the glass pin-heads, and at first glance, viewed from certain angles, the lamps appear to be alight. Realistic turned bezels could, if desired, be fitted in place of the tubes.

Pipe Couplings which Cause Derailments

When an engine, especially one with a long wheelbase, persistently runs off the road, don't blame the wheelbase, flanges, springing or track, nor start in to make radical alterations, without first examing the water pipe connections between engine and tender. The majority of small-gauge locomotives are fitted with a hand pump, and tender engines almost invariably have a stiff metal pipe connection to carry the water from the pump to the boiler. The pipe is usually of the stereotyped "coil" formation, the original designer of which proceeded on wrong lines altogether by making the pipe exceedingly free to swing from side to side, but entirely neglecting to provide for any movement in a fore and aft direction. Here you have a frequent cause of derailment. In order to enable the union to be easily coupled up, it is placed near one end of the buffer beam.

Now when an engine traverses a sharp curve, the lateral movement of the buffer beams is very small compared with the amount the ends approach to or recede from each other, which means that the distance between the fixed points of the feed pipe on engine and tender will vary a considerable amount. As the usual form of pipe will swing freely, but will not lengthen or shorten, it tries to go in the only direction it can—sideways—and either the engine or tender, or both, come off the road. The sketches (Fig. 8-25) explain the whys and wherefores.

Arrangements which will give Flexibility

If the pipe from the horizontal coil instead of being straight is bent as shown (Fig. 8-25) this will ensure a certain amount of play; another plan is to use two coils, one at either end of the tender. A third way is to bend the pipe in zig-zag or grid-iron fashion, which will allow the union end a comparatively free movement in any direction. A fourth method is to use a transverse coil. When an engine thus fitted traverses a curve, the pipe coils open and close "concertina" style, and this gives perfect freedom of movement. But for anyone who wants a really simple and easily fitted arrangement, a rubber or fabric hose connection fills the bill, provided it can stand the pressure of water necessary to feed the boiler. For engines of $2\frac{1}{2}$ in. gauge or thereabouts, the humble cycle inflator connection, obtainable at any cycle shop, can be utilised; and for larger engines the heavier hose, as used on automobile tyre pumps, will be found quite suitable. The only drawback, if it can be termed as such, is that hoses deteriorate after a time, and either burst or tear away from the couplings, as in real practice; but when a connector can be renewed in a few seconds at the cost of a few shillings, this is a small matter, and here is the way to do it.

Fig. 8-25   Diagrams illustrating causes of derailment.

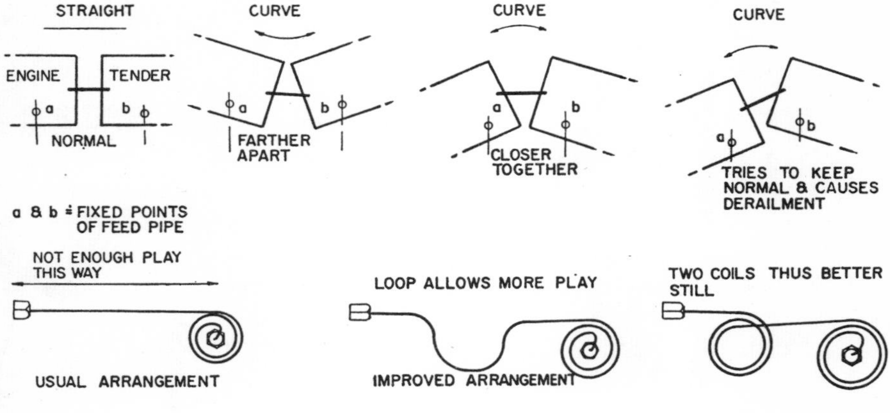

A Flexible Coupling Hose

The commercial cycle-pump connection is just the right size for a $2\frac{1}{2}$ in. to $3\frac{1}{2}$ in. gauge locomotive "feed-bag", as we called it on the L.B. & S.C. Railway in the days gone by. I have used the "Bluemel" type; this is $4\frac{7}{8}$ in. long overall, $\frac{5}{16}$ in. diameter, has male and female end both threaded $\frac{7}{32}$ in. Whitworth, and is made of rubber-and-canvas hose covered with a green braiding. This particular specimen has carried 180 lb. hydraulic pressure without fracture. Don't mutilate the connector in any way, but use it just as purchased; then, if one does by any chance go off pop, all you have to do is unscrew it and change the union adapter on to a new one, a few seconds' work at the outside. The tender end is a plain screwed socket, as shown (Fig. 8-26), sweated on to the end of the feed pipe leading from the pump. This is plenty strong enough, as the joint has no heat to withstand. For the engine coupling, make a union; $\frac{5}{16}$ in. by 26 or 32 threads is a handy size, but a smaller one will do if preferred. The lining and nut portion is attached to the engine feed pipe. The stem of the coned portion is threaded $\frac{7}{32}$ in. Whitworth, and screwed into the female end of the connector. That is all the fitting necessary. There are different ways of hanging the pipe; the usual method, shown at Fig. 8-26 (left) is not very satisfactory on a small engine, as the kinking is too pronounced when the buffer beams are at their closest position. Fig. 8-26 (right) is that adopted for ordinary hose connection on many small transatlantic engines and is quite all right. (Fig. 8-26 (bottom) is a compromise between the two and will be found generally satisfactory, especially if the union can be arranged to come just ahead of the engine footstep so that you don't have to grope between the buffer beams for it when coupling up in a hurry. For larger engines, use a piece of tyre-pump hose with an inch of tube and a union at each end.

Fig. 8-26   Cycle pump connector used as "feed-bag".

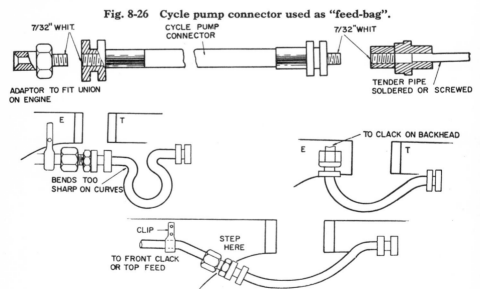

CHAPTER IX

Mechanical Lubricators

THE HIGH TEMPERATURE of the steam in a small locomotive with an efficient superheater makes a constant supply of oil to cylinders and steam-chests an absolute necessity; and mechanical lubrication is the only satisfactory means of ensuring that the valves and pistons never have a chance of running dry. In the early days, we depended on displacement lubricators, which were satisfactory up to a point. Every engine I have described has had provision for continuous oiling of valves and pistons. Whilst displacement lubricators— or hydrostatic lubricators, as they are sometimes called—will keep the valves and pistons oiled, their action is not regular. Sometimes they "gulp", the reason for this being that when steam is suddenly shut off, and the pressure in the steam-chests falls to zero—or even below, when valves remain on their faces and the pistons act as pumps driven by the momentum of the engine— the pressure remaining in the lubricator will force out every drop of oil remaining above the outlet, and this naturally floods the steam-chests and cylinders, with the result that when the regulator is opened again, the unfortunate driver gets an oily shower-bath from the surplus oil blown out of the chimney.

I spent a lot of time experimenting with displacement lubricators, until at last I got over the gulping trouble, and ensured a more or less constant feed, by copying the principle of the American "Nathan" hydrostatic lubricator in a small size. This has a special arrangement for regulating the oil feed, and a jet of steam from the boiler is introduced into the oil pipe to atomise the oil and force the spray or "emulsion" to the cylinders. However, this lubricator fed all the time, whether the engine was running or standing, and so I turned my attention to mechanical lubrication; and after trying out several different patterns, "standardised" on the oscillating cylinder type as being about the most reliable and the easiest to make. The lubricator specified has the same "works" that have given consistent trouble-free satisfaction on my own engines. The lubricator illustrated in Fig. 9-1, and described below, was fitted to a 2-4-0 engine of $3\frac{1}{2}$ gauge, with very little room available between cylinders and buffer beam; but it can be used on any two-cylinder engine, by varying the size of the oil tank to suit the particular type. On inside-cylinder engines, the oil should be fed to the steam-chest; with outside cylinders, feed into the cross pipe, opposite the point where steam enters

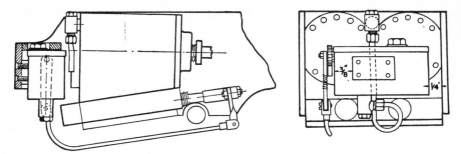

Fig. 9-1 Mechanical lubricator for inside cylinder engine.

from the boiler, so that both cylinders get their equal share. The ratchet lever may be driven from an eccentric on one of the axles, should that be more convenient.

Oil Tank

The container measures 2 in. long by $\frac{3}{4}$ in. wide by 1 in. high, and can be made from any metal except aluminium, the thickness being $\frac{1}{32}$ in. The easiest way to make it is to cut a strip of metal 1 in. wide and $5\frac{1}{2}$ in. long, bending this into a rectangle of the dimensions given. If the open corner refuses to close up, and shows a gap, tie a piece of thin iron wire around it, then stand the embryo tank on a flat piece of the same kind of metal a little over 2 in. by $\frac{3}{4}$ in., put the lot in the brazing pan and silver-solder around the bottom and along the open corner. If the container is steel, brass wire can be used, and the joints brazed instead of being silver-soldered. Clean up the job, and file the projecting edges of the bottom plate flush with the sides. The lid is made by cutting out a piece of metal (same kind as the tank) $2\frac{5}{16}$ in. by $1\frac{1}{16}$ in., snipping a $\frac{5}{32}$ in. square out of each corner, and bending a $\frac{5}{32}$ in. edge over on all four sides. This lid should be a nice snap fit.

On the centre-line of the bottom, and $\frac{5}{8}$ in. from one end, drill a $\frac{5}{32}$ in. hole. On the centre-line of that end, and $\frac{3}{16}$ in. from the top, drill a $\frac{3}{16}$ in. hole. On the long side of the tank which faces you when these holes are to your left, fix a piece of brass $\frac{5}{32}$ in. in thickness, $\frac{1}{2}$ in. wide, and about $\frac{7}{8}$ in. long. It should be $\frac{5}{16}$ in. from the bottom of the tank, and $\frac{3}{8}$ in. from the end with the hole in it, see illustration. Solder it in place, and put a couple of $\frac{1}{16}$ in. rivets through for extra security. For outside cylinder engines, a piece of angle can be substituted for attaching the tank under the buffer beam, as shown in Fig. 9-5.

Stand for Oil Pump

There are only two parts in the actual pump, the stand and the pump cylinder. The stand is made from $\frac{5}{16}$ in. square brass rod. Chuck a length truly in the four-jaw; face the end, centre, drill down a full $\frac{1}{8}$ in. with No. 30 drill, tap $\frac{5}{32}$ in. by 40, and part off an inch from the end. Alternatively, saw off a piece a little over 1 in. long; face one end and drill and tap as above with the piece held in the four-jaw, then reverse it and face the other end to bring it to 1 in. dead length. At the opposite end, mill or file a little step, $\frac{3}{32}$ in. deep and $\frac{3}{8}$ in. long. On the stepped side, drill the holes as shown. A $\frac{5}{32}$ in. hole is drilled right in the middle of the step, and this is tapped $\frac{3}{16}$ in. by 40. At $\frac{1}{2}$ in. below that, on the centre-line of the same side, put a No. 41 drill clean through. At $\frac{1}{8}$ in. from the bottom, make two small centre-pops each $\frac{1}{16}$ in. from the centre-line; that is, $\frac{1}{8}$ in. apart, and be mighty careful over this if you wish to avoid "blowback" in the lubricator. Now put a No. 55 drill through the right-hand centre-pop, and let it go right into the hole in the bottom of the column; and look out that the drill isn't beheaded when it breaks through, which it does on the angle. Drill the left-hand pop for about $\frac{1}{16}$ in. only; then with a weeny chisel made from a bit of silver-steel, or the broken end of a $\frac{3}{32}$ in. drill, chip a little groove from the blind hole to the bottom of the column, as shown in the illustration (Fig. 9-3).

It is very important that the bearing and trunnion holes go through the stand absolutely square, so don't drill these by hand on any account. If you haven't a bench drilling-machine, use the lathe; drill in three-jaw, with work help up against a drilling-pad or true bit of wood against the tailstock barrel. Next, file a recess about $\frac{3}{32}$ in. deep and $\frac{1}{4}$ in. wide, across the trunnion hole (No. 41 drill hole) just above the ports; and with a $\frac{1}{4}$ in. pin-drill having a $\frac{3}{32}$ in. pilot pin, open out the No. 41 hole on the opposite side, to a depth of about $\frac{3}{16}$ in. This allows a long spring to be used, and helps the sliding faces to keep in perfect contact. Finally, rub the port-face side on a smooth flat file laid on the bench, and finish off on a piece of emery cloth laid on a true surface.

Pump Cylinder

A piece of $\frac{3}{8}$ in. square brass rod $\frac{1}{2}$ in. long will be needed for the pump cylinder; either part it off the rod in the four-jaw, or saw off and face to length. Chuck truly in four-jaw, centre, drill right through with No. 32 drill, and follow up with $\frac{1}{8}$ in. parallel reamer. Open out to $\frac{3}{16}$ in. depth with

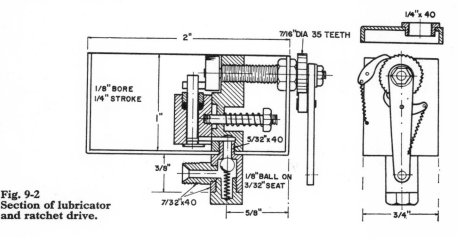

Fig. 9-2
Section of lubricator
and ratchet drive.

$\frac{3}{16}$ in. drill, and tap $\frac{7}{32}$ in. by 40. Make a little headless gland to fit. Mark off the positions of port and trunnion holes, as shown in Fig. 9-3; drill the port No. 55, and be careful when the drill breaks into the bore. Drill the trunnion hole No. 48, and *don't* break into the bore. Tap the latter hole $\frac{3}{32}$ in. by 60, or 7 BA if a "60" tap isn't available. Both port and trunnion hole must be dead true and square; so use drilling machine or lathe as before. Put the $\frac{1}{8}$ in. reamer through the bore again, to clear off any burring; then turn a little brass plug a tight drive fit for the end of the bore, drive it in, and solder it over. The outside of the cylinder can then be filed to the shape shown in the plan sketch, rounding off one side, and reducing the width to $\frac{5}{16}$ in. to match the stand. Face the port side truly as above.

The trunnion pin is a $\frac{3}{4}$ in. length of $\frac{3}{32}$ in. silver-steel or 13-gauge spoke wire. One end is screwed to match the hole in the pump cylinder, and the other end either same thread, or $\frac{3}{32}$ in. Whitworth. Screw it in very carefully, exactly at right-angles to the port face; if it isn't at right-angles the rubbing faces of cylinder and stand won't work oil-tight, and the lubricator will not feed. The pump ram, or plunger, is a piece of $\frac{1}{8}$ in. rustless steel or bronze rod $\frac{5}{8}$ in. long. It should be as near a perfect sliding fit in the pump cylinder as is possible to get it. At $\frac{3}{32}$ in. from one end, drill a No. 48 cross hole; a flat may be filed on the ram, to give the drill a fair start, as the hole must go straight through the centre, otherwise the ports will not open evenly. The ram is pushed into the pump cylinder, and the gland may then be packed with a few strands of graphited yarn; but don't screw the gland up tight enough to cause any binding of the ram. It has plenty to do, forcing oil past two spring-loaded check-valves against steam pressure, and any further addition to the load might severely strain the ratchet-gear.

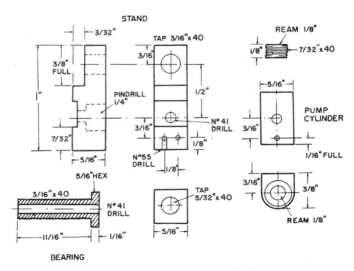

Fig. 9-3 Pump stand and cylinder.

Bottom Check Valve

This is made from $\frac{5}{16}$ in. round brass rod (Fig. 9-2). Chuck a length in three-jaw, face the end, centre, drill down about $\frac{5}{8}$ in. depth with No. 43 drill, open out with $\frac{3}{16}$ in. drill, and bottom with a $\frac{3}{16}$ in. D-bit to $\frac{5}{16}$ in. depth; tap $\frac{7}{32}$ in. by 40, and don't let the tap go in far enough to spoil the seating formed by the D-bit. Slightly countersink the end. Part off at $\frac{1}{2}$ in. full; reverse in chuck, turn down a full $\frac{1}{8}$ in. of the other end to $\frac{5}{32}$ in. diameter, and screw it $\frac{5}{32}$ in. by 40. Poke a $\frac{3}{32}$ in. parallel reamer through the central hole. If you haven't one, make a substitute. Take a couple of inches of $\frac{3}{32}$ in. silver-steel, and file off one end on the slant, the end looking like a long oval. Harden and temper to dark yellow, rub the oval face on a fine oilstone, and you're all set.

Drill a $\frac{5}{32}$ in. hole in the side of the fitting, and silver-solder a $\frac{7}{32}$ in. by 40 union nipple into it. To make the nipple, chuck a piece of $\frac{1}{4}$ in. rod and turn down about $\frac{1}{2}$ in. of it to $\frac{7}{32}$ in. diameter. Put $\frac{1}{4}$ in. length of $\frac{7}{32}$ in. by 40 thread on the end, using the die in the tailstock holder. Face the end, centre deeply with a centre drill, and drill down about $\frac{1}{2}$ in. depth with $\frac{3}{32}$ in. drill. Part off a bare $\frac{3}{8}$ in. from the end. Reverse in chuck, and turn down a $\frac{1}{16}$ in. pip on the other end, to a size that will drive tightly into the hole in the fitting. Squeeze it in, and silver-solder it. Either No. 1 grade (best) silver-solder and jeweller's borax as flux, or "Easyflo" and the special flux sold with it, are best for these small fittings. Simply apply a slight smear of the flux mixed with water to a paste, heat to dull red, touch with a thin strip of the silver-solder, let cool to black, pickle and clean up.

Incidentally, I use a circular wire brush to clean up all my small brazed and silver-soldered jobs. It consists of a large number of tufts of wire stuck into a circular wooden boss, with a hole through the middle. I mounted it on a short spindle, the end of which is turned to No. 1 Morse taper. A piece of 1 in. round steel 2 in. long, has one end bored No. 1 Morse taper and the other end tapped to screw on to my grinder spindle, outside the emery wheel. With this in place, and the brush spindle stuck into the taper hole, the brush revolves at nearly 3,000 r.p.m.; and any small fitting held against it, acquires a lovely bobby-dazzle. I use felt and calico polishing bobs also, mounted and driven the same way.

If you have a $\frac{1}{8}$ in. rustless steel ball, drop it into the hole, and seat it by holding a short bit of brass rod on the ball, and hitting the end one good sharp crack with a hammer. To support the check-valve whilst seating the ball, get a bit of flat steel bar, or a disc, or anything flat and $\frac{1}{4}$ in. or so in thickness, and drill a few holes in it, varying in size from $\frac{5}{32}$ in. upwards to about $\frac{3}{8}$ in. If this is placed on your anvil or bench block, the screwed end of the clack can be placed in the $\frac{5}{32}$ in. hole, and the threads won't be damaged by the "biff". This gadget often comes in very useful.

If you have only a bronze ball, use a $\frac{1}{8}$ in. cycle ball to form the seating. All we then need is a cap. Chuck a piece of $\frac{5}{16}$ in. hexagon brass rod, face the end, centre, and drill down about $\frac{3}{16}$ in. with $\frac{1}{8}$ in. drill. Turn down $\frac{5}{32}$ in. of the end to $\frac{7}{32}$ in. diameter, screw $\frac{7}{32}$ in. by 40, and part off $\frac{1}{4}$ in. full from the end. Reverse in chuck, and chamfer the hexagon slightly. Wind a bit of 24-gauge hard brass wire around a bit of $\frac{3}{32}$ in. silver-steel, to form the spring, which fits into the hole in the cap and holds the ball in place.

Assembly and Erection

The bearing, spindle, and crank are made as described for the twin-pump lubricator described immediately following, and the ratchet gear is also made in the same manner. The complete assembly is shown in Fig. 9-2, and one method of erection is shown in the preceding Fig. 9-1. In this particular case, the steam chest is underneath the cylinders; and to introduce the oil into the flow of steam through the vertical passage between the bores, a check valve (Fig. 9-4) was screwed into the cylinder block, a communicating hole being drilled into the steam way. The check valve was made similarly to that under the tank, except that the stem was screwed and countersunk for a union. This was connected to the check valve under the tank, by a $\frac{3}{32}$ in. pipe as shown.

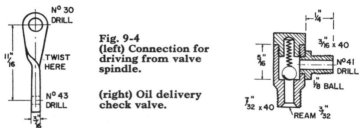

Fig. 9-4
(left) Connection for driving from valve spindle.

(right) Oil delivery check valve.

The drive was taken from one of the valve spindles, to the ratchet lever, by a rod made from $\frac{3}{32}$ in. silver steel and furnished with two forks. A connection, shown in Fig. 9-4, was attached to the valve spindle (Fig. 9-1) and this accommodated the driving end of the rod. The length of the ratchet lever was so proportioned, that the ratchet clicked one tooth when the engine was running fully notched up, with the minimum movement of the valve spindles. For outside cylinders, the drive shown in Fig. 9-5 would be quite satisfactory.

A V-Twin Mechanical Lubricator for 3-Cylinder Engine

The lubricator described below differs from anything hitherto specified by virtue of being what our motoring friends would call a V-twin, having two pumps of different bores. As the inside and outside cylinders are supplied by separate connections to the hot header of the superheater, and there is no central steam distribution point outside the smokebox into which a common oil supply could be fed, it will also be necessary to split up the oil feeds. The uninitiated will probably wonder why oil could not be supplied by a single pump to a three-legged spider fitting, thence by separate pipes

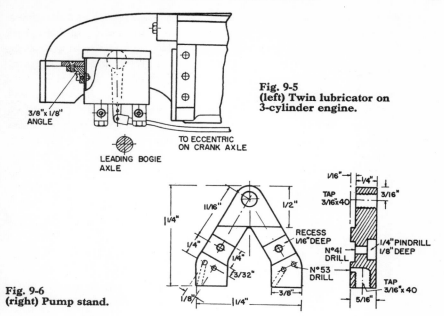

Fig. 9-5
(left) Twin lubricator on 3-cylinder engine.

Fig. 9-6
(right) Pump stand.

to each cylinder; but although this sounds feasible and would work up to a point, it suffers from a serious drawback. The oil delivered to the spider fitting would naturally be at a constant pressure during the delivery stroke; but as it would also naturally take the path of least resistance when leaving the spider, all three pipes would have to be exactly the same length and internal diameter, and if clacks were provided at the entry to the cylinders, the springs would all have to be exactly the same tension. Otherwise, the cylinder with a short pipe or a weak clack spring would get an extra supply of oil at the expense of the other two.

As I have found from practical experience that a pump, delivering into a plain tee with pipes of equal length to two outside cylinder, will feed satisfactorily, one pump in the twin will feed the outside cylinders only, and the other one will feed the inside cylinder direct. Naturally the inside merchant won't need as much oil as its two confreres outside; and so the pump feeding it can be made smaller in the bore. The two pumps work off one crank; and as the small ram or plunger needs a separate big-end bush to work on the crankpin, the two pumps have to be set at different centres to allow the two rams to clear. I guess that will explain the "whys and wherefores" to novices and beginners.

Oil Tank

The simplest way of making the oil tank, is to cut a strip of 18 or 20-gauge sheet brass 6 in. long and $1\frac{5}{16}$ in. wide, and bend it into a rectangle with $1\frac{1}{2}$ in. sides. Stand this on a piece of the same material a little over $1\frac{1}{2}$ in. square, in your brazing pan; then silver-solder all round the bottom, and down the open corner. Pickle and wash off, then file the bottom flush with the sides, and trim off the corner which is joined, if it needs it. Scribe a line right across the centre of the bottom plate; make a centre-pop $\frac{3}{8}$ in. from one side and $\frac{1}{4}$ in. from the other; drill them $\frac{3}{16}$ in. clearing. Drill another $\frac{3}{16}$ in. hole $\frac{1}{4}$ in. from the top of the right-hand side, for the bearing (Fig. 9-8). A snap-on lid can be made for the tank, either by flanging a bit of 18 or 20-gauge brass sheet over an iron former $1\frac{1}{2}$ in. square, or by cutting out a piece of brass $1\frac{7}{8}$ in. square, taking a nick $\frac{3}{16}$ in. square out of each corner, and bending $\frac{3}{16}$ in. of each side at right-angles, thus forming a shallow tray. The corners can be silver-soldered if you so desire.

Pump Stand

This may easily be cut from the solid; first, saw and file to the shape shown, from a $1\frac{1}{4}$ in. length of $1\frac{1}{4}$ in. by $\frac{5}{16}$ in. brass bar. All holes, except the oil inlets, should be drilled either on a drilling machine, or in the lathe against a drilling pad on the tailstock; it is essential that the holes for the bearings should go through dead square. At $\frac{3}{16}$ in. from the apex, drill No. 22 or $\frac{5}{32}$ in., and tap $\frac{3}{16}$ in. by 40 for the spindle bearing. Locating from this, mark off the trunnion holes and ports to sizes given on the illustration; drill trunnion holes No. 41, and ports No. 53, these only going halfway through the stand. Now note carefully: close to the left-hand edge of each foot or base, and about on the middle line, make a centre-pop, and from it drill a No. 53 hole into the left-hand port, as shown in dotted lines. Then, with a rat-tail file, make a "mouse-hole" in the wall, so that oil can get into the duct when the stand is in place at the bottom of the tank. At $\frac{1}{8}$ in. from the right-hand side of each foot, about on the centre-line, drill a $\frac{5}{32}$ in. hole $\frac{3}{16}$ in. deep, and tap it $\frac{3}{16}$ in. by 40; from the top of this, run a $\frac{3}{32}$ in. drill into the right-hand port.

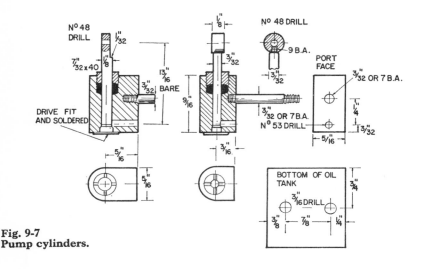

Fig. 9-7
Pump cylinders.

File or mill away $\frac{1}{16}$ in. of the face, from the apex to the point where the legs divide; then ditto repeato on each leg, from a point $\frac{3}{32}$ in. above the ports, to form a recess $\frac{1}{4}$ in. wide, see illustration. Form a circular recess, $\frac{1}{4}$ in. diameter and $\frac{1}{8}$ in. deep, at the back of each trunnion hole (see Fig. 9-6) the boy for this job being a pin-drill. The raised portions left after the recessing must be truly faced, but if you are using a casting, rub it first on a smooth file. Face by rubbing on a piece of fine emery cloth laid working side up, on any handy truly-flat surface, such as the lathe bed or drilling-machine table. After facing, be sure to wash all the chippings and emery dust out of the ports and oil ducts; recollect you are making a lubricator, not a valve and piston grinder!

Pump Cylinders

The bigger one needs a bit of $\frac{1}{2}$ in. by $\frac{5}{16}$ in. brass rod, and the smaller $\frac{3}{8}$ in. by $\frac{5}{16}$ in. ditto, both $\frac{9}{16}$ in. long after both ends have been squared off in the lathe. On the centre-line of the narrow end, make a centre-pop $\frac{5}{16}$ in. from the edge of the big one, and $\frac{3}{16}$ in. on the little one; chuck in four-jaw with the pop mark running truly, and drill the big one No. 33, following with $\frac{1}{8}$ in. reamer. Drill the small one No. 44 and finish with $\frac{3}{32}$ reamer. If you haven't any regular reamers these sizes, simply get a couple of bits of silver-steel about 2 in. long, file one end of each to a long oval, harden and temper to dark yellow, rub the oval faces flat on an oilstone to get rid of the file marks and any roughness of the edges.

Open out the ends of the bores to a bare $\frac{3}{16}$ in. depth with $\frac{3}{16}$ in. drill—it pays beginners to make pin-drills for jobs where two holes have to be concentric—and tap $\frac{7}{32}$ in. by 40. For the glands, use $\frac{7}{32}$ in. brass rod, and make them about $\frac{1}{8}$ in. long; cross-nick with a saw or file.

Scribe a line down the middle of each port face, centre-pop it $\frac{3}{32}$ in. from the end opposite gland, and also at $\frac{1}{4}$ in. above that. Drill the bottom hole No. 53, piercing the bore. Drill the other one No. 48 and *don't* pierce the bore; tap it 7 BA. Poke the reamers through again, to clean out any burrs, and then turn up two little plugs for the cylinder-ends as shown, from $\frac{1}{4}$ in. rod. These should be a tight drive fit in the bores; solder over the heads for the sake of "safety first". True up the port faces, and screw in the trunnions; these are $\frac{11}{16}$ in. lengths of $\frac{3}{32}$ in. round rod, screwed both ends, as shown in the illustrations.

The larger ram is a piece of $\frac{1}{8}$ in. round silver-steel, or rustless steel, $\frac{7}{8}$ in. long, with a No. 48 cross hole drilled at one end, and a flat filed on it to clear the big-end bush of the smaller ram. This is a piece of $\frac{3}{32}$ in. steel, one end turned down to $\frac{5}{64}$ in. and screwed 9 BA as shown in Fig. 9-7. The bush is a $\frac{1}{8}$ in. slice parted off a $\frac{7}{32}$ in. rod held in the three-jaw. Drill a No. 48 hole through the middle before parting off, and then drill a No. 53 hole in the edge, and tap it 9 BA. The distance from end of ram to the hole is approximately $\frac{13}{16}$ in. Pack the glands with graphited yarn, and round off the cylinders as shown in the plan view.

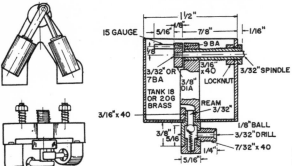

Fig. 9-8
Complete pump unit.

Bearing, Spindle and Crank

To make the bearing, chuck a piece of $\frac{5}{16}$ in. hexagon rod in three-jaw with 1 in. projecting. Turn down $\frac{7}{8}$ in. length to $\frac{3}{16}$ in. diameter, and screw $\frac{3}{16}$ in. by 40. Face, centre, and drill down 1 in. depth with No. 41 drill. Part off $\frac{15}{16}$ in. from the end, this leaving a $\frac{1}{16}$ in. head. Make a nut to suit, from the same size rod; face, centre, drill $\frac{5}{32}$ in. for $\frac{3}{16}$ in. depth, tap $\frac{3}{16}$ in. by 40, chamfer the corners, and part off a $\frac{1}{8}$ in. slice.

The spindle is a piece of $\frac{3}{32}$ in. silver-steel, approximately $1\frac{7}{16}$ in. long, with $\frac{1}{8}$ in. 7 BA thread on each end, and carries a ratchet wheel $\frac{7}{32}$ in. diameter, $\frac{3}{32}$ in. wide, with about 35 to 40 teeth. The wheel should be drilled No. 43 and forced on to the spindle, so that $1\frac{1}{16}$ in. projects from the bearing side. Press an over-length bit of silver-steel through the wheel first, then cut to length and screw the ends afterwards; this saves a lot of trouble, as you don't have to shift the wheel any more, when once it is on. *And* be careful it is on the right way; with the long end of the spindle away from you, the vertical side of the teeth should point left, the sloping side right; the lubricator works clockwise, looking at the ratchet end.

The crank is only a few minutes' work. Chuck a bit of $\frac{3}{8}$ in. round rod in the three-jaw; face, centre, drill $\frac{3}{16}$ in. deep with No. 48 drill, and tap to match the spindle. Part off a $\frac{1}{8}$ in. slice. At $\frac{1}{8}$ in. from centre, drill and tap a 9 BA hole (53 drill) and screw in a piece of 15-gauge spoke wire, so that $\frac{5}{16}$ in. projects from the crank disc.

Check Valves or Clacks

Chuck a bit of $\frac{5}{16}$ in. round rod in three-jaw; face the end, and turn down $\frac{3}{16}$ in. length to $\frac{3}{8}$ in. diameter; screw $\frac{3}{16}$ in. by 40, and part off $\frac{3}{8}$ in. from shoulder. Reverse in chuck, centre, drill right through No. 44, open out with $\frac{3}{16}$ in. drill and bottom with $\frac{3}{16}$ in. D-bit to $\frac{5}{16}$ in. depth. Tap the end of the hole $\frac{7}{32}$ in. by 40, taking care not to let the tap run into the seating and spoil it. Countersink the end slightly, then run a $\frac{3}{32}$ in. reamer through the remnants of the No. 44 hole. Drill a $\frac{5}{32}$ in. hole in the side, half-way along the body. Chuck a bit of $\frac{1}{4}$ in. rod in three-jaw, turn down about $\frac{3}{8}$ in. to $\frac{7}{32}$ in. diameter, and screw $\frac{1}{4}$ in. of it $\frac{7}{32}$ in. by 40. Face the end, centre deeply, drill down $\frac{3}{8}$ in. depth with $\frac{3}{32}$ in. drill, and part off $\frac{5}{16}$ in. from the end. Reverse in chuck, turn the blank end to fit the hole in the clack body, squeeze it in, and silver-solder it.

Pickle, wash, and clean up; then seat a $\frac{1}{8}$ in. ball on the $\frac{3}{32}$ in. hole. Make a little cap from $\frac{5}{16}$ in. hexagon brass rod, to fit the clack body; but before parting off, centre and drill it a bare $\frac{1}{4}$ in. deep with No. 30 drill. Wind up a little spring from steel wire about 26-gauge, around a bit of 15-gauge cycle-spoke, or something about the same diameter; when this is released, it will spring out to a nice sliding fit in the No. 30 hole. Square off the end that presses on the ball, by holding it for a second or two against the side of a fast-running emery wheel; then cut to such a length that it just starts to compress as the cap is screwed home.

Assembly

Poke the pump-cylinder trunnion pins through the holes in the stand, put springs on them, and secure with ordinary commercial nuts. The springs can be wound from 22 or 23-gauge steel wire, around a bit of $\frac{3}{32}$ in. rod; compression should be just enough to allow the cylinders to be pushed off their faces about $\frac{1}{16}$ in. before the spring is fully compressed. The cylinders should have freedom to oscillate, but at the same time should not be easy enough to allow oil pressure to force them off the faces instead of passing the clacks against steam pressure.

Put the stand in the tank, and screw in the clacks through the holes in the bottom of tank; these hold the stand vertically in position, the bearing forming an additional stay. Poke it through the hole in the tank side, put on the nut and screw it into the hole in the top of the stand, until the head just touches the side of the tank; then run the lock-nut back against the inside of tank, and tighten it, as shown in the side view of the ratchet-gear. Put the crankpin through the holes in the rams, and hold it with the centre hole in line with the centre of the bearing; then put the spindle through the bearing,

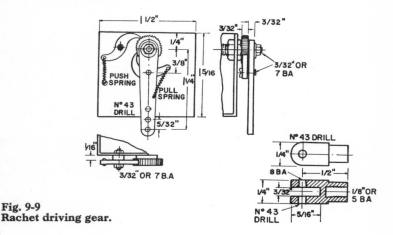

Fig. 9-9
Rachet driving gear.

and screw it home into the crank. The spindle, when right home, should have just the weeniest bit of end ·play. The lubricator can now be tested by putting some oil—autcmobile engine oil will do—in the tank, and turning the ratchet wheel clockwise with your fingers. A distinct resistance should be felt as the rams take the downward stroke and the oil forces the clack balls off their seatings. Put your thumb over each outlet in turn; and if the lubricator is O.K., no matter if you are as strong as Samson and have a grip of iron, you won't be able to prevent the oil coming out when the ratchet wheel is turned. These weeny lubricators have been tested to pump against 450 lb. pressure; and that wasn't the limit, the tester was afraid of straining his master gauge!

Ratchet Gear and Erection

All that remains is to fit a waggler to operate the ratchet wheel, and erect the lubricator on the engine. The ratchet lever is filed up from $\frac{3}{32}$ in. by $\frac{5}{16}$ in. steel strip, to dimensions given; the pawls are filed up from the same stuff, to the shape shown in the illustrations. Drill the tails $\frac{1}{16}$ in., and the pivot holes No. 41. Both pawls are case-hardened. The moving pawl is pivoted on a screw turned up from $\frac{3}{16}$ in. silver-steel, with enough plain left under the head to allow free movement when the screw is right home. The stationary pawl works on one end of a double-sided stud.

Chuck a bit of $\frac{3}{16}$ in. steel rod, and turn down one end of it to $\frac{3}{32}$ in. diameter for $\frac{3}{16}$ in. length, putting $\frac{3}{32}$ in. of thread on the end. Part off at $\frac{1}{4}$ in. from the shoulder; reverse in chuck, and repeat operation, but this time screw full length. Put this end through a No. 41 hole drilled in the tank at position shown, put a nut on the inside, and tighten it, cutting off the superfluous thread close to nut, which effectually locks it, as the thread beyond the nut will be too distorted for the nut to slack accidentally. Then put the pawl on, and see it remains free when the nut is right home. The springs are wound from 24-gauge steel wire; note, one pulls and the other pushes. If a spot of thin oil is applied to pawls and pivots, and the lever waggled back and forth, the ratchet-gear should work perfectly, clicking one tooth when the bottom of the lever swings about $\frac{2}{8}$ in. overall movement.

The lubricator is erected by attaching it to the front buffer-beam by a piece of $\frac{3}{8}$ in. by $\frac{1}{8}$ in. angle, $1\frac{1}{2}$ in. long. This is fixed across the front of the lubricator by three $\frac{3}{32}$ in. by $\frac{1}{4}$ in. brass screws, nutted inside the tank, the angle being placed $\frac{3}{8}$ in. below the top of the tank and, of course, level; the ratchet-gear is on the right-hand side. Drill a No. 41 hole in the middle of the top of the buffer-beam, and $\frac{1}{4}$ in. from the edge, and another $\frac{1}{2}$ in. each side of it; countersink all three. Hold the lubricator in the position shown in Fig. 9-5, close to the beam and in centre of same; run the 41 drill through the holes, making countersinks on the angle; drill through No. 48, tap 7 BA, and attach by three countersunk screws.

Make up an eccentric and strap to fit the crank-axle, but instead of slotting the lug, tap it $\frac{1}{8}$ in. or 5 BA. Make up a fork or clevis to the dimensions given in Fig. 9-9 and attach it to the ratchet lever by an 8 BA screw with $\frac{3}{16}$ in. plain under the head; this can be turned from a piece of $\frac{3}{16}$ in. steel rod. Connect up the fork and the eccentric strap by a piece of $\frac{1}{8}$ in. steel rod, the exact length of which can be obtained from the actual job. Put the eccentric at half-stroke, and the ratchet-lever vertical; measure the distance between the end of the fork and the lug .of the eccentric-strap, allowing about $\frac{1}{4}$ in. each end extra for screwing into the lug and fork respectively. Screw the rod into the eccentric-strap and the fork on the rod; bend the rod slightly to clear the inside cylinder, and re-connect. The ratchet should click one tooth for every turn of the wheels; if it doesn't, and adjusting the fork on the rod doesn't produce the desired effect, shift the fork to a hole higher up the ratchet-lever. It is better for the pawl to overrun the teeth slightly, than risk missing a tooth; good lubrication is vital with superheated steam.

CHAPTER X

Further Thoughts on Valves

A GLOBE-VALVE is just as easy to make as an angle-valve, and a section of a typical one is shown in the detailed illustration (Fig. 10-1). The working part of the valve is just the same as on any other type of screwdown-valve of the pin or conical pattern; simply a recess in the body, with a seating formed at the bottom of it, the plug carrying the valve-pin or spindle being screwed into the recess. Holes are drilled slantwise from the ends of the body, into the recess; one slopes upwards to the space above the valve, and the other slopes down to the space below the seating. The latter should be the inlet side, as this relieves the gland from continuous boiler pressure. The ends of the valve body may be made to any desired pattern, with internal or external threads, and countersunk for unions if needed.

The bodies of the globe-valves used on full-sized locomotives are made from castings, and it is a good wheeze to follow suit on the weeny editions, as a chucking-piece can be cast on, opposite that part of the body in which the valve seating is formed. *Model Engineer* advertisers can supply these little castings in several sizes, and in every case, the machining is the same; so if I briefly run through the construction of the valve shown in the sectional illustration, the same method can be followed for any other size.

Chuck in the three-jaw by the piece provided, and face the boss on the body. Centre, and drill nearly through with No. 24 drill. Open out and bottom to half the depth of the body, with $\frac{9}{32}$ in. drill and D-bit; tap $\frac{5}{16}$ in. by 32 or 40. Run a $\frac{5}{32}$ in. parallel reamer into the blind hole as far as it will go. Rechuck by one end; face the other end, centre deeply, and turn the outside to $\frac{3}{8}$ in. diameter for $\frac{1}{4}$ in. length. Screw it $\frac{3}{8}$ in. by 32. Reverse and

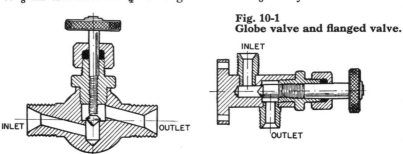

Fig. 10-1
Globe valve and flanged valve.

INLET

INLET   OUTLET

OUTLET

rechuck in a tapped bush, to ensure the other end running truly, and repeat operation. Be careful over the next bit, which is to drill a No. 30 hole from one end, into the recess above the D-bitted seating, and a similar hole from the other end, into the hole below the seating. The method used for passage-ways in cylinders, from bore to port, can be followed with advantage here, taking care that the hole slanting upwards, doesn't come out close enough to the valve seating to cut into it.

To make the gland fitting, chuck a piece of $\frac{7}{16}$ in. hexagon rod in the three-jaw. Face, centre, and drill down with No. 30 drill, to a depth of $\frac{5}{8}$ in. full. Open out with No. 21 drill to $\frac{1}{8}$ in. depth. Turn down $\frac{3}{16}$ in. of the outside to $\frac{1}{4}$ in. diameter, and screw $\frac{1}{4}$ in. by 40. Part off at $\frac{1}{2}$ in. from the end. Reverse and rechuck in a tapped bush, to make certain that the hole runs truly. Turn down $\frac{3}{16}$ in. of the outside to $\frac{5}{16}$ in. diameter, and screw $\frac{5}{16}$ in. by 32 or 40 to suit body. Tap the hole $\frac{5}{32}$ in. by 40, or 3 BA; if quick action is needed, use the coarser thread. Make a $\frac{1}{4}$ in. by 40 gland nut, from $\frac{3}{8}$ in. hexagon rod; this is just the same as a union nut.

The valve spindle can be made from $\frac{5}{32}$ in. rustless steel or phosphor-bronze rod; if the former, make quite sure that it is rustless, as I've received samples of so-called "rustless" steel from readers, which had both rusted and pitted. I have also seen cycle balls which had been sold as "rustless". A rough-and-ready test is to try a magnet on the steel; a child's toy magnet will do quite well. If the steel flies to the magnet like sweethearts after a long separation, don't use it; rustless steel is non-magnetic—anyway, the stuff I use myself, treats a magnet with contempt! For the valve illustrated, a piece $1\frac{1}{8}$ in. long is required; file a square on one end, using the chuck jaw as a guide. Reverse in chuck, and screw $\frac{5}{32}$ in. or 3 BA to match the tapped hole in the gland fitting, for about $\frac{1}{2}$ in. length. Face the end, centre, and drill No. 43 for about $\frac{3}{16}$ in. depth; fit a handwheel, any size you fancy, on the squared end. The wheel can be turned from brass, dural, rustless steel, or anything else available; a fibre one could be used for operation by tender fingers. There is also the age-old "cool handle"; for this, just turn a half-round groove in the rim of a metal wheel, wind up a small spiral spring, from steel wire, to a size which will just fit the groove, bend it into a circle, spring it into the groove, and secure with a touch of solder.

Just Like the Kitchen Tap!

Screw the spindle through the gland fitting, and in the end of it, fit a conical valve with a stem turned to a tight push fit in the hole in the spindle, like the jumper on the kitchen tap; only this one won't be needing new washers every five minutes or so! To make the valve, chuck a bit of $\frac{7}{32}$ in. or $\frac{1}{4}$ in. round bronze or rustless steel rod in the three-jaw, face the end, and turn down a bare $\frac{3}{16}$ in. length to fit tightly in the hole in the spindle. Part off at $\frac{5}{16}$ in. from the end. Reverse in chuck, grip by spigot, and turn the outer end to a cone point about 45 deg. angle, skimming the outer edge down a wee bit under $\frac{7}{32}$ in. diameter. Push the spigot into the hole in the spindle, and assemble the valve as shown in the illustration, packing the gland with a strand of graphited yarn, and putting a smear of plumbers' pipe jointing on the threads of the gland fitting. Don't get any in the recess! The valve can be seated steamtight, merely by screwing it down tightly when first assembling; afterwards, it will be quite O.K. with quite a moderate pressure of the screw.

The size of valve given above, is quite all right for most purposes on $3\frac{1}{2}$ in. and 5 in. gauge engines; it can be enlarged within reason, or reduced to almost microscopic dimensions, the method of construction remaining the same. Just to pull somebody's leg, I made one only $\frac{3}{16}$ in. overall length; valve and spindle were in one piece, made from a domestic pin, the head being turned to form the valve. It was threaded full length by aid of a watchmaker's screwplate, and the hole in the gland-fitting tapped full length. The handwheel was screwed on to the end of the spindle, and a touch of solder prevented its coming unstuck. The tiny thing worked! I told the "donee" to get it silverplated, and use it for a watch-chain charm.

Flanged Valve

This is a first cousin to the globe-valve, and can be used with advantage in places where the inlet and outlet don't of necessity have to be in line, and where a support is handy (such as the boiler backhead) to which the flange can be attached. Several of my own engines have valves of this kind on the backhead, taking steam from the turret, or an elbow, on top of the wrapper. As the steam inlet isn't in direct communication with the boiler, there is no need to fit the valve high up, level with the steam space; it can be placed in any available spot between the rest of the fittings. The outlet union can be at right-angles, or indeed at any angle, to the inlet; on my L.M.S. "Pacific", for example, the valve is situated half-way down the backhead, by the firehole door. Steam enters the top union via a pipe from the turret, and the outlet is at the side, the pipe going direct to a donkey-pump on the right-hand side of the firebox. Another instance is the blower-valve on my *Britannia*.

The whole issue can be made from rod material, preferably bronze or gunmetal, though brass will do at a pinch; the union screws are silver-soldered into the body. Dimensions can be arranged to suit the job in hand. By way of variety, I have shown a one-piece valve and spindle; but if desired, the valve and spindle can be made in the same way as described and illustrated for the globe-valve. If a coarse-threaded spindle is used, a full opening can be easily obtained with only one turn of the handwheel; this is mighty handy for injector steam valves which are operated when the engine is running.

Large Valve with Small Spindle

It sometimes happens that a valve is needed with a big steam or waterway through it; and if made normally, with a proportionate-sized spindle and handwheel, it would look unsightly among the other backhead adornments, probably project too far, or else be awkward to fit in, and difficult to operate.

Fig. 10-2   Small spindle valve and "Easyclean" water-gauge blowdown valve.

In that case, a valve such as is illustrated here could be used. It has a big steam passage, and a separate cone valve to match; but instead of the valve having a spigot to fit a hole drilled in the spindle, a la the kitchen tap, the arrangement is reversed, the valve being drilled to receive the end of a small spindle passing through the gland fitting. This is furnished with a small handwheel and gland nut to match. The relative sizes can be anything within reason. The same arrangement of valve and spindle could be used with either of the valves described above. There is no need to detail out the construction, as this is practically the same as the other valves described in this book; and anyway, the drawing is self-explanatory.

Water-Gauge Blowdown

Complaints occasionally come in, that with my "standard" type of water-gauge, when used in districts where the water is hard or "dirty", there is difficulty in keeping the blowdown valve steam and watertight, and at the same time easy to operate. Little bits of scale and grit not only get stuck in the valve seating, causing a leak or blow, but they get jammed around the end of the valve-pin, and also get into the threads, making the spindle very stiff to turn. A good remedy for that is to make the blowdown valve as shown in the accompanying drawing. Instead of the bottom fitting being drilled and tapped direct for the valve spindle, it is opened out in a similar way to the valves described above, and a plug made to fit. This plug is drilled and tapped to take the valve spindle, which is screwed through it as shown. This arrangement ensures quite a big recess around the valve seating and pin; and if the blowdown pipe is made a bit larger than usual, any scale or grit coming through the valve, will be blown clean away, instead of choking the waterway, damaging valve and seating, and getting into the threads.

Boiler Blowdown Valve

The trouble mentioned above, sometimes occurs with the screwdown type of boiler blowdown valve, especially if the boiler is allowed to run for too long a period without washing out. Dirt and scale which settles on the foundation ring, invariably finds its way to the outlet, so it is advisable to take precautions; and it can easily be seen, that any valve with the outlet opening in the ring itself, would be rendered useless before you could say— (deleted by censor)—anyway, you'd probably say it afterwards, probably adding an encore!

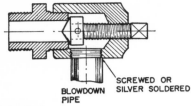

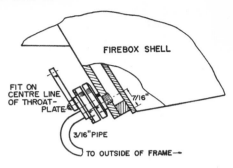

FIREBOX SHELL

FIT ON
CENTRE LINE
OF THROAT-
PLATE

7/16"

BLOWDOWN
PIPE

SCREWED OR
SILVER SOLDERED

3/16"PIPE

TO OUTSIDE OF FRAME—

Fig. 10-3
Boiler blowdown valve with large
waterway and "Everlasting" blowdown
valve fitted to 4-6-2 boiler.

The sectional illustration shows a boiler blowdown valve which, while not as effective as the "Everlasting" type (which is absolutely the cat's whiskers) is a pretty good cousin to it. The valve body is merely a double-ended nipple with a big hole through it, the size depending on the boiler, into which one end is screwed. A long nut, like a glorified union nut, goes over the outer end, and carries a valve made as shown; the spindle is screwed full length, the outer end being squared for key or box-spanner operation. The hole in the end of the nut is tapped to suit the spindle. A coned valve is fitted to the inner end of the spindle, which is screwed into it and pinned. The blowdown pipe, which should be the largest size that the nut will accommodate, can either be screwed in as shown, or silver-soldered. Two or three threads will give plenty of hold for the pipe, as there is no pressure to withstand; the end of the pipe is left open. Any leakage at the screw doesn't matter a Continental.

"Everlasting" Blowdown Valve

For the benefit of readers who are not acquainted with the "Everlasting" blowdown valve, I might mention here that it is about the most trouble-free gadget of its kind ever used in full-size practice; and is widely used in this country, U.S.A. and other parts of the world. It provides one of those few instances where a little copy of the full-sized article can be made to work satisfactorily without modifications, the reason being the simplicity and reliability of the big one. The valve body is made in two halves, one of which forms a portface. The other half is recessed, to carry the valve and operating arm. Normally, the circular valve covers the port, and the full pressure of the boiler keeps the valve tight against the portface. The handle is attached to a spindle, which operates an arm inside the recess; and as the arm carries the valve, a slight movement of the handle causes the arm to slide the valve off the port, allowing the water (and any sludge or other residue in it) to blow clean through the valve, without having to negotiate any corners. Another slight movement of the handle, closes the valve, steam and water-tight. Rather a different proposition to trying to close a screw valve with the body of same full of grits and scale, which stops the pin from seating properly.

Valve Body

Model Engineer advertisers may be able to supply little castings for the valve body. Also $\frac{7}{8}$ in. rod material can be used. Make the recessed half first; this is the inlet side. Chuck a short bit of rod in the three-jaw; face off, and form a recess $\frac{1}{2}$ in. diameter and $\frac{5}{32}$ in. deep, with a $\frac{1}{2}$ in. D-bit, held in tailstock chuck. This is the easiest and quickest way, though some folk may prefer "boring technique". Now cut back the face very slightly, so as to leave a ring, a bare $\frac{5}{8}$ in. diameter, around the hole (see section). This ring forms a steam and watertight joint with the portface. Part off at $\frac{7}{16}$ in. from the end; reverse in chuck, and turn down a bare $\frac{9}{32}$ in. length to $\frac{5}{8}$ in. diameter. Use a tool with a rounded-off tip, so as to leave a radius at the end of the cut.

The parting tool should have left the true centre on the piece of metal. At $\frac{1}{8}$ in. from this, make a centre-pop and chuck the piece in the four-jaw with the pop-mark running truly. Open it out with a centre-drill, and drill right through into the recess, with No. 30 drill. Turn down a bare $\frac{1}{4}$ in. length to $\frac{3}{8}$ in. diameter, using the rounded-off tool again; then, with an ordinary knife-tool, turn down a bare $\frac{3}{16}$ in. length to $\frac{1}{4}$ in. diameter, and screw $\frac{1}{4}$ in. by 40. If castings are used, they will be of the correct shape, and there won't be all this fallal to bother about. Never mind about the holes for the screws yet, nor filing the outside to shape as shown.

Chuck the bit of rod again, face off truly, and turn down $\frac{5}{32}$ in. length to $\frac{7}{16}$ in. diameter. Part off at $\frac{5}{16}$ in. from the end; reverse in chuck, and take a $\frac{1}{32}$ in. skim off the face, to true it up. The tool again will indicate true centre; and through this, scribe a line right across the face, also another, parallel to it, but $\frac{1}{16}$ in. away. Scribe another line at right-angles to the first one. On the off-centre line, at $\frac{1}{8}$ in. above and below the horizontal line, make two centre-pops. Chuck in four-jaw with the upper one running truly; open the pop-mark with a centre-drill, and drill through with No. 34 drill. Counterbore with a $\frac{3}{16}$ in. D-bit to $\frac{1}{16}$ in. depth, and poke a $\frac{1}{8}$ in. parallel reamer through the rest of the hole. Rechuck with the lower mark running truly, open as above, and drill through with No. 30 drill. Remove from chuck, open out the other side of the hole for $\frac{1}{8}$ in. depth with $\frac{5}{32}$ in. drill, and tap $\frac{3}{16}$ in. by 40.

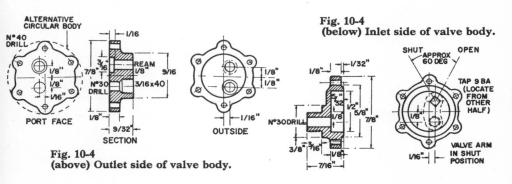

ALTERNATIVE CIRCULAR BODY

Nº 40 DRILL

PORT FACE

SECTION

Fig. 10-4
(above) Outlet side of valve body.

OUTSIDE

Fig. 10-4
(below) Inlet side of valve body.

Nº 30 DRILL

SHUT   APPROX 60 DEG   OPEN

TAP 9 BA (LOCATE FROM OTHER HALF)

VALVE ARM IN SHUT POSITION

Now, on a circle $\frac{23}{32}$ in. diameter ($\frac{5}{64}$ in. from the edge) set out and drill
the six No. 48 holes for the screws. Put the two halves of the valve body
together in such a position that the No. 30 holes line up; done in two wags
of a dog's tail, by putting the No. 30 drill through the two holes, lining up
the two halves of the body with the drill in position, and putting a toolmaker's
clamp over them. Run the No. 48 drill through the holes in the drilled half,
making countersinks on the undrilled half; follow with No. 53, and tap
9 BA. Put the screws in temporarily (steel screws, any head you fancy) and
remove the clamp; then, if you aren't as lazy as I am, file out the metal between
the screws, and make the whole doings look pretty, as per the illustrations.
If you *are* lazy, leavy the body circular; it doesn't make a farthingsworth of
difference to the working of the valve, and as it is hidden between the frames,
on the throatplate of the boiler, nobody will be any the wiser. What the eye
doesn't see, the heart doesn't grieve over!

Valve and Arm

On a bit of $\frac{1}{8}$ in. brass plate about $\frac{1}{2}$ in. long and $\frac{5}{16}$ in. wide, scribe a line
down the middle; and on this, make two centre-pops $\frac{1}{4}$ in. apart. Drill the
top one right through with a $\frac{7}{64}$ in. or No. 36 drill, and either file the hole
square, or drive a square punch through it. The latter could be made from
a bit of $\frac{1}{8}$ in. square silver-steel, as quickly as most folk could file the hole,
and is useful for other things; I keep a collection of various sizes. Drill the
other pop-mark a little way in, with a $\frac{5}{32}$ in. drill, and finish with a $\frac{5}{32}$ in.
D-bit to $\frac{3}{32}$ in. full depth; watch your step here, as there is very little metal to
play with. Finally, file the piece to the outline shown around the holes.

To make the valve, chuck a piece of $\frac{1}{4}$ in. round bronze rod in three-jaw;
turn down $\frac{1}{8}$ in. or so, to $\frac{7}{32}$ in. diameter, face the end, and cut a recess
$\frac{1}{32}$ in. deep, in the face, with a $\frac{1}{8}$ in. D-bit. The exact diameter doesn't matter;
it is only a clearance recess, to help the valve to keep a true face. At $\frac{1}{32}$ in.
from the face, run in a parting-tool, until the rod is a bare $\frac{5}{32}$ in. diameter;
then part off at $\frac{1}{16}$ in. from the face. The $\frac{5}{32}$ in. part should be an easy fit
in the recess in the valve arm.

Lever and Post or Spindle

The lever is filed up from a bit of $\frac{1}{4}$ in. by $\frac{3}{32}$ in. mild-steel strip, just like
a lever or link in the valve gear; the illustration gives dimensions. The small
boss is drilled No. 48, and the larger one $\frac{3}{32}$ in. or No. 42, the hole being
filed or punched square. Note that the square is set over approximately
30 deg.; this is to give the lever an equal movement each side of the vertical

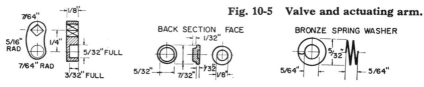

Fig. 10-5   Valve and actuating arm.

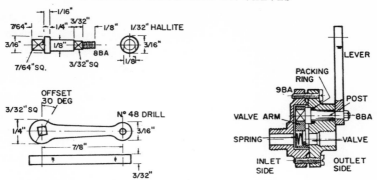

Fig. 10-6 Lever and post and section of valve assembled.

position, when the valve is shut or fully open, as shown diagrammatically, on the illustration of the inlet half of the valve body.

The spindle, or post, as the makers of the full-sized valves call it, is turned from $\frac{1}{4}$ in. round bronze or rustless-steel rod, held in three-jaw. Face the end, and turn down the first $\frac{1}{8}$ in. to a bare $\frac{3}{32}$ in. diameter, screwing it 8 BA. Next, turn down $\frac{11}{32}$ in. diameter, an exact sliding fit in the $\frac{1}{8}$ in. reamed hole in the outlet side of the valve body. Push the rod back into the chuck until only $\frac{3}{32}$ in. of this turned part is projecting from the jaws, and file it to a $\frac{3}{32}$ in. square, using one of the chuck jaws as a guide.

Pull it out again, turn down about $\frac{1}{4}$ in. to $\frac{3}{16}$ in. diameter, and part off at a bare $\frac{3}{16}$ in. from the shoulder. Reverse in chuck, and file a square on the end, $\frac{7}{64}$ in. long, to fit nicely in the square hole in the valve arm. Line up the two squares on the post, or the lever will be all cockeyed when the valve is assembled.

Face the two halves of the body (portface and ring) also the valve, by rubbing on a piece of fine emery or other abrasive cloth, laid business side up on something dead flat. Put a washer of $\frac{1}{32}$ in. Hallite, or similar jointing, made to size shown, on the post behind the collar; push the post through the hole in the valve body (see assembly section) so that the washer and collar enter the counterbore. Put on the lever, and secure with a nut. Put a small bronze spring washer of the kind shown (commercial article, used in radio and electrical fittings) in the recess in the valve arm, and put the spigot of the valve in the recess over the spring; then place the arm in position, with the square on the post entering the square hole in the arm. Put a smear of plumber's jointing around the faced part of the ring on the other half of the body, put the two halves together, secure with the six screws, and Bob's your uncle.

If the lever doesn't move equally both sides of the vertical position, you have got it on the wrong side out, as the kiddies would say; turn it over.

All that is needed to erect, is to drill a $\frac{7}{32}$ in. hole in the centre of the throat plate, $\frac{7}{16}$ in. from the bottom, tap it $\frac{1}{4}$ in by 40 and screw in the spigot of the valve, with a taste of plumber's jointing on the threads.

CHAPTER XI

North-Eastern Compounds

IT IS SURPRISING how few enthusiasts attempt the building of compound locomotives. The old North-Eastern had quite a number of two-cylinder compound engines, notably those designed by Mr. Worsdell, so here are some notes an how to build a small edition: they should appeal especially to readers up in the north-east corner.

I have often been asked for drawings and a few notes on this subject, especially after the success I had in eliminating the faults and failings of the Webb three-cylinder compound engines. So I schemed out a design which should suit almost any type of Worsdell engine. The dimensions on my drawings are suitable for $3\frac{1}{2}$ in. gauge, but can easily be scaled up for 5 in. gauge by anybody who wants to build a North-Eastern two-cylinder compound in that size.

The cylinder casting would be about the same size as that specified for my $3\frac{1}{2}$ in. gauge North-Western *Mabel*, but there the resemblance ends, for this one has the two bores of very different diameter, viz. 1 in. and $1\frac{1}{2}$ in., with pistons and cylinder covers to match, the latter being of the ordinary type, as I have described many times in the past. The ports of the larger (low pressure) cylinder are also larger, with a corresponding increase in the size of the slide valve. The piston rods, valve spindles and glands are the same on both cylinders.

Owing to the difference in working pressure of the two cylinders, the steam chest has to be divided into two sections, each with its own steam entry and with separate exhaust ways through the steam chest wall. There is not much room left for the dividing wall, but though only $\frac{1}{8}$ in. thick, it is $\frac{5}{8}$ in. deep and should keep quite steam-tight against the top and bottom jointing gaskets, provided that the top and bottom of the steam chest are truly faced off when machining. The machining and fitting up of the cylinders presents no more difficulty than those specified for the more usual inside cylinder high pressure engine, the principal difference being that there are two 'entrances to the way out' (says Pat), which are drilled from the sides of the casting and the ends plugged as shown.

In the drawings I have shown a boiler $3\frac{1}{2}$ in. diameter, which is the same as that on my Webb three-cylinder compound and would be quite O.K. for most of the North-Eastern compounds. The boiler has two superheater flues, one at each top corner of the firebox, with a single element in each. The high pressure steam pipe starts from the wet header as usual and proceeds via the first element direct to the smaller chamber of the steam chest. The exhaust goes out through the side passage in the steam chest into an intercepting valve, which is hand operated from a lever in the cab and has two outlets. One of these leads to the bottom of the blastpipe and the other to the element of the second superheater, the other end of which is connected to the larger chamber of the steam chest. These connections can be plainly seen in the front view of the pipes inside the smokebox. The exhaust steam from the larger chamber goes out through the side wall of the steam chest through a pipe connecting it to the bottom of the blastpipe. A hand operated valve on

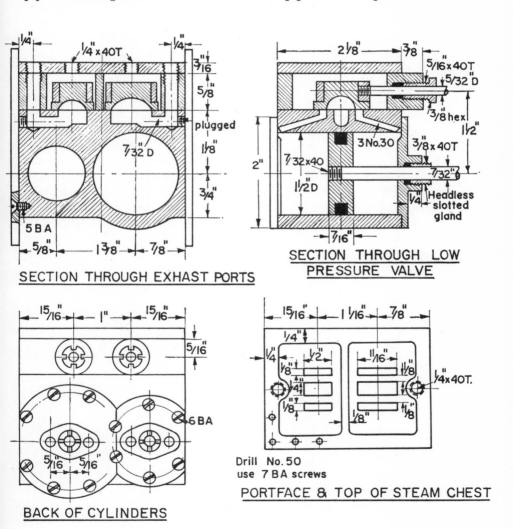

SECTION THROUGH EXHAST PORTS

SECTION THROUGH LOW
PRESSURE VALVE

BACK OF CYLINDERS

Drill No. 50
use 7 BA screws

PORTFACE & TOP OF STEAM CHEST

the side of the smokebox has two pipes, one of which is connected to the high pressure superheater just above the steam chest; the other is connected to the second superheater, which is really an exhaust steam reheater, close to the point where it enters the superheater flue.

Starting from Cold

Now suppose that the engine is blowing off and just about to start, the cylinders not being at full working temperature. Incidentally, they won't be "stone cold" as the steam chest cover is actually the bottom of the smoke-box, as on my *Mabel*, and other similar engines which I have built and therefore the steam chest becomes heated while the engine is getting up steam. The lever operating the intercepting valve is first pulled back, so that the valve closes the port leading to the reheater and the port leading to the blast-pipe is wide open. The starting valve is turned so that the flat plate on its plug bridges the two pipe openings in the body of the valve, as shown in the section. The reversing lever should be in full gear before starting.

On opening the regulator, steam rushes through the high pressure super-heater direct to the smaller (high pressure) chamber of the steam chest. Steam also goes through the connecting pipe to the starting valve through the flat on the plug, thence through the other connecting pipe to the reheater, passing through this and collecting plenty more heat in the process, which then goes down to the larger (low pressure) chamber in the steam chest and builds up to boiler pressure in two wags of a happy dog's tail. With both chambers of the steam chest at boiler pressure, the engine will then start readily, whatever position the cranks happen to be in and as long as the intercepting valve and starting valve are both left in the position mentioned above the engine will work as an ordinary "simple". The exhaust from the high pressure cylinder will take the short cut from the intercepting valve

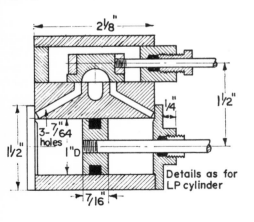

SECTION THROUGH HIGH PRESSURE CYLINDER

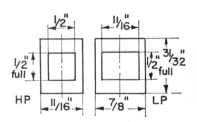

VALVE FACES

direct to the blastpipe and that from the low pressure cylinder will go through its own connection to the same destination. Owing to the difference in the size of the cylinder bores, the exhaust beats won't be all of the same intensity, but will alternate, one loud then one softer, with the usual four beats per revolution of the driving wheels.

After running a little distance to get the cylinders warmed up, the engine can be changed over to compound working by giving the starting valve half a turn and pushing the lever of the intercepting valve forward, so that the outlet to the blastpipe is closed and the outlet to the reheater open. Steam from the boiler then goes via the high pressure superheater to the smaller chamber of the steam chest only, as it cannot pass the starting valve. The exhaust from the high pressure cylinder goes out through the first port in the intercepting valve to the reheater, where it picks up some more heat and all moisture from any condensation is thoroughly dried out of it; then it goes into the larger chamber of the steam chest, does a spot of overtime in the low pressure cylinder and finally escapes to the blastpipe through the side passage in the steam chest wall and the connecting pipe shown in the front view of the pipe connections. From then on there will only be two comparatively soft beats per revolution of the driving wheels, which is plenty to keep the fire going at sufficient intensity to provide lots of steam for compound working.

As long as the high pressure crank does not stop on or very near dead centre, the engine will re-start after a service stop on opening the regulator, same as an ordinary "simple" engine. If, however, it *does* stop with the high pressure crank on dead centre, a flick of the starting valve should let enough steam into the low pressure chamber of the steam chest to allow her to get going again. It does not need much steam against that big piston to persuade it to get a move on.

An Error

There was an error in the big engines for they were sluggish starters and one of the reasons for this was the provision of an automatic intercepting valve. The driver could move it by hand to admit live steam to the low pressure cylinder if the engine stopped with the high pressure crank on either of the dead centres, but he could not keep it there. Consequently, the darn thing shifted itself back to the position for compound working as soon as the engine moved off from the high pressure dead centre and if the engine had been standing long enough for the cylinders to cool off a little, the effect of trying to get away on a mixture of wet steam and water—the engines had no super-heaters—can better be imagined than described!

This state of affairs was found out and corrected on Continental railways, running two-cylinder compounds on the Von Borries system, by fitting non-automatic intercepting valves, so that the driver could start away and run the engine as a "simple" until she became properly warmed up. It was also a big advantage to be able to use live steam in both cylinders if the engine showed signs of running out of breath with a big load on a heavy grade. With the arrangement I have shown here you can work the little engine just as you please.

Incidentally, I schemed out an intercepting valve for my Webb three-cylinder compound engine *Jeanie Deans* one night in the air raid shelter during the latter part of the war. It has worked perfectly ever since it was fitted and the one shown here is just a modification of it to suit the Worsdell type of compound, so it should give the same satisfaction.

Notes on Construction

The methods of machining up and putting together a set of $3\frac{1}{2}$ in. gauge cylinders of the usual type can be used for the little Worsdell, so there is no need of repetition. The steam chest and cover are held in place by screws in the outside walls only; there is no need to put any screws in the dividing wall, provided that the faces are true and the jointing gasket quite sound, but be sure to trim the edges so that the backing does not catch against the slide valves. Also, make certain that there is no obstruction in the exhaust ways at each side of the steam chest.

The intercepting valve is quite a simple job, the whole issue resembling the steam chest of an ordinary single-slide valve cylinder. The body of the valve is made from $\frac{1}{2}$ in. by $\frac{1}{2}$ in. bronze or gunmetal—brass can be used at a pinch—the steam chest part from $\frac{1}{2}$ in. by $\frac{1}{4}$ in. material, slotted out as shown and the cover from $\frac{1}{16}$ in. hard-rolled sheet, which should be true enough to make a steam-tight joint without any machining. The ports are plain round drilled holes, with corresponding holes drilled in the side of the block; these may be tapped to take unions or short pieces of pipe may be silver-soldered in. The slide valve face has no cavity, the back being slotted to take a flat filed near the end of the $\frac{3}{32}$ in. valve spindle, which should be either rustless steel or bronze. A $\frac{3}{16}$ in. fork can be screwed on to the end projecting beyond the gland and connected to a small lever in the cab. To keep the diagrams as simple as possible, I have not shown any fancy joints in the pipework and so builders can fit anything they please; I used plumbers' running joints when assembling *Jeanie*.

There is just one other thing to point out. When assembling the intercepting valve, put a thin flat brass or gunmetal spring between the underside of the cover and the back of the valve, to make sure that the valve is always in close contact with the valve face. If it was accidentally blown off the face, it would be a dickens of a job to get it back again and there is only exhaust pressure to keep the faces in contact.

The starting valve can be made from $\frac{5}{16}$ in. round or hexagon gunmetal or bronze, first drilled number 24 and a $\frac{5}{32}$ in. parallel reamer put right through it, so that the bore is parallel throughout. The end is closed by a plug pressed in and soldered over, the same as I specify for the pump cylinders of little mechanical lubricators. The two union nipples for the 'short-circuiting' pipes are silver-soldered in and go through two corresponding holes in the side of the smokebox, with a distance piece of flat brass

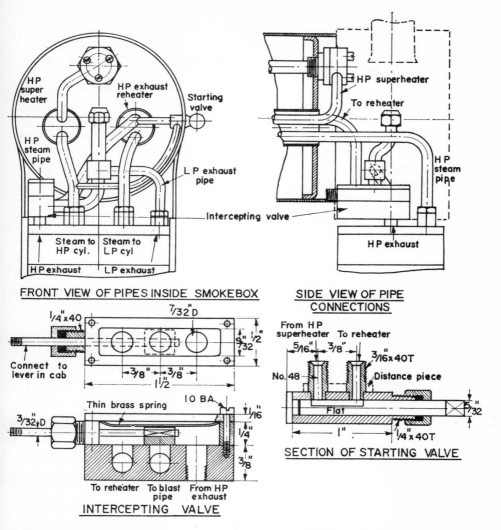

FRONT VIEW OF PIPES INSIDE SMOKEBOX

SIDE VIEW OF PIPE CONNECTIONS

INTERCEPTING VALVE

SECTION OF STARTING VALVE

between the valve and the smokebox and locknuts inside the smokebox. The valve plug is just a piece of $\frac{5}{32}$ in. rustless steel or phosphor-bronze, which should be an exact fit in the valve body. It has a flat filed or milled on it, so that when in the position shown in the drawing the flat part forms a connection between the two nipples, allowing steam to pass, while half a turn of the plug closes both openings. The outer end of the plug is squared and fits in a squared socket on the end of the handrail, the outer end of which passes through the cab front and is furnished with a little hand-wheel or handle inside the cab. As the handrail is perfectly free to turn in the knobs on the boiler, the valve is easily operated by turning the wheel or handle.

For lubricating the cylinders, a "mini-check valve" should be screwed into the front wall of each chamber of the steam chest. A small mechanical lubricator can then be fitted in front of the cylinders and a tee-piece fitted in the delivery pipe. The two outlets of the tee-piece are then connected to the check valves by $\frac{3}{32}$ in. pipes and unions, so that each chamber of the steam chest gets its share of the oil delivered.

I have shown the cylinder covers arranged for guide bars at the sides, but top-and-bottom bars may be substituted if desired and any type of connecting rod preferred by the builder fitted. As to the valve gear, Worsdells' engines on the North-Eastern had Joy valve gear and this would be most suitable for the little one. I described a $3\frac{1}{2}$ in. gauge Joy valve gear many years ago for a North-Eastern "R" class 4-4-0, which was called "Miss 10 to 8". A number of Webb compounds have been built to my notes, so I hope that there will be a few Worsdells to keep them company.

CHAPTER XII

Mini Steam Engines

MANY BUILDERS OF small locomotives are interested in vertical-boilered engines, so maybe a few notes on this subject won't come amiss. One of the first engines to run on an American railroad had a vertical boiler, the celebrated *Tom Thumb*, which worked on what is now part of the Baltimore and Ohio system. Naturally, it did nothing worth writing home about, but being such a little thing and its builders having no locomotive experience to talk about to draw upon, it was really remarkable that it was able to run at all. Other odd engines have been built from time to time with vertical boilers, but it was eventually found out that this type of boiler was not really suited to locomotive work and they have all long since disappeared.

The vertical-boildered engine has also been tried out in this country. I used to have an old book showing a picture of one and some particulars of its anatomy. The book went into ecstasies over it, calling it a completely efficient locomotive, especially suitable for contractors' use. Among its peculiar features were wheels with double flanges, so that the top of the rail was gripped and, as the average contractors' railway is anything but true to gauge or level, the wheels were not pressed on to the axles, but were allowed to move sideways between rubber collars. Some form of differential gear was evidently provided, as it was stated that the engine would negotiate sharp curves without any wheel slip on either side. The drive was by keys in the axles and corresponding keyways in the wheel bosses; according to the illustration, the four wheels were coupled by ordinary coupling rods.

The engine itself looked rather like an ordinary two-cylinder launch engine and was located transversely just in front of the boiler. It didn't drive the leading axle direct; a small gear wheel was fitted at each end of the crankshaft, meshing with two larger ones on the leading axle. The book didn't say how the differential drive was allowed for.

The boiler was described as being of the "new firebox with hanging tubes design", the latter presumably being field-tubes, and was arranged vertically, to prevent the crown of the firebox being uncovered by the water when either end of the engine was lifted, due to sudden variations in the level of the line. It was also claimed that this boiler possessed all the advantages of the locomotive type boiler, was a better steamer and was much cheaper and easier to construct and maintain. There was a plate on the side

179

frame, bearing the inscription "Chaplin's patent"; but as the engine was built long before Charlie's time, we can't blame *him* for the design!

Incidentally, the last locomotive to do regular service on the old broad gauge was a four-wheeled engine with a vertical boiler. This operated for quite a number of years at one of the South Wales docks, after the broad gauge had ceased to exist on the rest of the Great Western system.

Small Variations

There doesn't seem to be any reason why a 3½ in. or 5 in. gauge vertical-boilered four-wheeler should not be a complete success. There are quite a number of modern ones still at work. For example, the firm who was responsible for the Sentinel steam waggons brought out a steam shunting engine as a competitor to the diesels when the latter first came into vogue and had it not been for the craze of so-called modernisation and the idea that steam power was old-fashioned, there might have been an exceedingly good market for them.

The boiler was a small vertical high-pressure generator of the water tube type and could be fired either by oil or any kind of solid fuel; the boiler feed was automatic.

A small high efficiency engine drove the axles through gearing. I know of one firm at least who considered the Sentinel geared locomotives to be superior to the diesels in reliability, maintenance and performance. Before the closing of the line, a steam railcar with a similar engine, boiler and geared drive worked the Southern line between Brighton and the Dyke very successfully. I remember quite well seeing it one Sunday morning pass the back of our house on its way down from the makers and it was going at quite a good speed.

The frames of a little-four-wheeler could be much the same as those I specified for *Tich*, or outside frames could be used like those of a tender with four wheels instead of six. The same sort of springing could be used; with outside frames the wheels could be coupled by rods working on outside cranks. The boiler should be of large diameter, as it isn't very high, and have a water space around the firebox; but as a single flue wouldn't be much good for locomotive purposes, a nest of small tubes should be provided, like those on the test boiler which I described many moons ago. The top tubeplate should be, in the case of a 3½ in. gauge job, about ¾ in. below the top of the boiler barrel and a snap-on lid made from steel with a deep flange would make a nobby smokebox.

The steam pipe, which could be attached to the top tubeplate by a flange and screws, should have three or four coils in it, right over the top of the flue tubes, the regulator being an ordinary screw-down valve outside the boiler shell. The usual fittings, such as steam and water gauges, feed clacks and so on, could be attached like those on a stationary vertical boiler. Firing could be by oil or coal; if oil is preferred, a burner like those fitted to Primus stoves could be used and these are commercially obtainable, saving the trouble of making a burner. Alternatively, one of the propane burners could be used.

Engine and Transmission

The engine can be arranged vertically, horizontally or diagonally, as preferred. If vertical, it could be made up from one of the sets of castings advertised for launch or stationary engines and mounted on suitable brackets. Alternatively, the "works" of one of my inside cylinder engines could be turned up on end and used, complete with its valve gear, a bracket at each end taking the place of the side frames of an ordinary locomotive.

Where the vertically-arranged engine is used, I recommend a geared drive, a pinion on the end of the crankshaft meshing with a larger gear wheel on one of the axles. Another alternative would be to mount the engine longitudinally, as in the usual type of motor car, and drive through a worm and wheel. In that case, a small single-cylinder engine with loose eccentric gear would be found quite powerful enough to haul one or two passengers on $3\frac{1}{2}$ in. gauge.

With inclined or horizontal cylinders, the drive may be either geared or direct, as preferred. If geared, a pair of cylinders $\frac{5}{8}$ in. bore and $1\frac{1}{4}$ in. stroke would be ample for a $3\frac{1}{2}$ in gauge engine. They should be located ahead of the leading axle and attached to the frames in the same way as those on a conventional outside cylinder locomotive and drive on to a cross shaft located ahead of the driving axle and having an outside crank at each side, on which the big-ends of the connecting rods would work. The eccentrics for operating the valve gear would be mounted on the shaft and it should have a gear wheel in the middle, with a corresponding gear wheel on the driving axle; but an idler gear would have to be used between them, as the driving wheels would prevent the cross shaft being placed near enough to the driving axle to allow the gears to mesh direct. The eccentric for driving the boiler feed pump should be fitted on the leading or driving axle and not on the cross shaft.

A very good vertical boilered locomotive could be made by building a *Tich* chassis and fitting it with a vertical boiler instead of a locomotive type boiler. The boiler shell should be the full width between the frames, with a $\frac{3}{16}$ in water space around the firebox. The boiler tubes could be $\frac{5}{16}$ in diameter, which would be quite permissible, as there would be no risk of them becoming choked with ashes or cinders. Either coal or a Primus burner or a propane burner could be used for firing.

A Mini Steam Engine

Here is a farewell design, which should appeal to any reader who has a young hopeful interested in steam engines. I remember once, the boy who lived next door, the son of a bobby, brought in to show me a weeny steam engine which he had acquired and asked if I could make it go. It was a pretty little thing, an oscillating cylinder marine engine, complete with two eccentrics and link motion, like those used in the old paddle steamers; it was mounted on a plinth of glazed tiles of very small size. I examined it closely and found that it was apparently not intended for working under steam, the motion being far too flimsy, especially the curved link, which looked as though it would crumple up under the slightest stress.

The lad was somewhat disappointed, as he apparently thought that I could make *anything* work, so I determined right away to make a similar size engine with an oscillating cylinder that *would* go. The accompanying drawings show how I did the trick. The cylinder was nothing more nor less than the pump cylinder of one of my mechanical lubricators, the ram or plunger being enlarged to $\frac{1}{8}$ in. diameter and forming the piston. No gland or cover was needed, a little brass big-end being screwed direct on the end of the ram. The cylinder support and one of the bearings for the crankshaft was made from a single piece of $\frac{1}{2}$ in. by $\frac{1}{8}$ in. brass angle, the ports and the hole for the trunion being drilled at one end, as shown. This was mounted on a base made from 18 gauge steel, bent to a channel shape, flanges being left at the bottom by which the base was attached to the stand on which the whole box of tricks was mounted. The other crankshaft bearing was bent up from sheet brass and screwed to the top of the support.

The crankshaft itself was made from $\frac{3}{32}$ in. round steel, with a disc crank the same as I specified for the lubricators, allowing for a stroke of $\frac{7}{32}$ in. It was pressed on to the shaft, the other end of which carried a 1 in. diameter flywheel and a $\frac{1}{4}$ in. diameter grooved pulley turned from the solid. The steam and exhaust pipes were silver-soldered into little counterbores at the back of the ports, the steam pipe being $\frac{3}{32}$ in. diameter and the exhaust $\frac{1}{8}$ in. A displacement lubricator $\frac{1}{4}$ in. diameter was fitted on the steam pipe, midway between the cylinder and the boiler.

The Boiler

The boiler was a piece of 22 gauge copper tube $1\frac{1}{2}$ in. diameter and $1\frac{3}{4}$ in. high, not including the firebox. The top and bottom plates were of 18 gauge copper, flanged and silver-soldered in. The centre flue was $\frac{1}{2}$ in. diameter and 22 gauge, silver-soldered into holes in both top and bottom plates and projecting far enough to form a chimney. The circular firebox was rolled up from 18 gauge soft mild steel on my Diacro 12 in. bench roller, which made such an accurate job of the circle that it ran quite truly when I chucked it to counterbore it for a depth of $\frac{3}{32}$ in., so that the boiler could sit in the counterbore. A row of $\frac{5}{16}$ in. holes was drilled all around, close to the bottom, for admission of air to the spirit lamp and three more were drilled close to the top, to give extra ventilation to the lamp when starting up from all cold. The exhaust steam, which was discharged into the chimney, kept a current of air flowing through the firebox when the engine was working.

Little bronze bushes tapped $\frac{5}{32}$ in. by 40 were silver-soldered into the top plate and side of the boiler and I had one larger bush tapped $\frac{3}{16}$ in by 40 for the safety valve, which was of the same type that I always specified for locomotives. This had a $\frac{1}{8}$ in. ball on a $\frac{3}{32}$ in. seating and was pressed to 20 p.s.i. The steam regulator was a weeny plug cock, with a number 53 hole through the plug. I didn't fit a little wheel valve, as the boy's fingers weren't exactly as fire-proof as my own, and the valve naturally became very hot when the boiler was in steam; but he was able to operate the plug cock quite safely by means of an extension handle fitting over the cock handle. There was a swan-necked pipe going from the plug cock to the superheater, the

BSC'S Mini steam plant.

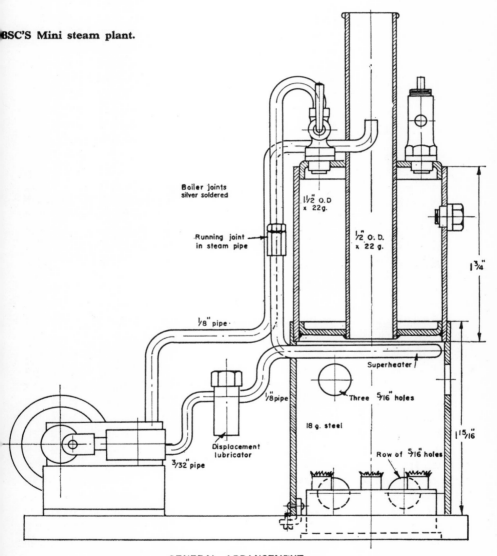

Boiler joints
silver soldered

Running joint
in steam pipe

$\frac{1}{8}$" pipe

$1\frac{1}{2}$ O.D
x 22g.

$\frac{1}{2}$" O. D.
x 22 g.

$1\frac{3}{4}$"

$\frac{1}{8}$"pipe

Superheater

Three $\frac{5}{16}$" holes

18 g. steel

$1\frac{15}{16}$"

Displacement
lubricator

$\frac{3}{32}$" pipe

Row of $\frac{5}{16}$" holes

GENERAL ARRANGEMENT

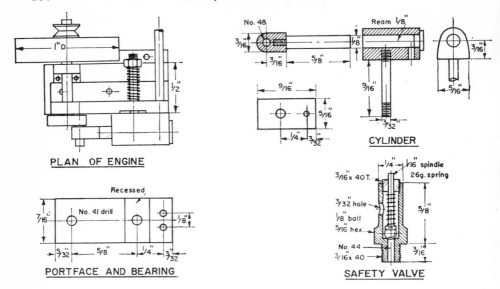

PLAN OF ENGINE

CYLINDER

PORTFACE AND BEARING

SAFETY VALVE

latter being a piece of $\frac{1}{8}$ in. copper tube entering the upper part of the firebox and running around it just below the tubeplate, emerging through the oval hole where it went in and from thence it went to one side of the cylinder lubricator.

The exhaust pipe from the cylinder went up the side of the boiler and was bent over to enter the chimney, as shown. At first, I fitted a test cock in the bush on the side of the boiler, but I replaced it with a plain screwed plug in case it became inadvertently turned on when the boiler was in steam, resulting in the boy scalding his fingers. When filling the boiler, the plug was removed and water was poured in through the safety valve bush until it ran out of the hole. The spirit lamp had three small wicks and the whole box of tricks was mounted on an 18 gauge sheet steel stand.

When the boiler was filled with hot water, I was able to raise steam in about a minute and the tiny engine went at a tremendous speed when all out, buzzing like a hornet. It is hardly necessary to add that the boy was delighted with it.

L.B.S.C. LOCOMOTIVES

"L.B.S.C." has passed on a wealth of practical experience in many hundreds of articles in MODEL ENGINEER, and most of the locomotives listed below have been "written up" at one time or another. All are, except where otherwise stated, coal-fired, passenger-hauling models. You are advised to consult the current PLANS HANDBOOK No 3 for latest prices and amendments.

L.O.	**50**	**"SIR MORRIS DE COWLEY." 1¼ in. gauge 4-6-2 tender locomotive.** (Vols. 54-55). This free-lance engine is suitable for spirit or coal firing.
Sheet	1	General arrangement, frames, bogie and cylinders etc.
	2	Boiler and smokebox details, mechanical feed pump, etc.
	3	Cab and running boards, and tender details.
L.O.	**51**	**"MOLLYETTE." 1¼ in. gauge 0-6-0 L.M.S. tank locomotive.** (Vol. 89). Fitted with single cylinder and spirit-fired boiler.
Sheet	1	General arrangement, cab and tank construction and burner.
	2	Arrangement of frame showing cylinder and boiler in position.
	3	Cylinder, axles, valve gear, lubricator and coupling rods.
L.O.	**52**	**"BAT." 1¼ in. gauge 4-4-0 locomotive and tender.** (Vols. 81-83). This engine has outside cylinders, and is based on the S.R. "Schools" class. It is suitable for spirit or coal-firing.
Sheet	1	General arrangement, frames, cylinders, valve gear, lubricator, guide yokes.
	2	Boiler details, cab arrangement, tender, etc.
L.O.	**53**	**"JULIET." 1¾ in. gauge 0-4-0 tank locomotive of freelance design.** (Vols. 95-97). Suitable for spirit or coal firing.
L.O.	**54**	**"CHINGFORD EXPRESS." 1¾ in. gauge 0-6-0T. of L.N.E.R. type.** (Vol. 90). A simple spirit-fired model with single inside cylinder. Drawing gives full details of frames, wheels, boiler, valve gear, lubricator, etc.
L.O.	**55**	**"DOT." 1¾ in. gauge 4-6-0 model based on the Stanier class "5."** (Vols. 101-102). It is spirit-fired, and has outside cylinders and slip-eccentric valve gear.
Sheet	1	General arrangement, frames, beams, coupled wheels, bogie details. Guide yokes, connecting rods, cross heads, eccentrics, valve gear details.
	2	Cylinder details, lubricator, steam and exhaust fittings, smokebox saddle. Boiler details, sections, backhead, regulator, blower, safety valves.
	3	Tender, frames, wheels, beams, axles, hand pump.
L.O.	**56**	**"DIANA." 1¾ in. gauge 4-6-2 coal-fired freelance Pacific model.** (Vol. 102).
Sheet	1	General outline, frames, wheels, axles, axleboxes, bogie frames, coupling rods, etc. Valve gear details, guide yokes, crossheads, and pony truck details.
	2	Cylinder details, smokebox, steam and exhaust connections, safety valve, lubricator and regulator. Boiler feed pump, stay and eccentrics, diagram of pipe connections, ashpan fixing, fire box bracket, and cab footplate.
	3	Full boiler details with sections, combustion chamber, etc., backhead details, ashpan and grate.
L.O.	**57**	**"SOUTHERN MAID." 2½ in. gauge. A simple 0-6-0 S.R. type tender locomotive.** (Vols. 75-78). Coal-fired with outside cylinders.
Sheet	1	General arrangement, frames, wheels, coupling rods, mechanical and hand pump, etc.
	2	Cylinders, boiler, smokebox, valve gear and steam connections.
	3	Tender details, frames, wheels, axles, loco cab details
L.O.	**58**	**"VICTORIA." 2½ in. gauge simple single-cylinder 0-4-4 tank locomotive.** Oil-fired.
Sheet	1	General arrangement, frames, oil burners, boiler etc.
	2	Wheels, cylinder, valve gear, regulator, cab details, etc.
L O.	**59**	**"AUSTERE ADA." 2½ in. gauge, 2-8-0 "Austerity" type tender locomotive.** (Vols. 88-91). With outside cylinders and Walshaerts valve gear.
Sheet	1	General arrangement, frames, pony truck, wheels, axles, etc.
	2	Cylinders, valve gear, mechanical lubricator details.
	3	Boiler details, smokebox, cab arrangements.

| | 4 | Tender details, frames, pump, etc., and boiler backhead details. |
| | 5 | Mechanical feed pump, platework, cab and tender. |

L.O. 60 "OLYMPIADE." 2½ in. gauge 4-6-0 tender locomotive based on the L.M.S. 5XP type. (Vol. 79). Three cylinders and Walschaerts valve gear.

Sheet	1	General arrangement, frames and bogie details.
	2	Cylinder details, steam pipe connections, mechanical lubricator.
	3	Arrangements and details of inside and outside valve gears.
	4	Boiler and smokebox details and boiler fittings.
	5	Tender details, frames, pump, etc.

L.O. 61 "PURLEY GRANGE." 2½ in. gauge 4-6-0 tender locomotive based on the G.W.R. "Grange" class. (Vols. 76-78). Outside cylinders, with inside Stephenson link valve gear.

Sheet	1	General arrangement, frames, wheels, bogie, coupling rods, etc.
	2	Cylinder and valve gear details and mechanical pump.
	3	Boiler, smokebox, lubricator, reverser, regulator, etc.
	4	Tender, frames, beams, wheels, hand pump, cab details.

L.O. 62 "JULIET." 3½ in. gauge 0-4-0 tank locomotive. (Vols. 95-97). A free-lance contractor's type of engine, with outside cylinders and either slip-eccentric or Stephenson valve gear.

Sheet	1	General arrangement, frames, wheels, axles, buffer beam details.
	2	Cylinder details, coupling rods, displacement lubricator, guide yokes.
	3	Valve gear, mechanical pump.
	4	Stephenson's link motion arrangement, lubricator and reverser.
	5	Boiler details, smokebox, hand pump.
	6	Cab details, pipe connections, boiler fittings.

L.O. 63 "JEANIE DEANS." 3½ in. gauge, 2-2-2-0 L.N.W.R. compound locomotive. Three cylinders.

Sheet	1	General arrangement.
	2	Frames, buffer beams, wheels, axleboxes, crank-axle, L.P. motion plate.
	3	H.P. and L.P. motion arrangement and reverser.
	4	H.P. and L.P. cylinder details and valve gear, motion plate, etc.
	5	Pipe connections, intercepting valve, drain cocks, etc.
	6	Boiler details, ashpan, grate, regulator and smokebox.
	7	Footplate arrangement, front view, running boards, etc.
	8	Tender details, hand pump, etc.

L.O. 64 "JULIET No. 2." 3½ in. gauge 0-4-0 tank locomotive. This model is similar to L.O. 62, but is fitted with Baker valve gear.

Sheet	1	Arrangement of lococmotive, main frames and driving crankpins.
	2	Assembly and details of Baker valve gear.
	3	Cylinders and details, eccentric rods, return cranks, reverse lever and connections.
	4	Side tanks, injector connections, injector steam valve, erection of lubricator, exhaust pipes, steam pipes and oil check valve, crossheads and ashpan.
	5	Buffer beams, hornblocks, axles, wheels, axleboxes, hornstays, leading crankpin and washer arrangement, also details of mechanical water feed pump and details of mechanical lubricator.

For boiler and cab details, customers are advised to purchase sheets 5 and 6 of L.O. 62.

L.O. 66 "HIELAN LASSIE." 3½ in. gauge 4-6-2 tender locomotive, based on the Thompson rebuild of the L.N.E.R. Pacific. (Vols. 94-97, reprinted Vols. 121-126). Three cylinders, with choice of piston or slide valves, and Walschaerts or Baker valve gear.

Sheet	1	General arrangement, frames, horns, etc.
	2	Wheels, axles, crank-axle, mechanical feed pump.
	3	Bogie details and trailing axleboxes.
	4	Cylinder details, side valve and piston valve.
	5	Walschaerts valve gear details.
	6	Baker valve gear details and reverser.
	7	Mechanical lubricator and pipe connections.

	8	Boiler and smokebox details.
	9	Boiler fittings and tender hand pump.
	10	Cab and running boards, backhead arrangements.
	11	Tender details with brake gear, etc.

L.O. **67** **"RAINHILL." 3½ in. gauge 0-2-2 locomotive and tender based on Stephenson's famous "Rocket."** (Vol. 84).

Sheet **1** General arrangement, frames, wheels, axles, mechanical pump, cylinders.

2 Boiler details, tender details, hand pump and valve gear.

L.O. **68** **"MOLLY." 3½ in. gauge 0-6-0 tank locomotive.** (Vols. 85-87). Standard L.M.S. class "3F" shunting engine, with inside cylinders and Stephenson valve gear.

Sheet **1** General arrangement, frames, wheels, motion plate, etc.

2 Cylinders, crank-axle.

3 Valve gear, reverser and brake details.

4 Boiler details and hand pump.

5 Running boards, splashers and cab details.

L.O. **70** **"MAISIE." 3½ in. gauge 4-4-2 locomotive and tender.** (Vols. 72-76). Based on the famous Ivatt G.N.R. "Atlantic" type, this model has outside cylinders, with inside valve gear, and a wide-firebox boiler with alternative designs.

Sheet **1** General arrangement and frames.

2 Buffer and drag beams, and bogie details.

3 Boiler details, etc.

4 Cylinder and valve gear details.

5 Smokebox, mechanical pump, lubricator, etc.

6 Tender details, pump, running boards and splashers, etc.

7 Modified boiler and superheater layout plus Doris type lubricator.

L.O. **71** **"PETROLEA." 3½ in. gauge 2-4-0 locomotive and tender.** (Vols. 89-94). This model is based on Holden's G.E.R. design and has inside cylinders with Stephenson valve gear.

Sheet **1** General arrangement, frames, buffer beams, horns, coupling rods.

2 Wheels, cylinders, crank-axle, motion plate details.

3 Valve arrangement, reverser details, cylinder drain cocks, hand pump.

4 Boiler fittings, regulator, grate, etc.

5 Lubricator details, tender brake arrangement and details, oil burner.

6 Engine brakes, running boards, splashers and cab details.

7 Full tender details, alternative for oil burning loco.

L.O. **72** **"DORIS." 3½ in. gauge 4-6-0 locomotive and tender.** (Vols. 98-101). Based on the famous L.M.S. Stanier class "5 MT," this model has outside piston-valve cylinders and Walschaerts valve gear.

Sheet **1** General arrangement, frames, buffer beams, bogie bolster, pump stay, etc.

2 Driving and bogie wheels. axles, bogie details, mechanical pump, horns, etc.

3 Piston valve and cylinder details, mechanical lubricator.

4 Valve gear arrangement and reverser.

5 Boiler details, etc.

6 Regulator arrangement, superheater and main steam pipe arrangement, grate and ashpan, lubricator, check valve and pipe arrangement.

7 Backhead arrangement, injector, whistle valve, bypass valve, top feed fitting, delivery clack valve, everlasting blowdown valve, washout plug, backhead clack, snifting valve, injector steam valve, water gauge.

8 Running boards, cab steps, etc.

9 Tender arrangement, and tender frames, etc.

10 Tender details.

L.O. **73** **"PAMELA." 3½ in. gauge 4-6-2 locomotive and tender of free-lance design.** (Vols. 102-104). Outside piston-valve cylinders and Walschaerts valve gear. The boiler is of the wide-firebox type with combustion chamber.

Sheet 1 General arrangement and frames.
2 Cylinders and motion.
3 Smokebox and superheater.
4 Boiler, firebox and saftey valve.
5 Steam pipe assembly and regulator.
6 Boiler erection, backhead fittings, exhaust pipe assembly.
7 Tender and details.
8 Tender pump, brake column, drawgear, brake gear.

L.O. **80** **"MAID OF KENT." 5 in. gauge locomotive and tender.** (Vols. 97-101). This model is based on the Southern Railway Maunsell "L.1" class. It can be built with inside or outside cylinders and Stephenson valve gear, or with inside cylinders and Joy valve gear.

Sheet 1 General arrangement, frames, buffer beams, bogie bolster, etc.
2 Cylinder details, crank-axle, hornblocks, etc.
2a Bogie details, coupled wheels, coupling rods, etc.
3 Stephenson's valve gear arrangement and details of motion plate, etc.
4 Outside cylinder details, guide bars, motion brackets and connecting rods.
5 Joy valve gear arrangement and details, motion plate.
6 Mechanical lubricator, drive and reverser details.
6a Link motion, valve gear and details, feed pump.
7 Boiler details, superheater.
8 Backhead arrangement, whistle and turret valve, injector, steam valve, steam gauge syphon, safety valve, injector bypass valve, blowdown valve, and alternative snifting valve, pipe connections, clack valves, washout plug.
8a Pipe connections for outside cylinders, grate and ashpan, blast pipe, whistle and tender connections.
9 Footplate, cab, steps, etc.
10 Tender arrangement and frames.
11 Tender details.
12 Steam brake details.
13 Revised Stephenson valve gear for the inside-cylinder engine. By K. N. Harris.
14 Revised valve gear for the outside-cylinder version, with feed pump details.
15 Further details for outside-cylinder version.

L.O. **81** **"BRITANNIA." 3½ in. gauge 4-6-2 locomotive and tender.** (Vols. 104-109). A large and powerful model based on the B.R. class "7" Pacific. Outside piston-valve cylinders, Walschaerts valve gear and wide firebox boiler.

Sheet 1 General arrangement.
2 Mainframe details, stays, buffer beams, hornblocks, coupled wheels, axles, axleboxes, coupling rods, pump and lubricator eccentrics and crankpins.
3 Bogie frames, wheels, axleboxes, equalising beams, springs, bogie slide assembly and details.
4 Pony truck frame, pony axleboxes, wheels and axles, roller brackets, king-pins, screw couplings, buffers, erection of pony truck and pump.
5 Position of cylinders, details of cylinders, piston valves, etc., mechanical lubricator and details.
6 Guide bars, crossheads, connecting rods, guide bar brackets, valve crossheads, elevation and plan of valve gear, combination levers and union links.
7 L.H. and R.H. motion brackets, expansion links and die blocks, radius rods, position of motion brackets.
8 Reversing screw and nut, L.H. lifting and reversing arms, R.H. lifting arm, return cranks, lifting links eccentric rods, steam brake arrangement and details.
9 Boiler and firebox.
10 Firebox (further details) and smokebox.
11 Footplate fittings.
12 Injector, grate and ashpan, pipe connections.
13 Whistle valve, blower valve, alternative slide valve regulator, steam gauge.

14 Firehole door and details. Safety valves , blowdown valve and clackbox.
15 Cab and superstructure details.
16 Cab brackets, footplate, injector water valve, reversing gear shaft and universal joints and reversing gear.
17 Pipe connections, cylinder drains, hand pump clacks.
18 Tender and details.
19 Tender details, arrangement of driver's brake valve.
20 Tender details, hand pump, wheels and axles.
21 Tender details, brake gear, pull rods, buffers, steps, grabrail.

L.O. 82 **Oil Burner.** One sheet giving three alternative types, with oil tank and control valve.
L.O. 83 **Holcroft Valve Gear for 2¼ in. gauge.** One sheet giving full details of links, etc.
L.O. 84 **Westinghouse Brake.** One sheet giving full details of pump, reservoir, brake valve and engine and tender brake cylinders.
L.O. 86 **Vertical Test Boiler.** One sheet showing vertical cross-section of boiler, firebox tubeplate and arrangement of superheater.
L.O. 87 See under "Workshop Equipment." No. W.E.10.
L.O. 88 **Cylinders for 5 in. gauge "Doris."** (Full size).
L.O. 89 **"TITFIELD THUNDERBOLT." 3½ in. or 5 in. gauge 0-4-2 locomotive based on the famous "Lion" (No. 57) of the Liverpool and Manchester Railway.** (Vols. 108-110).
Sheet 1 General arrangement, frames, axleboxes, trailing wheels and axle, coupled wheels, axles and springs (3½ in. and 5 in.).
2 Motion plate, crank-axle, eccentrics, coupling and connecting rods, guide bars, crossheads (3½ in. and 5 in.).
3 Gab motion, cylinder arrangement, eccentric straps and rods and slide valve (3½ in.).
3a Cylinder, steam chest, guide bars, motion plates, buckles and spindles, trailing horns (5 in.).
4 Eccentric valve gear, eccentric strap and rod. Rocker assembly, reverse lever details (3½ in. and 5 in.).
4a Gab motion, rocker shaft, eccentric straps, rods and gabs, lubricators, oil pump (5 in.).
5 Crosshead pump and details, mechanical lubricator and details, and arrangement for 3½ in. gauge engines (3½ in. and 5 in.).
6 Arrangement and details of boiler, arrangement of superheater and regulator (3½ in.).
6a Arrangement and details of boiler (5 in.).
7 Arrangement and details of smokeboxes, arrangement and details of safety valves (3½ in. and 5 in.).
7a Arrangement and details of superheater, arrangement of regulator and details (5 in.).
8 Arrangement and details of boiler fittings, including steam gauge, whistle valve, water gauge, injector steam valve, injector, location of injector, hand pump clack, longitudinal stays, etc. (3½ in. and 5 in.).
9 Diagram of pipe connections, ashpan and grate, brackets for firebox shell, smokebox and barrel. Steam and oil pipe connections, pipe brackets on drag beam. Front coupling, steps, oil check valve, fenders, footplate, buffers, splashers, drawbar, bracket, by-pass valve, oil check valve, etc. (3½ in. and 5 in.).
10 Details of tender and water pump.
11 Brake gear details.

L.O. 90 **"NETTA." 3½ in. gauge 0-8-0 locomotive and tender, N.E.R. Worsdell design.** (Vols. 110-113). Outside cylinders with inside Stephenson valve gear. Numbers L.O. 91-94 are 5in., 2½ in., 1¾ in. and 1¼ in. gauge versions of this engine—in each case the general arrangement drawing (L.O. 90 sheet 1) is the same.
Sheet 1 General arrangement of engine and tender (for all gauges).
2 Main frames and details.
3 Cylinders, coupling rods, connecting rods, guide bar brackets, crossheads.
4 Reversing lever and rod, junction block and oil check, steam and exhaust flanges, mechanical lubricator and details, pipe and lubricator assembly, lubricator drive arrangement, blast nozzle.

	5	Arrangement of link motion, valve gear details.
	6	Arrangement of boiler and details.
	7	Arrangement of smokebox and details, regulator and superheater and details.
	8	Footplate fittings and footplate arrangements, arrangement of grate and ashpan and details.
	9	Diagram of pipe connections, by-pass valve, cab side and roof, running boards, buffers, tender drawhook and coupling, engine and tender coupling.
	10	Section of tender, tender details and brake work.

L.O. **91** **"NETTA." 5 in. gauge.**
Sheet

1. (See L.O. 90, sheet 1).
2. Main frames, frame details, wheels, axles, hornblocks and axleboxes, coupling rods, crankpins.
3. Arrangement of outside motion, guide bars, crossheads, cylinders, guide bar brackets, connecting rods.
4. Steam and exhaust pipes, lubricator, steam pipe assembly, oil check valve, exhaust pipe assembly, blast and blower nozzle, cylinder lubricator and details, feed pump and details.
5. Arrangement of link motion and details, lubricator drive arrangement.
6. Reversing lever and details, safety valves, injector steam valve, blower valve and nipple, smokebox.
7. Arrangement of boiler and details.
8. Arrangement of regulator, superheater and boiler details.
9. Arrangement of grate and ashpan and details, regulator and details, boiler expansion brackets.
10. Footplate fittings, cab sides and roof, diagram of pipe connections, whistle, by-pass valve, injector steam valve, blowdown valve, boiler feed clacks, running boards.
11. Tender details.

L.O. **92** **"NETTA." 2½ in. gauge.**
Sheet

1. (See L.O. 90, sheet 1).
2. Main frames, pump and frame stays, hornblocks and axleboxes, coupled wheels and crankpins, valve gear and pump eccentrics, axles, buffer beams, crossheads, guide bar brackets.
3. Coupling rods, feed pump, lubricator and details, cylinders and details, arrangement of pump, connecting rods.
4. Arrangement of valve gear and details, lubricator drive.
5. Pipe and lubricator assembly, smokebox and details, blower valve and nipple, reverser and details.
6. Boiler and details, regulator and superheater and details.
7. Arrangement of grate and ashpan and details, footplate fittings.
8. Running boards, etc., whistle, by-pass valve, arrangement of pipes, cab sides and roof, injector water valve.
9. Tender and details.

L.O. **93** **"NETTA." 1¾ in. gauge.**
Sheet

1. (See L.O. 90, sheet 1).
2. Main frames, crankpins, loose eccentrics, wheels and axles, crossheads, guide bar brackets, connecting rods, eccentric assembly, frame details.
3. Arrangement of valve gear, cylinders and details, valve gear, lubricator, steam and exhaust connections.
4. Arrangement of boiler and details of fittings, smokebox details.
5. Spirit burners, alternative vaporising burners, cab.
6. Tender and details, engine running boards, etc.

L.O. **94** **"NETTA." 1¼ in. gauge.**
Sheet

1. (See L.O. 90, sheet 1).
2. Main frames and frame details, wheels, axles, valve gear details, cylinders, coupling rods, crossheads, connecting rods, guide bars.
3. Arrangement of valve gear, boiler, lubricator, boiler fittings, steam and exhaust connections.
4. Running boards, cab, tender details.

L.O. **95** **"VIRGINIA." 3½ in. gauge 4-4-0 locomotive and tender.** (Vols. 115-116). This model is based on a typical American express engine of the 1870-80 period. It has outside cylinders and inside Stephenson link valve gear.

Sheet 1 General arrangement.

2 Cylinders, port face and steam chests, pump, eccentric straps and rods, link motion and Walschaerts valve gear.

3 Reversing gear, pump cylinder, lubricator, section of boiler and alternative throat plate, door plate for firebox.

4 Superheater and throttle, smokebox for straight top boiler, smokebox for wagon top boiler.

5 Cab and fittings, pilot, dome, pipe layout, water gauge, blowdown valve, safety valve, cab deck, by-pass valve, boiler mountings, grate and ashpan, check valves, steam valve.

6 Tender, tender trucks, wheels and axles, smoke stack. blower, snifting valve, whistle, injector.

7 Tender details, pump, brakes, bell, and lighting system.

L.O. **96** **"PANSY." 5 in. gauge 0-6-0 tank locomotive.** (Vols. 118-120). This is an accurate model of the well-known G.W.R. "57xx" class Pannier tank. It has inside cylinders with Stephenson valve gear.

Sheet 1 General arrangement, main frames, buffer beams.

2 Wheels, axles, axleboxes, horns, framestays, coupling rods and cylinders.

3 Cylinders and attachments, valve gear, eccentric straps and rods, connecting rods, reversing lever and bracket.

4 Regulator, superheater, crosshead pump, lubricator drive assembly, arrangement of pump, steam and exhaust pipes.

5 Boiler and details of smokebox and its assembly.

6 Backhead fittings, water gauge, blower, dome, grate, ashpan, smokebox arrangement and boiler brackets.

7 Brake gear, steam chest draincock, arrangement of tanks, buffers, drawhook, pumps, etc.

8 Running boards, splashers, injector water valve, leading sandbox and guard iron, trailing footsteps, top feed connections.

9 Cab and bunker details, trailing sandboxes, hand rails and pillars, lamp irons and small footsteps.

L.O. **97** **"MABEL" by LBSC. 3½ in. gauge L.N.W.R. 2-4-0 Locomotive.**

Sheet 1 General arrangement and frames.

2 Cylinders and details, connecting rods, crank-axle.

3 Motion plate, valve gear, eccentric straps and rods, reversing gear.

L.O. **98** **"MABEL" 5 in. gauge version.**

Sheet 1 Main frames, buffer and drag beams, crank-axle, main and leading horns and axleboxes, leading, driving and coupled wheels, coupling rods.

M.M. **922** **"MONA." Simple 0-4-2 inside cylinder tank engine, London Chatham, and Dover Railway.**

Sheet 1 Side view, 3½ in. gauge, frames for 3½ and 1¾ in., wheels, axles, pony truck, 3½ and 1¾ in., coupling rods, cylinders, 3½ in., rods and crank-axle 1¾ in.

2 Motion details, 3½ in., alternative loosee ccentric valve gear, 3½ in., cylinder, 1¾ in., lubricator for 3½ in., boiler for 3½ in.

3 Operations in boiler construction, reversing lever, 3½ in.; motion details, 1¾ in., blower and firebox stays; boiler for 1¾ in., dome, smokebox, hand pump etc. for 3½ in.

4 Boiler components for 3½ in., tanks, cab, and bunker, 3½ in., boiler fittings for 3½ in., final details, 3½ in and 1¾ in., lamp for 1¾ in.

M.M. **923** **"BETTY." A 2-6-2 outside-cylinder locomotive in 3½ in. gauge to the proposed N2 Southern class of 1934, itself a development of the 2-6-0 S.E. & C.R. N class or "mongoliper".**

Sheet 1 Full side elevation, main and cradle frames, wheels, axles, coupling rods, eccentrics, etc., pump, pony truck, trailing axleboxes and and springs, frames erected, cylinders.

2 Valve gear, motion details, valve gear parts, reverser, lubricator, pump, pipework, boiler.

3 Smokebox, regulator, superheater, cab, grate, ashpan, running boards etc., tender, complete.